GENTLEMAN OF
THE RING

Also by Bob Lonkhurst

MAN OF COURAGE: *The Life and
Career of Tommy Farr*

GENTLEMAN OF THE RING

The Life and Career of Jack Petersen

Bob Lonkhurst

Published by
BL Associates

Published by
BL Associates
6 Drayton Avenue
Potters Bar
Hertfordshire

First published 2001
© Bob Lonkhurst 2001

Typeset and designed by
Typecast (Artwork & Design)
Yeovil, Somerset

Printed in Great Britain by
Chiltern Press Ltd.
Bicester, Oxfordshire.
Part of MFK Group Ltd

Bound in Great Britain by
Petam Bookbinding Co. Ltd.
Waltham Abbey, Essex.
Part of MFK Group Ltd

A catalogue record for this book is
available from the British Library

ISBN 0-9540271-0-8

DEDICATION

This book is dedicated to all British boxers who, in general, represent a hard, controversial sport with great courage and dignity. They are a special breed and I regard it as a privilege to have known and worked closely with fighters of all levels for more than a decade.

Handsome, smartly dressed, Jack had an irresistible smile.

CONTENTS

FOREWORD

A book about Jack Petersen has been long overdue. For a man who so dominated British boxing during a particular period of the sport, very little has been written, and certainly a complete work has never before been attempted. This excellent book serves to remedy that omission, and carefully and eloquently documents Jack's boxing career, accomplishments, and what followed after his career as a professional boxer was so tragically curtailed.

In the days long before television, Jack Petersen was such an incredible attraction that crowds of more than 60,000 went to see him fight at the White City and other venues. He was a man of enormous charisma – a dashing, debonair, handsome young man, and when he knocked out Reggie Meen with an immaculate right hand to win the British heavyweight championship, he became a national hero.

Jack had originally wanted to become a doctor, but when he realised how accomplished he was as a boxer, he changed direction and followed a career in boxing. Unfortunately, he was plagued with fragile eye tissue and was prone to cuts. It was due to this condition that he was obliged to retire from boxing at the unusually early age of 25.

I well remember listening to the commentaries of his contests with Walter Neusel, and hoping and praying I would not hear the commentator say the words 'Petersen is cut.' Sadly, he was, and his injuries contributed to defeats in all three contests against the German.

When I first met Jack at the Board of Control where he was a Steward, I was amazed to find that he was still as handsome as ever, tall and upright, and with a beautifully spoken voice. It was an education to see young boxers appear before the Board after committing some kind of misdemeanour. Many resented the fact that they were to be judged by people who, in their opinion, had little or no knowledge of boxing and were therefore ill-equipped to deal with them.

Jack's presence, however, changed all that. A whispered caution from their older manager or trainer pointed Jack out, and from that moment the lack of respect vanished to be replaced by a polite regard, and indeed, veneration.

When Jack became President of the Board, I was Chairman. I changed the time of Board meetings simply because of the pressure of business. Jack, however, would leave Cardiff on a train which arrived to accommodate the old time. As he walked in apologising for his lateness, I would always invite members of the Board to stand to greet the President, and then ask, 'Will you take the chair Mr. President?' To this he always replied with a charming smile, 'No thank you Mr. Chairman. Please carry on.' Little wonder that when the Board were finally able to purchase their own building, it was named *Jack Petersen House*.

Jack was a gentleman in every possible meaning of that word. This fact is underlined in every page of Bob Lonkhurst's excellent book which so capably accommodates the need for Jack Petersen to be recalled and remembered with regard and affection.

Leonard 'Nipper' Read
President of the British
Boxing Board of Control.

ACKNOWLEDGEMENTS

I owe thanks to many people for making the publication of this book possible. I mention in particular, John Petersen, Jack's eldest son, who outlined his father's life away from boxing. Without his help, so much would have been missing.

I am grateful to Leonard 'Nipper' Read, the President of the British Boxing Board of Control who kindly agreed to provide the foreword. A friend for many years, 'Nipper' held tremendous affection for Jack, and has fed me with a steady stream of interesting tales. Special thanks go to Larry Braysher, another long-time friend, who provided an abundance of high quality photographs to help illustrate the book. Harold Alderman, an enthusiastic and respected boxing researcher, provided me with valuable information concerning Jack's father, 'Pa' Petersen, and also loaned photographs.

Journalists, Gareth Jones and Ron Olver, advised their readers of my project which resulted in a supply of newspaper cuttings and photographs from Petersen enthusiasts. My thanks also go to Ray Gunn, Brian Lee, Charles Giles, Dudley Waters, Dave Allen, Chas Taylor and Derek O'Dell for their kind contributions.

The staff of the National Newspaper Library at Colindale as always gave excellent service in providing me with countless items required to thoroughly research Jack's life and career. I was also helped greatly by the staff of Cardiff Central Library and the National Army Museum at Chelsea, to whom I am extremely grateful.

Special thanks also go to Claude Abrams, editor of *Boxing News*, for allowing me access to his photograph collection and also to Derek Rowe who provided rare photographs of Jack Petersen in later life.

Reg Gutteridge, OBE, one of the world's most respected boxing writer's and broadcaster's, kindly offered to read the contents before going to print. His advice and guidance were of paramount importance. I consider myself extremely fortunate that a man of Reg's standing is willing to guide a mere novice like myself, and I extend my gratitude to him.

ACKNOWLEDGEMENTS

Finally, I thank once again, my good friend Barry Hugman, a highly successful author of sporting publications, for his continual advice and guidance towards publication.

INTRODUCTION

When Jack Petersen was elected President of the British Boxing Board of Control in 1986, it was a tribute to one of Britain's most respected sporting personalities. A giant of a man in every sense, he was the ultimate role-model to every young boxer, and indeed sportsman.

During my early days as an Inspector for the Board of Control, I met Jack on a number of occasions, yet cannot claim to have known him. That was my misfortune. As an observer, however, I was tremendously impressed by the esteem in which he was held by people from all walks of life. Polite and well spoken, he acknowledged everyone who spoke to him, whether it be at a boxing arena or in the street. During the course of extensive research I have conducted over the past two years, everyone I have spoken to has described Jack as being an absolute gentleman. Such consistency, therefore, made selecting the title of this book a formality.

I first became interested in Jack's career whilst researching my previous book, 'Man of Courage', the biography of his fellow Welshman, Tommy Farr. As an ardent boxing fan, I knew he was highly respected, but had little knowledge of his early career and life outside the sport. Some preliminary research, however, soon convinced me that publication of his story was long overdue. I was amazed it had not been written before.

Jack Petersen came to prominence in the bleak years of the early 1930's when, with mounting unemployment, Wales sorely needed such an imposing figure. From the day he turned professional at the age of 20, people were warmed by the sheer magnetism of his personality. He was an exceptionally exciting fighter, and his devastating punching power brought him quick victories over Alf Noble (30 seconds), Jim Campbell (22 seconds), Tom Wailes (60 seconds), Dick Power (21 seconds), which gained him the Welsh heavyweight title, and Charlie Smith (16 seconds).

Jack was a brave, fiery, yet extremely polite and cheerful fighter who never complained nor bore any grievance. In a short but exciting career, he established himself as the most popular heavyweight since Bombardier Billy Wells 20 years earlier.

Incredibly, he topped the bill in every one of his fights, a record that will surely never be equalled in the history of British Boxing.

His exciting style and immense courage attracted crowds in their thousands because they knew he would fight from the first bell to last. More than 70,000 saw his fights at the White City against Jack Doyle, Len Harvey and Larry Gains, 60,000 flocked to Wembley Stadium on a damp evening in 1936 to see his second fight against Walter Neusel, and 53,000 packed into Ninian Park for his fight with Heine Muller when he had been a professional for less than three years.

Although he was able to command huge purses, Jack still made money for the promoters. Sir Arthur Elvin, who staged boxing at Wembley before the war, once claimed that the only time he made a profit was when Jack Petersen was on the bill.

Described by many people as the 'new Carpentier', some critics believed he could bring the world heavyweight title to Wales. Such predictions, however, were rather optimistic because physically he was only a light-heavyweight, and frequently gave away up to 28lbs.

Jack always showed tremendous courage and desire in the ring, but unfortunately he took too much punishment. His brave heart and natural appetite for aggression became his eventual downfall because he couldn't resist a fight. At times when he should have boxed he got drawn into punch-ups which often led to him being cut around the eyes. Even many of his winning fights were wars, and consequently the damage took its toll. Serious eye problems eventually brought about his premature retirement from boxing at the age of 25.

Tall, handsome, charming and articulate, Jack was a credit to British boxing. The ultimate gentleman both in and out of the ring, he was totally unaffected by the savagery of his chosen sport. Although a lack of capable sparring partners often hindered his preparations, and severe cuts around the eyes put him under the most terrible pressure, he never once complained. Even in defeat he was magnanimous. He retired from boxing with tremendous respect, and a reputation of being one of the most courageous of British heavyweight champions.

Jack's popularity was incredible, and this was clearly demonstrated in June 1934, the night he attempted to regain his British heavyweight title from Len Harvey. Crowds waiting outside newspaper offices throughout South Wales awaiting the result of the fight, were so large that traffic was brought to a standstill.

The popularity was not just confined to the fans. During, and after his ring career, praise was heaped upon Jack by former opponents, a number of whom remained his firm friends for life.

'Jack Petersen was one of the best heavyweights Britain has ever had,' said Larry Gains, himself a top class heavyweight during the 1930's. 'A good puncher with both hands, he had tremendous courage and a lot of style.'

When Jack announced his retirement in March 1937, Len Harvey, whom he fought three times, said 'He was a splendid sportsman, both in and out of the ring. His retirement is a great loss to British boxing.'

Jack also impressed the ladies. 'I think his personality is greater than that of Carpentier,' said the wife of Australian heavyweight George Cook on the eve of her husband's first fight with Jack in June 1933. 'Petersen is gifted with glamour, and he must have considerable character to have done what he has for a young man.'

Jack, however, never thought of himself as anything other than an ordinary young man. As champion, he became tired of being a hero. Consequently, he avoided walking along main streets as much as possible because he found the continual pointing, hand-shaking and autograph hunting tedious.

He once said of himself when discussing his career, 'When I have done my job, I am just like any other young man, for I have interests outside and far removed from the ring.'

He had little time for the loud, sporting set, preferring instead the company of people he knew. He loved going to taverns in the Welsh hills and valleys, mixing in particular with miners, many of whom walked miles to see him fight.

Although his retirement was sudden and heartbreaking, Jack had the character and ability to adjust and move on. He spent many years in the Army, served in local government, was Chairman for a number of prestigious sporting bodies, and became a boxing columnist for a Sunday newspaper.

This man of simple tastes loved children, and was an ardent supporter of the scout movement. He was dedicated to health and physical fitness, and spent years developing sporting facilities for youth, particularly in South Wales. In 1978, his hard work and dedication was officially recognised, when he was awarded an O.B.E. for outstanding services to sport.

Throughout his busy life, Jack remained closely involved with boxing. For a number of years, he ran the Glamorgan Army Cadet team with great success. He was President of the Welsh Area Council of the British Boxing Board of Control, and also the Welsh Ex-Boxers' Association. After acting as both a representative and an administrative steward of the Board, he reached his pinnacle in 1986 when the national governing body elected him President.

In recognition of his immense popularity and service to the sport, the Board of Control subsequently named their new headquarters in South London, JACK PETERSEN HOUSE. It was the fitting tribute to 'Gentleman Jack' a truly wonderful fighting man.

This book is a true labour of love written essentially as a boxing story. Whilst acknowledging Jack's considerable achievements and contribution elsewhere, it was in boxing that he first came to prominence. As an ardent supporter of the sport, I am convinced that his achievements should be chronicled and become part of the history, not only of boxiana, but also Wales.

There are many fine men in boxing and I believe Jack's story endorses that. I sincerely hope I have done him justice and portrayed him as the wonderful man he was.

Bob Lonkhurst
Potters Bar, 2001

1

EARLY DAYS

As daylight faded on a mid-May evening during 1933, only a skeleton crew remained aboard a huge German naval vessel as she rocked at anchor in Cardiff docks. Hundreds of other sailors, and officers too, had scrambled ashore some hours earlier and headed for Ninian Park, the venue for an open-air fight of tremendous interest.

German boxer, Heine Muller, was a former heavyweight champion of Europe, and had been brought to Cardiff to test the ability of a tall, good-looking young Welshman whose exciting style of fighting had captured the hearts of his countrymen.

Although only 21 years old, Jack Petersen had won the light-heavyweight and heavyweight championships of Great Britain in consecutive fights within the space of just 51 days. He was in his third year as a professional, and had won all of his 21 contests.

Petersen was idolised in Wales, and on this warm May evening, a crowd of more than 53,000, believed at the time to be the largest ever to attend a boxing match in Europe, packed into Ninian Park to see him face Muller.

Throughout the day, the whole of Wales had been gripped with fight fever. Special steamer excursions from ports all along the Bristol Channel brought fans flocking to Cardiff in their thousands. Special trains ran from destinations within a radius of 80 miles right into Ninian Park Station. There were dozens of extra bus services, and the proprietors of private coach companies were inundated with reservations for return trips to all parts of South Wales.

Petersen was already being described as the 'new Carpentier', and fans throughout Britain believed he had the punch and ability to bring the world heavyweight title back to Britain after more than 30 years.

* * *

Jack was born on 2 September 1911, at 52, Monthermer Road, in the Whitchurch area of Cardiff. He was christened John Charles, although on his birth certificate the family name is spelt 'Peterson'. This is thought to have been human error because throughout the greater part of his life the spelling was 'Petersen', as was that of his father.

Nevertheless, the situation did prompt speculation. One theory was that there was a mis-spelling early in his career because a promoter believed Jack to be of Scandinavian parentage. Early newspaper articles often referred to him as being a 'Welsh-Norweigian', 'Welsh-Dane,' or 'the Cardiff boy born of Swedish ancestry.' All were totally inaccurate because he was as true a Welshman as any other person born in the prinicpality.

Jack's grandfather on his father's side of the family, Arthur Petersen, was in fact Norweigian. He was a ship's carpenter and sailed all over the world aboard wind-jammers. He had a reputation of being very handy with his fists, whether it be at sea or in port. During his travels he met an Irish lady when he visited Cork. They eventually married, and some years later moved to South Wales.

Much of the subsequent confusion concerning Jack's true nationality came about as a result of remarks made to the press by his father, John Thomas Petersen. A volatile character known affectionately as 'Pa', 'Pop' or 'J.T.', depending on who was referring to him, he occasionally remarked that Jack had inherited the Irish fire, Norse hardiness and Welsh heart for a good fight.

Born at Cork in 1886, Pa moved to Cardiff with his parents in the mid-1890's. He had two brothers, Charlie and Lew, both of whom became fighters. In his day, Pa was no mean performer in the ring, and over the years many differing stories circulated concerning his achievements. Some claimed he was never beaten. Boxing, however, was not well reported in Wales during the early 1900's, largely because it was disapproved of by the Chapel. Consequently, many claims made by particular fighters remain unsubstantiated. Pa Petersen fell into that category.

In January 1934, the *South Wales Post* published a story about Pa, and listed contests he was believed to have had. Although the record was more detailed than one produced years earlier in *'Mirror of Life'*, no dates or venues were given.

Reference was made to Pa having boxed a draw with Jim Driscoll. Although it was generally believed that they fought at Cardiff in the early 1900's, there is considerable confusion regarding

2

the actuality of the event. In some quarters, it was claimed they boxed a draw over six rounds, whilst other reports indicated it was a no decision contest.

A small reference appeared in *Sporting Life* on 3 February 1903 advising that Jim Driscoll (Cardiff) would meet Young Petersen (Cardiff) over 20 rounds at the Theatre Royal, Cadoxton, on 16 February. Petersen was described as being ex-amateur 8 stones 6 lbs champion of Wales. No further reference was ever made to this contest. The indications are that Pa and Driscoll met much earlier. Jim became a professional in 1901, and although there is no reference in any record to show he and Petersen met, he is known to have taken part in hundreds of booth fights.

Some years later it was claimed in a Welsh newspaper that they met at Queen Street Hall, Cardiff, in 1900. Petersen, said to have been amateur bantamweight champion of Wales, was awarded the decision by referee, Dan Meredith, but Master of Ceremonies, Harry Wheeler declared it a draw. Years later, top referee, Mr. C. B. Thomas, in an article about his experiences in the ring, also referred to Pa having boxed a draw with Driscoll in 1900 but provided nothing further to that already written.

A number of newspaper articles referred to Pa as Welsh amateur bantamweight champion. This claim was also unsubstantiated because in those days there was no controlling body, and many boxing shows were privately run. The Welsh Amateur Boxing Association was not formed until 1910, and no official records existed before that date.

In April 1904, a story appeared in *'Mirror of Life'* concerning 'Young' Petersen of Cardiff, described as the 8 stones 6 lbs amateur champion of Wales, who wished to turn professional at 9 stones. He challenged any man for a side-stake and best purse, and stated that Billy Barrett (New York), 'Kid' Davis (Denver, Colorado) or Billy Morgan (Swansea) were preferred. A photo of 'Young' Petersen illustrated the article.

In May the following year, *Mirror of Life* reported that Jack Petersen (Cardiff) had supposedly turned to wrestling. The article was illustrated by a photograph and brief record of claimed contests, although no dates or venues were given.

In July 1914, Petersen challenged Freddie Welsh (Pontypridd) to a fight at ten stones (140 pounds), for £100 plus a side-stake of £100. Welsh had won the world lightweight title earlier that month by outpointing Willie Ritchie (US) over 20 rounds in London. Described as Professor Jack Petersen of Cardiff, it was claimed he had substantial backing to stage the contest. His challenge was, however, ignored by Welsh who returned to America to pursue his career.

Although some areas are unclear, there can be no doubt that Pa Petersen was a very prominent figure in Welsh boxing during the early 1900's. In March 1918, when British middleweight champion, Pat O'Keefe, boxed an exhibition at the Theatre Royal, Barry Dock, the referee was listed as Professor John (Jack) Petersen of Cardiff.

Pa also had great interest in medicine, having studied and trained in Norway. He beame a specialist in the cult of health, fitness and massage, and in 1905 purchased the Lynn Institute at St Johns Square, Cardiff. Practising his skills in physiotherapy, osteopathy and manipulation, he turned it into a highly successful business which attracted many rich clients. Often described by the media as the best physical culture specialist in Wales, he also became a visiting lecturer in physio and osteopathy at Cardiff Medical School.

Boxing, wrestling and self-defence were also taught by Pa at the Lynn Institute, and during the First World War he taught ju-jitsu to hundreds of policemen. When the Welsh Amateur Boxing Championships were first staged in 1910, six lads he trained reached the finals. Three became champions.

Pa also enjoyed considerable success as a promoter and match-maker, running many shows at the Lynn Institute. A smart dresser who invariably wore spats on his shoes, he was very much 'a man about town'. Consequently, he made friends with prominent people, many of whom became his clients. He once boxed a six rounds no decision bout with the Chief Constable of Glamorgan, Captain Lindsay, before an audience of prominent Cardiff businessmen.

The Lynn Institute became a central meeting place for sportsmen and businessmen of Cardiff, and many a dispute was settled there in the ring. Journalist, Charles Barnett, once referred a fight there between a ship owner and the proprietor of a coal business. The prize was a champagne supper paid for by the loser.

* * *

Pa married Malinda Laura Rossiter at the Parish Church of St John the Baptist, Cardiff on 13 September 1909, and they set up home in the Whitchurch district. They had three children, Jack being the second. The family were Catholics, and many problems subsequently arose when Jack's mother left home when he was quite young.

4

Times became very lonely for Jack, and he had an unhappy childhood. His sisters Kathleen and Doreen, (the youngest), were sent away to Convent School, but he lived at home with Pa who worked long hours at the Lynn Institute. Consequently, Jack often returned home to an empty house and became known as a 'latch-key child.'

He hated his home and greatly missed not having a mother. The situation was made worse by the fact that his grandparents did not figure in his life. It was a very dark period which Jack never forgot. In order that his own children would have a secure family life, he rarely talked about his own childhood until he was much older.

Eventually, Pa sent Jack to Convent School but he soon became very homesick. After about six months he was so ill that Pa took him home and nursed him back to fitness.

During the evenings, Pa spent hours telling Jack about the great Welsh fighters of the early 1900's. He also loved listening to Pa and his sporting friends recalling the old days of fights on the mountainsides, in the booths and the Welsh valleys.

The stories had atmosphere and excitement, and impressed Jack to the extent that all the romance in the world appeared to be centred around fighters. It made no difference whether it was for the love of a scrap or the few shillings which meant so much to them in times of great hardship.

Jack was taught the basics of self defence at a very young age. In an interview in later life, he said he was always led to believe that he was as young as two when he first had the gloves on. A photograph existed as testimony of the fact that he was little more than a baby when he first stuck out his left hand and put his feet in the position indicated. He would quietly smile whenever he came across that picture.

From an early age, Pa was very strict with Jack, and as he grew up demanded that he earned his keep by doing cleaning work and other chores at the Lynn. This turned out to Jack's advantage because by watching his father at work, he quickly became interested in both medicine and fitness training.

Pa always hoped that one day Jack would become a doctor. With that in mind he sent him to St. Illtyds College to get the best possible education. Although he knew medicine would be a good career, Jack was not so keen. He wanted action rather than study, but although his heart was not in it, he became a good scholar.

At school, he was a mild, inoffensive lad. Although he wasn't quarrelsome, he loved to get the gloves on and have a few rounds boxing with his mates. Rumours of his ability filtered back to Pa, but he dismissed them as schoolboy stories. He did, however, notice how Jack was growing, but accepted his evasive answers about gymnastics and physical training.

Jack loved physical culture as much as his father, and developed a strict fitness routine at quite a young age. Pa was delighted to see he wanted to develop his body along scientific lines so he encouraged him to use the equipment at the Lynn as often as possible.

From that point, Jack went to the gym everyday and, whether it was from home or school, he ran all the way. He loved keeping fit, and in his mid-teens put in an hours training each day using dumb-bells, weights and developers, and punching the ball.

At the age of 15, Jack was almost six feet tall but very thin. One day Pa suggested that a sea-cruise would do him good and help build him up. Nothing could have delighted Jack more because one of his real joys as a schoolboy, was roaming around Cardiff docks. He loved looking at ships of different nationalities, chatting to the crews and finding out where they were headed. It opened his mind to the romance of travel and adventure.

The docks and sea-front, and his training sessions were the real and genuine things in life for Jack. They considerably eased the unhappiness and loneliness of his childhood. He was, therefore, absolutely thrilled when Pa eventually said he had arranged a trip for him aboard the merchant vessel 'Fairwater' which was headed out of Cardiff docks for South America. Although it was only a small tramp steamer not built for speed, Jack thought the 'Fairwater' was the most wonderful craft afloat. Captain Horsfield and his crew were a fine bunch of men, and made him extremely welcome. The youngster quickly took to the rough life of a seaman, and although the food was poor, he at least had a comfortable bunk.

Whenever he felt like it, Jack got involved in work on the deck, chipping, filing, and pulling on the salty hand-searing ropes. He also worked in the stokehold and helped the firemen keep up a good head of steam.

The work hardened Jack up considerably, but in the company of rough and ready sailors, he was fair game for a joke. Sometimes things got rough and he had a few scraps. Despite his age, he more than held his own and soon earned the respect of everyone on board.

The cruise lasted for three months, and when he returned to Cardiff, Jack was physically and mentally stronger than when he went away. This excited him, and he was soon back in the gym doing his daily work-outs. He also spent a great deal of time running on Porthkerry sands on the coast near Barry and Penarth. The dunes were particularly good for improving his wind and leg strength.

Jack was often accompanied by Pa who, by this time, had married a lady who lived nearby. Although she became Jack's step-mother, they did not get on because he still desperately missed his natural mother.

Meanwhile, his interest in boxing grew rapidly, although in his mid-teens he would never have struck anyone as a champion in the making. He was in his element whenever he had the gloves on with any of Pa's clients or assistants at the Lynn. With the customers, however, there was a strict rule – he was not allowed to hit back. Many were wealthy businessmen who took liberties and hit Jack hard and often.

The one-sided state of affairs turned out to be an advantage because it taught him good defensive skills. Jack took everything in good heart and thought boxing was by far the finest sport and exercise in the world. There came a time when he hated hearing the words, 'That's enough for today my lad!'

Although Pa bought Jack a tiny pair of boxing gloves when he was a small boy, he was strongly opposed to him making any serious attempt to take up the sport. Jack, however, loved boxing far more than his studies. So, full of determination, and without Pa's knowledge, he went along to Bob Downey, a tough, one-legged character who had a tiny gym in the notorious Tiger Bay district.

Bob was also the landlord of the Bute Castle public house at Angelina Street, and in 1935 would become Vice-President of the Welsh Area of the British Boxing Board of Control. He walked with a crutch which he used for a multitude of purposes. He rested on it, walked with it, pointed out fighters faults, and even used it to maintain order in the bars. He had been involved with many good fighters over the years, including Jim Driscoll, Gentleman Joe White, Bat McCarthy, Phoenix Emmanuel and Blind Frank Reid. All had at some stage sparred in his ring.

The first thing Downey taught Jack was how to punch. For nine months he went to the gym daily and spent his entire training period hitting the bag. He was never allowed to put on a boxing glove, let alone fight.

'He was as raw as a carrot when he first came to me,' Bob recalled years later. 'I knew the only way he'd ever do anything in the ring was to keep right on at that bag and learn how to time and deliver a punch.'

Jack's only other sporting interest was rugby but this did not meet with Downey's approval. 'Boy, if you want to become a boxer, it will be a whole-time job,' he told him. 'You won't have time for other games. Besides, there's the danger of being hurt on the field, and that might set you back months in your training.'

There was no arguing with Bob Downey as any rough-neck from Tiger Bay would confirm. When he bellowed orders with his wild Irish voice, he was obeyed.

For month after month, Jack obeyed. He punched the bag with increasing ferocity, and all the time wore only small mitts to cover his knuckles. Yet he was craving for a fight, something which would have astonished people who knew him as a gentle, docile young man. He pleaded with Downey for more action but the trainer wouldn't budge.

Jack stuck at it for as long as he could, but then after nine months, threw instructions aside. One Saturday afternoon he played rugby but got a bit of a kicking. When Downey found out, he was furious and their relationship came to an abrupt halt.

Back at the Lynn Institute, Jack seized every opportunity to get into the ring and have a good set-too. He had fallen in love with boxing, and for him it was the supreme thrill of life.

Pa recognised that his son was deadly serious, so instead of discouraging him, he sometimes stripped off and got into the ring with him. He had a wealth of experience, and being much shorter than Jack, was elusive and light on his feet. Although he had serious reservations about Jack becoming too involved in the sport, Pa was an excellent tutor and taught him a great deal.

* * *

Jack's development impressed many of Pa's friends and clients and there were plenty of suggestions that he joined an amateur club and enter local competitions. Although he had plenty of self-belief, Jack was not so certain of his potential as some of his admirers. Nevertheless, believing he might have an outside chance of doing well, he joined the nearby Gabalfa Amateur Boxing Club which was run by Fred Yates, a friend of Pa's, who was also trainer of the Welsh amateur international team.

Full of enthusiasm and determination, Jack entered the 1929 Welsh Amateur Championships. Being tall for his age, he could only consider entering the middle, light-heavy or heavyweight divisions. Despite not having had a single competitive contest, he entered all three, thereby creating a record for the championships in Wales.

Great interest was shown in Jack's debut at Cardiff Drill Hall on

11 March, and despite him being only 17½ years old, he was already attracting the attention of the local newspapers. The *South Wales Echo* reported;

> Great interest is being shown in the debut of J. C. Petersen, who bears a name well known in the sport. He is one of the genuine 'dark-horses' yet to be introduced into boxing in Wales.

The report also mentioned Pa in favourable terms, thus indicating the high esteem in which he was held in Welsh boxing circles.

Jack's baptism into competitive boxing was not a particularly happy one. Although there was no denying his gameness, he made the mistake of mixing it with two vastly more experienced opponents. Consequently, he went away empty-handed.

The first man Jack faced was Albert Donovan in the middleweight division semi-final, but found him too clever and experienced, and lost on points after a good, competitive fight. Donovan would go on to be Welsh ABA champion in 1930, 31 and 32.

Although he was completely exhausted at the end of the fight, Jack had not suffered any physical damage. He therefore declared himself fit to box in the light-heavyweight division. A bye took him straight into the final against Police Constable Rhys Howells, a top-class amateur and reigning Welsh champion at the weight. He had also won the middleweight title in 1923, 24 and 25, and was losing British ABA finalist at middleweight in 1925. He held the Welsh light-heavyweight title for three consecutive years from 1926, and was losing British ABA finalist in 1927.

It was too much to expect a 17 year old, one fight novice to beat Howells, and it came as no great surprise when the referee stopped the fight in the second round, resulting in Jack withdrawing from the heavyweight division. Nevertheless, he went out of the championships with great credit. He had shown a good left hand and an abundance of courage, a feature he would demonstrate throughout his professional career.

The *South Wales Echo* reported his fights and commented;

> a feature of the championships was the entry of Jack, the son of John Thomas Petersen, a well-known exponent of the noble art …

Such set-backs would be enough to discourage most youngsters, but Jack was made of stern stuff. Above all, he had tremendous determination, so rather than allow disappointment to effect him, he got straight back into training. Although he boxed for the Gabalfa Club, he continued to train at the Lynn Institute under the supervision of his father.

At first he boxed as a middleweight, but being over six feet tall and still growing, he soon developed into a natural light-heavyweight. Most of his amateur opponents were fairly prominent fighters, amongst them being Police and Services champions.

In almost every contest Jack gave away a lot of weight. One of his opponents was Jack Mellins of the Glamorgan Constabulary who was Welsh ABA heavyweight champion in 1929. He was a big, rugged fighter, but despite giving away about two stones, Jack beat him twice. After their second meeting, Mellins remarked, 'Jack, you have the makings of a grand fighter. I never thought you could beat me, but you did my boy. I can see you at the top of the amateur tree.'

An indication of the progress Jack was making was seen during a fine points victory over six two minute rounds over Pat Floyd at the Masonic Hall, Haverfordwest in 1930. Pat was a top class fighter having won the A.B.A. heavyweight title the previous year. The way in which the young Petersen beat him convinced critics that he was also destined for national honours.

During the build-up to one of Jack's important amateur contests, Pa persuaded Frank Moody, the Pontypridd professional, to travel to the Lynn Institute one evening to give his son a serious try-out over five rounds. Moody was a top class fighter, having been a professional since 1914, and had held the British middle and light-heavyweight titles.

Jack put up a good show, and afterwards Frank told him he was considerably better than he had expected. Coming from a man of Moody's standing, it was a tremendous compliment and gave the youngster great encouragement.

Although he didn't fight very often, Jack was building himself a big following. After his sensational first round victory over London heavyweight Dave Kevern in October 1930, the *South Wales Echo* headlined a story in the sports pages: 'WELSH AMATEUR IS A FUTURE HOPE.'

The following month, Jack was selected to box for a Welsh Amateur Boxing Association team invited to take part in a series of matches in Demark. His first fight was at Copenhagen against Danish Amateur champion, Jacob Michaelson, a huge man, who earlier that year had won the European amateur heavyweight championship in Budapest. Believing the fight to be over six rounds, Jack boxed carefully at the beginning in order to save himself for the later rounds. Then to his amazement, the referee awarded the decision to Michaelson at the conclusion of round three. Even though he believed he should have been declared the winner, Petersen made no protest, accepting that he had made a mistake.

Two days later, a Friday evening, Jack faced another Dane, Eberhardt Hansen, in Copenhagen. He was similar in size and style to the Welshman, and after a hard battle, Petersen got the decision. He faced Hansen again two days later at Aarhus in the final match of the series, and again won on points.

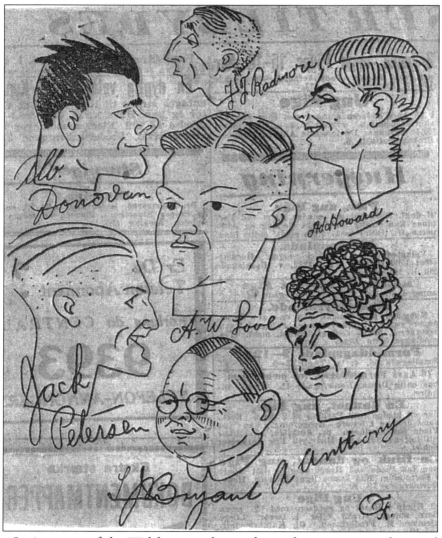

Caricatures of the Welsh team drawn by Jack Petersen, and signed by each member.

11

Jack's victories contributed to the success of the Welsh team in each match. The team consisted of Trevor Radmore (Cymmer), Austin Anthony (Glynreath), old opponent Albert Donovan, Albert Love and Leslie Howard, who like Jack, were all from Cardiff. They won 13 contests against just five defeats, and were described by Danish boxing critics as 'the finest British team ever seen in Denmark.'

Jack captured his first title at Cardiff Drill Hall on 23 February 1931. He took barely 20 seconds of the opening round to knock out Guardsman Penny to win the Welsh ABA light-heavyweight title. The third punch he landed put the soldier down for the full count. Later that evening he was awarded the Welsh heavyweight title on a walk-over, there being no other entrants in the division.

Although he was extremely proud, Jack refused to get carried away, knowing what he had achieved was only the first step towards his goal of an ABA title.

Two weeks later, he boxed in the main event of the evening at the Glamorgan Police Annual championships at Pontypridd Town Hall. His opponent was Police Constable J. Rodda of Nottingham. The contest was a disappointment because Rodda had injured his hand in a fight 24 hours earlier, and was no match for the new Welsh champion. Although Jack was wild with his right hand, he still managed to put the policeman down in the first and second rounds before knocking him out in the third. The victory, however, was still news, and the *South Wales Echo* carried a headline, 'ANOTHER EASY WIN FOR JACK PETERSEN', across the sports page.

Being a natural light-heavyweight, Jack sensibly elected to pursue the national title at that weight rather than the more prestigous heavyweight crown. His progress continued to attract media attention and there was speculation about him turning professional. In an interview with the *South Wales Echo*, Pa Petersen insisted that they were concentrating on winning the ABA title and nothing else. He did, however, add: 'It is just possible Jack will go over to the paid ranks if he fails to win the ABA title.'

Petersen trained hard but sensibly at the Lynn Institute under the close supervision of his father and trusted aide, Billy Diamond. He was determined to give his very best, not only for himself, but for Wales. The only concern was, that having had only 17 amateur contests meant he had not been seriously tested at the very top level. Everything possible was therefore done to ensure that he was ready for the biggest night of his career.

More than a dozen heavyweights were contacted to assist in the preparations. With two weeks to go before the ABA finals, experienced professional, Jack Stanley, was considered to be the best man to put Jack through his paces. He had a reputation of being a real hard man, and in 1927 had taken Frank Moody 11 rounds. He was, therefore, engaged to box with Jack daily.

The following week, Marine Smith was also engaged as a special sparring partner as training built to a peak. Jack showed his punching power one evening when he and Smith were having a three rounds try-out. Before a small select audience, they set a gruelling pace, and from beginning to end it was give and take. Despite only being an amateur, the skill was undoubtedly with Petersen as he used his left jab with great force and his right was like a battering ram.

Towards the end of the final session, they put everything behind vicious short arm punches. Then with half a minute to go, Jack caught Smith with a perfectly delivered right. The marine crashed to the floor, slowly got to his knees only to fall flat on his face. He was clearly knocked out. The fact that they were wearing 16 ounce gloves demonstrated the power the young Welshman had in his right hand. He was more than ready for the task ahead.

* * *

The ABA championships were held at the Royal Albert Hall in London on 25 March 1931. Boxing commenced at 10.30am with the heats, semi-finals and finals all taking place on the same day.

In his first contest, Jack made short work of R. Parsons (Northern Counties) whom he knocked out in the opening round. In the semi-final he stopped F. Dove (Battersea) in round two.

In the final, he faced a formidable task in Joe Goyder, a City of London policeman, who had won gold at the British Empire Games in Canada the previous year. A very experienced man, he had also won the ABA light-heavyweight title in 1929 and been losing finalist in 1928.

In a rousing contest, the young Welshman was too fast and too busy, and had Goyder in trouble on several occasions. The ex-champion's experience, however, kept him in the fight to the end, and although Petersen was awarded the decision it was on the casting vote of the referee.

The ovation Jack received from the Welsh fans was incredible, and something he never forgot. 'I was walking on air as I made my way back to the dressing room,' he recalled. 'It was the most memorable night of my amateur career.'

2

TURNS PROFESSIONAL

After becoming ABA champion, Jack took another holiday. This time he contented himself with a few days at Weston-super-Mare, and a similar spell at Porthcawl. As soon as he was refreshed, he was back at the Lynn Institute assisting his father.

Becoming ABA champion had made Jack restive and uncertain about his future. He had reached a crossroads, and the virtue of fighting was now in his blood. He felt that nothing else mattered, and wanted to turn professional as soon as possible.

Pa, however, did his best to discourage Jack by saying he would never make any money from boxing. He strongly advised him to pursue a career in medicine instead. Having become a visiting lecturer in osteopathy and physiotheraphy at Cardiff Medical School, he even went ahead and arranged for him to attend as a student.

Had Jack been seriously considering higher education with a view to a professional career, it would have been a wonderful opportunity. Going to university did not, however, particularly appeal to him. Although Pa was prepared to do whatever he could to help, he was insistent that Jack made up his mind. This put the youngster in a difficult position because of his urge to become a professional fighter.

Jack was a determined young man with a strong character, and after giving the situation a great deal of thought, he eventually told Pa exactly what he wanted to do with his life.

'Jack my boy, put that notion out of your head,' retorted Pa when he told him. 'I would not care to see any son of mine become a professional fighter. I know too much about the game. It's the hardest, cruelest game in the world. It is full of pit-falls and disappointments, and the rewards are few.'

Pa tried everything to get Jack to put the idea out of his head. 'The prize-ring is a hard task-master,' he continued. 'While in this country it is clean compared with what it was in my early years, it is one of the very last professions I would recommend any boy to take up.'

'Forget all about it,' continued Pa. 'I'll send you to college. Your boxing can do you no harm there.'

Jack listened carefully to everything his father said, and tried to accept his advice and forget all about turning professional. It was no use. He was now a fighter, and a fighter he wanted to be.

He pleaded with Pa to see things from his side, and give him twelve months. 'If I am not a champion within that time,' said Jack sincerely, 'I will concentrate on studying and forget about boxing.'

Pa was not convinced, and over the next few months refused to discuss the situation whenever Jack raised it. His attitude demoralised the youngster, and caused him to lose interest in his work at the Lynn. Nevertheless, he kept training religiously because he was determined never to neglect it. To feel really fit meant everything in life to him.

As the weeks passed by, Jack suddenly sensed a wavering on Pa's behalf. Whenever he appeared to be in particularly good humour, Jack would light-heartedly say, 'Well, what about my first fight as a pro? Be a sport and fix it up for me!'

Instead of getting angry, Pa would smile and urge his son to wait a little while longer. 'There's no immediate hurry is there?' he would reply. Then, in August 1931, five months after he became ABA champion, a series of events occurred in South Wales which would change the whole course of Jack's life and help him realise his ambitions.

* * *

The boxing fraternity and sporting media were convinced it was only a matter of time before Jack Petersen became a professional. In early September 1931, the *South Wales Echo* claimed that efforts were being made behind the scenes to match him with established professional, Dick Power, who had been recognised as Welsh heavyweight champion since 1928.

Unbeknown to the media, a group of wealthy sportsmen were in private negotiations with the Petersen's to form a syndicate which would provide financial backing to enable Jack to turn professional. The first steps were taken during the summer of 1931 on a golf course at Porthcawl.

Cardiff businessman, Harry Jones, one of Pa Petersen's closest friends, had watched Jack in the gym since he first put the gloves on. He had seen most of his amateur contests and was convinced that, with proper care and backing, he could develop into a world class heavyweight. During a round of golf, Jones suddenly asked his playing partner, William Blackwood, a London journalist and businessman, if he believed there was such a man as a 'real heavyweight champion'.

'Maybe, why do you ask?' enquired Blackwood.

'Because I know a lad who I have seen grow up from being a child, who looks like that very bird,' said Jones.

Blackwood was extremely interested, so by arrangement with Pa, Jones took him to the Lynn Institute a couple of days later. He was introduced to Jack who stripped off, went through some exercises and did a session of ball-punching. They all then sat down and had a long and friendly conversation. Although he was convinced Jack had exceptional talent, Blackwood said almost the same things to him as Pa had about the professional game. He pointed out the dangers of physical injury, the hardship, the worries and disappointments which were inevitable for 95 per cent of professional boxers.

Blackwood urged Jack to remember that not one fighter in a thousand ever got to the top of the tree, or made any real money. 'Do you relaise all this?' he asked. 'Are you still anxious to have a go?'

As the discussion continued, Blackwood asked Jack if he was ready to sacrifice all his other prospects in life on the off-chance of making good in the most difficult, thankless and arduous game in the realms of sport. 'It is too serious a matter for a light-hearted decision,' he insisted.

He implored the youngster to think the matter over carefully and give him and Jones a decision later. Jack looked at his father whose face was more solemn than he had ever seen it before. Pa didn't utter a word, so Jack made his decision on the spot.

'I want to become a professional fighter,' he said. 'I don't need time to think about it.' Blackwood then made a remark which pleased Jack immensely. 'I saw you beat Goyder at the Albert Hall, and think you have a wonderful chance of becoming British champion,' he remarked with sincerity. 'You have much in your favour – youth, strength, perfection of body, and obviously a natural aptitude for the game.'

Blackwood invited Jack to travel to London for a try-out at the Stadium Club. He was overjoyed, and Pa could see it. After looking at him for a few seconds, Pa said he would object no longer. 'In any event,' he remarked, 'there is no harm in Jack having a trial with a good professional.'

Jack did not quickly forget his first ever trip to London one morning at the end of August 1930. He and Pa arrived at the Stadium Club at about 12 noon for the try-out, and an hour later when the members were seated for lunch, Jack stepped into the ring to face Ted Coveney, a strong, well built professional. Not as tall as the Welshman, he was a stone or so heavier, but quite genial. Nevertheless, he was there to do a job for the syndicate.

They had a real set-to for three rounds, although Ted did take things easy in the opening session. In rounds two and three, however, he really opened up. The diners stopped eating and some even rose excitedly from their seats and clustered around the ring. At the end of the three rounds there was generous applause.

Coveney was a true pro, and after having a bath, went to Jack's dressing room.' Young fellow, I don't know anything about you,' he said, 'but you hit me harder and cleaner than any man I've fought for months.'

'Where the devil do you get that punch from?' he continued. 'You'll beat far more than will beat you, and I don't care where you pick 'em.'

'I like the look of the boy.' Blackwood told Pa immediately the try-out was over. 'Say the word and we will join forces to give him every chance to make good.'

After further discussions, a three year contract was agreed. During that period the syndicate would receive one third of all Jack's earnings out of which they would pay all the costs of training, travel and entertainment.

Clauses in the contract stipulated that; Jack would have ten fights under the direction of the Stadium Club, mostly on a Monday evening; he would always be top of the bill, and receive a purse of £5 for each fight; and he would continue to train with his father at the Lynn Institute. It was agreed that Jack would travel to London by train for each contest and return to Cardiff the same night.

Each member of the syndicate had specific skills – Jones and Blackwood the know-how, influence, money and desire to produce a world-class heavyweight boxer merely for the pleasure of it; Pa Petersen, the manipulative skill and knowledge of training, and Jack the ability to fight. Fred Howard, who was Managing Director of the Stadium Club, subsequently joined the syndicate and worked throughout the period of agreement.

Over the years, a great deal was written about the syndicate but according to Jack most of it was rubbish. There were occasions when certain difficulties had to be overcome, but in the world of

18

professional boxing there are inevitably more obstacles to be faced than in almost any other profession.

Once everything was agreed, Blackwood took Jack aside. 'Always go straight, train for your fights, live clean and fight clean,' he implored. 'Improve your mind and your mental outlook because there are far more things in this game than even you or your father think.' Although they were the men with the money, Blackwood and Jones always made it clear they had only one desire – to produce a young man who was a clean, well-behaved fighter who would bring credit to British heavyweight boxing.

* * *

The Stadium Club was situated at Holborn close to the west end of London, and had staged many great contests in the past. When Jack made his professional debut there on 28 September 1931, it was packed to capacity and the London pressmen were out in force.

Jack's opponent was Bill Partridge from Poplar, a huge man with a weight advantage of more than three stones. This, however, counted for nothing because the young Welshman turned in a solid performance, stopping Partridge in the fourth round.

Varying his attacks cleverly, Jack completely bemused the Londoner who could do little against accurate, powerful shots to both head and body. In the fourth round, tremendous punches to the head put Partridge down for a count of 'seven'. On rising, he was immediately clubbed to the floor for 'eight'. Although he bravely climbed to his feet, he was at the Welshman's mercy and the fight was stopped.

As Jack was escorted back to his dressing room by his father, they were joined by Charlie Barnett, a Welsh journalist. Although Jack was still quite tense, he relaxed and smiled as soon as they reached the dressing room. As emotion came to the surface, he playfully punched his father on the chin, and Pa responded by throwing his arms around Jack and kissing him on the cheek.

At an appropriate moment, Barnett quietly took Pa aside and suggested that in future, Jack should be matched with smaller men.

'No, we want them big,' responded Pa angrily. 'The bigger the better.' In years to come, however, those words would bring Pa Petersen's judgement into question because physically Jack was only a light-heavyweight.

* * *

JACK PETERSEN

FORM No. 4

British Boxing Board of Control (1929).

BOXER.

APPLICATION FOR LICENCE.

(*Office Use only.*)

Application Record.

Fee ; 5s. 0d. per Annum.

Received **30 MAR. 1932**

Received payment. 5/•

30 MAR. 1932

Checked ....

Photos *16. 4. 32*

Receipt sent.

Date approved **30** MAR 1932

Licence No. *4709*

– 7 APR 1932

Reg. No. *B 2054*

OK Welsh Branch

Name {
  Professional *JACK PETERSEN*
  in full { Private *JOHN CHARLES PETERSEN*

Address *6 ST JOHNS SQUARE 24. Tydraw Road Roath Park* *CARDIFF*

PHONE: TRAINING: *CARDIFF 4350* *CARDIFF*

PRIVATE: *CARDIFF 7111* *SOUTH WALES*

Age *20* Nationality *BRITISH*

Exact Fighting Weight at the }
time of application for Licence } *12 STONE 8 LBS.*

Name of Manager *JOHN T. PETERSEN*

I hereby apply for a Licence as a Boxer, and if this Licence is granted me I declare to adhere strictly to the Rules of The British Boxing Board of Control (1929) as printed, and abide by any further Rules or alteration to existing Rules as may be passed. I agree to pay the Fee in accordance with the above.

Date *March 10th 1932.* Signed *Jack Petersen*

Witness *Harry T. Jones*

Address *13 The Hayes Cardiff*

(Two Passport Photographs, full face without a hat, must accompany this application.)
(Manager's name to be filled in only when a contract has been entered into and signed.)

MUST BE WRITTEN IN INK.

HG8214-30

Jack Petersen's application for a professional boxing licence.

Many experts were impressed by the way in which Petersen beat Partridge, and predicted that he had a tremendous future. Jack impressed even more two weeks later when, in his second contest, he beat Alf Noble, an experienced London heavyweight, in just 30 seconds of the first round.

A left hook to the jaw floored Noble for a count of 'two'. When he rose, there was a brisk exchange of punches at close quarters before the Welshman landed a hard right to the chin. Noble sank to his knees, fell forward on to his face and was counted out.

Just seven days later, Jack scored an even quicker victory, the fight lasting only 22 seconds. His opponent was 'Big' Jim Campbell, a giant of a man from Camberwell in South London, who stood six feet four inches tall and weighed over 17 stones. Just four punches were needed for Petersen to score the quickest ever ending to a heavyweight contest at the Holborn Stadium.

Campbell advanced at the opening bell in a crouch, but as he attempted to throw a left, Petersen, beautifully poised, smashed two terrific rights to the jaw. Campbell crashed to the floor for a count of 'seven'. On rising, he was very groggy and an easy target for the ambitious young Welshman who hammered two more rights to the chin. The Londoner fell to the floor, rolled over, and was counted out.

Ex-guardsman, Jeff Wilson from Windsor, was Petersen's next opponent. They met at Holborn Stadium the following week, and Jack scored another relatively easy victory. Conceding half a stone in weight, he soon had his opponent in trouble, flooring him for a count of 'three' in the opening round.

Wilson, however, withstood everything that was thrown at him, causing Petersen to become wild and over-enthusiastic as he strove to land a knockout punch.

It wasn't until round four that the ex-guardsman was in trouble again. Then after forcing his man to the ropes, Jack landed some telling blows. Wilson held on desperately, but as they broke from a clinch, he was bleeding badly from a gash above his left eye. It was a nasty injury which forced him to retire at the end of the round.

Seven days later, Jack was taken the distance for the first time. His opponent, George Porter of Nottingham, was a rugged, experienced man who had been a sparring partner to Len Harvey.

For the first time as a professional, the Welshman enjoyed a weight advantage, but it counted for nothing. It was not until the final round that he succeeded in flooring Porter. The Nottingham man took a count of 'eight' but survived until the bell. Although Jack won every round, he failed to land a single damaging punch.

In his next fight, Petersen was taken the distance again, this time by substitute, George Brown of Stepney. During the contest, the young Welshman showed the first signs of weakness in his make-up as a fighter. He had always looked good when he got his opponents going early, but against Brown, a lack of early success caused his technique to desert him.

Brown, a former London policeman, was never in serious trouble at any stage of the fight. In the second round, Petersen was caught with some particularly heavy shots, and fought the next three rounds in a complete daze. He became disorientated, and at times was at a loss as how to deal with his cagey opponent.

As Pa Petersen was getting his son off the stool for the start of the last round, Jack mumbled something about the third round always being a poor one for him. 'Third round be blowed,' snapped Pa, 'this is the sixth and last, and you've got to win it or lose the fight.'

Although he attacked throughout the round, Jack made no impression on the tough Londoner and had to be content with a points victory. The fight, however, stuck in his mind for years to come because he realised how close he had come to losing.

In those early days, Jack was billed as the Stadium Club protegé, and received a great deal of public attention. He met many prominent gentlemen who extended great kindness and encouragement to him at all times. They included Douglas Furber the playwright, Lord Castlerosse, Joseph Hislop the tenor, Lupino Lane and Sir Harry Lauder. Several never missed a night at the club whenever Jack was boxing.

The young Welshman also became a favourite with the club chef, Mr. Sullivan, and at every visit for months, his appetite was well looked after.

* * *

Jack's performances against Porter and Brown had not been impressive, and caused his backers some concern. Pa and Billy Diamond were convinced their man needed some sharpening up if he was to progress.

Four days after the fight with Brown, two special contests were arranged for Jack against experienced London heavyweights, Joe Mullins and Ted Mason. Both were for real but behind closed doors at the Lynn Institute before a strictly private gathering of local sportsmen.

Both fights were scheduled for ten rounds, and Jack was really fired up. He faced the stockily built Mullins first, and in the opening round showed onlookers what tremendous progress he had made since turning professional. The Londoner was bewildered by the speed of Petersen's punches, and in the second round was knocked out by a tremendous right to the point of the jaw.

Ted Mason did not provide any sterner opposition as Jack again showed tremendous speed to drive him around the ring. Midway through the second round he delighted the audience when he landed a solid right hook to score his second knockout in a matter of minutes.

* * *

Back at the Stadium Club three days later, the Welshman looked much sharper as he faced Tom Waites of Blackheath. Showing tremendous power in both hands, he soon had the Londoner in trouble. When two solid punches to the chin had Waites reeling, the fight was stopped after just 60 seconds of the opening round.

Jack was back at the Holborn Stadium Club the following week to face Jack Stratton of Highbury in what was his stiffest test to date. He acquitted himself well and was not extended at any time during the fight. Using his advantage in reach, he scored easily with his left, and boxed with more restraint than in previous fights. At the end of the six rounds, he was a good points winner.

On 7 December, Petersen had a return fight with George Brown who had frustrated him four weeks earlier. Again the tough man from London's east end survived the Welshman's heavy punching and Jack had to be content with another points victory. In effect, it was a perfect workout for the most important fight of his career, scheduled for just seven days time.

* * *

Although Jack's professional career had got off to a thoroughly satisfactory start, there was great disappointment amongst boxing fans in Wales. They were anxious to see him in action and felt cheated that he was on show in London instead of his native Cardiff. Enthusiasts followed his progress with great interest, but it was not until 14 December 1931 that the new 'golden boy' of Welsh boxing was given a hometown contest.

By that time he had progressed steadily, winning all of his nine contests within the space of nine weeks. His handlers decided to move him up in class, and matched him with Leo Bandias, the experienced light-heavyweight champion of Australia at Greyfriars Hall. A large charity promotion was being organised by a committee comprising of staff and heads of department of the *Western Mail, South Wales Echo,* and *South West* newspapers. Proceeds from the event would be donated to the Newspaper Press Fund, and a top of the bill contest featuring Petersen would guarantee a sell-out house.

The chance to fight in front of his own people meant a great deal to the young Welshman, and he trained with exceptional enthusiasm. There was an added incentive that this would be his first fight for real money, his share of the purse being £100 which he viewed as a tremendous amount.

The event attracted a great deal of interest, and massive preparation was therefore required to cater for the crowds expected to attend. A willing army of helpers considerably transformed Greyfriars Hall in order that spectators would get a good view of the ring from wherever they sat.

The Great Western Railway and Rhondda Tramway Company made special arrangements to cope with the anticipated flood of fans from throughout South Wales. The last train from Cardiff Queen Street to the Rhymney Valley would be delayed to allow fans to stay at the venue until the end of the fight. Buses to the Rhondda, Ferndale and Treherbert would be delayed until after 11pm.

Petersen had really captured the imagination of the Welsh public. One newspaper compared his appearance in Cardiff with that of Jack 'Kid' Berg topping a bill at the Royal Albert Hall in London.

On the night of the fight, the doors of Greyfriars Hall were opened at 5.15pm in order to cope with the capacity crowd of 8,000. Although boxing was not due to commence until 7.15pm, those fans arriving early were entertained by a band.

The fight was a fitting climax to one of the greatest nights in the history of Welsh boxing. Many distinguished sportsmen and businessmen were in attendance, and had the priviledge of witnessing one of the most absorbing heavyweight fights staged at Cardiff for many years.

As the principals climbed into the ring, they appeared to be well matched physically. Petersen was taller with a longer reach. Bandias, seconded by the good Australian heavyweight, George Cook, was stocky and much thicker set. He was a first-class fighter of considerable experience, and an ideal opponent for the Welshman at this stage of his career. The only opponent they had in common was Jack Stratton who Petersen outpointed on 23 November. Bandias, however, had stopped Stratton in three rounds a week earlier.

At the opening bell, Petersen shot from his corner and launched a whirlwind, two-fisted attack on the bemused Australian. Although the fight was scheduled for ten rounds, Jack did not let up and bombarded Bandias with lefts and rights throughout the round.

Another big attack had the Aussie reeling in round two, and an early ending looked imminent. Bandias, however, was an extremely tough character and countered well with good shots to the body.

In the third, the Welshman unleashed a tremendous right cross which staggered Leo. A similar punch seconds later floored him for a count of 'eight'. Jack tried desperately to finish the fight, but his experienced opponent stayed clear of trouble until the bell.

A thunderous right to the temple at the start of round four stunned Bandias. Although he swayed noticeably, he remained upright, soaked up the punishment, and again survived to hear the bell at the end of the round.

The Australian held his own during some hard, close-quarter exchanges in the fifth. One hard right from Petersen was very low but referee, William E. Allen, was unsighted. Despite being in obvious pain, Bandias carried on without a word of protest. It was a demonstration of true sportsmanship which won him the admiration of everyone who saw what occurred.

Bandias fought back well during the middle rounds and gave as good as he got. There was no clinching or mauling, and in the eighth they traded punches in a tremendous melee which had the huge crowd roaring with excitement.

The Australian was in a bad way in round nine, but battled on courageously. In the last round, Petersen battered him around the ring with sustained volleys of punches. Bravely and resolutely, Bandias stayed on his feet. He had nothing left but pride, but this kept him upright until the final bell.

After ten wonderful rounds, Jack was the clear winner on points. He had fought his way into the hearts of the sports' loving Welsh public with a display like a warrior of old. As his arm was raised, the Greyfriars Hall was a scene of turbulent emotion because people saw him, not only as a fighter, but as a local hero.

Bandias had played his part in a magnificent fight, displaying courage and stamina of the highest quality. As they left the ring, the massive cheers were as much for him as the local hero.

Within a few days, Bandias challenged Jack to a return. London promoter Charlie Rose wrote to William E. Allen, Boxing Editor of the *South Wales Echo*, stating that whilst the Australian accepted defeat, he was used to fighting over three minute rounds. The contest had been over two minute rounds, and Leo claimed that he had not been able to get properly warmed up. He therefore challenged the Welshman to a return over 15 three minute rounds.

The Bandias fight had shown Jack to be a heavyweight of great potential, and, therefore, very hot property. He had beaten the Australian convincingly so his handlers saw no advantage in agreeing to a return.

* * *

Pa Petersen used to tell an amusing story in connection with the Bandias fight. The morning after the contest, he was stopped by a man who asked where Jack lived. 'Whitchurch at present.' replied Pa, 'but we are going to Porth-y-Castell.'

The man clearly didn't understand what Pa had said, and instantly remarked, 'Bought a castle have you? Well, that's not bad after a few fights. Hope you're not beginning to fancy yourselves.'

* * *

Seven days after beating Bandias, Jack was back at the Holborn Stadium Club in what posters described as his first public appearance in London. Previous contests had been fought exclusively in front of members of the Stadium Club.

His opponent was former British Army champion, Gunner Bennett, now a boxing instructor at Eton Public School, and the contest, promoted by Sam Russell, was over ten rounds.

Bennett, a clever, experienced man, put up an aggressive display, and was always looking to land a knockout punch. Petersen therefore had to change tactics and not mix it in the way to which he was accustomed. His defensive skills were superb, and his accurate left jab which he used throughout the contest, gradually wore Bennett down.

Solid right hooks to the jaw in round three and again in the sixth, did have the former Army champion in trouble, but he gallantly refused to go down.

The pace of the fight would have done justice to lightweights, and by the end of the seventh, Bennett looked exhausted. Realising he faced a durable opponent, Jack still took no chances and sensibly stuck to his jab to win the fight on points by a wide margin.

MAKE A NOTE OF THIS DATE

FIRST LONDON PUBLIC APPEARANCE OF JACK PETERSEN

BOXING

THE STADIUM CLUB, 85, HIGH HOLBORN, W.C.1

(By courtesy of the Committee).

Doors open 7.15 p.m. **MONDAY, DECEMBER 21st, 1931** Commence 8 p.m.

Promoted by SAM RUSSELL.

GREAT TEN ROUNDS HEAVY-WEIGHT CONTEST.

JACK PETERSEN v GUNNER BENNETT

(Undefeated). (Windsor).

SPECIAL TEN ROUNDS CRUISER-WEIGHT CONTEST.

EDDIE PHILLIPS v JACK STRATTON

(Undefeated), (Bow). (Stepney).

TICKETS may be obtained from Keith Prowse and Co., Ltd. (all branches); Alfred Hays and Co., Ltd. (all branches); The District Messenger and Theatre Ticket Co., Ltd. (all branches); and from the Stadium Club, 85, High Holborn, W.C.1. (Telephone: Holborn 6763).

LADIES SPECIALLY INVITED.

PRICES: 24/-, 12/-, 6/-: Unreserved, 2/6 (all including Tax)

A LIGHT-WEIGHT COMPETITION WILL BE HELD ON MONDAY, JANUARY 25, 1932, FOR THE STADIUM CLUB LIGHT-WEIGHT CHAMPIONSHIP.

AND HEAVYWEIGHT COMPETITION

Between eight men picked from the following:— (The competition will finish the same evening.)
Ex-Guardsman Gater, Leo Bandias, Phil Barnes, George Porter, Ted Mason, Tony Arpino, Jeff Wilson, Jim Savage, Jack Langford, Jack Marsh, Seaman Tim Foley, Ex-Marine Smith, Ex-Marine Trinder, Arthur Fowler, George Smith, George Brown, Seaman Harvey, Frank Fowler.

FREE COMPETITION FOR BOXING FANS.

Leave in list eight names and cross out the remainder. Put X against the one you nominate as the winner. If your selection agrees with the majority list selected by the Press and you also nominate the winner you win a £5 prize. In the event of a tie prize will be divided. Cut out and post your list to Boxing Competition, 85, High Holborn, W.C.1, before 12 p.m. Sunday.

Name ....

Address ....

Date ....

Poster advertising Jack Petersen's fight with Gunner Bennett.

Petersen was highly regarded in London, and the backers of the Stadium Club announced elaborate plans for him to be used as the cornerstone of a scheme to find a future heavyweight champion. The night he beat Bennett, a heavyweight competition was staged. It was planned to match the winner with Petersen for a purse of £100. In the final, Seaman Harvey of Chatham beat Leo Bandias on points, but for undisclosed reasons a fight with the Welshman was never staged.

* * *

Outside boxing, Jack Petersen was a Rover with the Rhiwbina Scout Troop in East Glamorgan. On 22 December 1931, the Scout Council staged a boxing tournament at the Rhiwbina Scout Hall. Although he had taken part in a gruelling contest against Gunner Bennett the previous evening, Jack boxed an entertaining three rounds exhibition with Andrew Pettigrew, a promising young Welsh amateur heavyweight from St. Fagans.

27

Jack's appearance ensured that a capacity crowd was in attendance and in appreciation of his efforts he was presented with a silver replica of a boxer. It was later announced that he would be donating a fine silver cup known as the 'Jack Petersen Cup' to be boxed for at an Inter-Troop competition between scout troops throughout East Glamorgan.

3

STEP UP IN CLASS

For his next contest, Jack was back at Holborn Stadium where, on 11 January 1932, he faced Jack Newitt of Birmingham. Although he scored an easy first round knockout, he did have to endure a period of some anxiety.

A powerful right to the jaw sent Newitt crashing to the floor, his head striking the boards heavily. He bravely rose at the count of 'four' but was quickly sent down again from another vicious right.

The full count was a mere formality, but Newitt looked seriously hurt. He was carried unconscious to his corner, and as Petersen looked on anxiously, his seconds worked frantically to revive him. Newitt showed no signs of recovery, and was eventually carried from the ring. It was only after lengthy attention from a doctor that he regained his senses.

The power of the Welshman's punching was making him a real threat in the heavyweight division. Knowing his popularity, his backers issued a challenge through the *South Wales Echo*, to any man in the country. Jack himself particularly wanted to pit his skills against British light-heavyweight champion, Harry Crossley. He also issued challenges to Eddie Steele, Don Shortland and Jack Pettifer, to be supported by side-stakes of any amount.

Meanwhile, Pontypridd idol, Frank Moody, stated that he had plenty of fight left in him. Backed by a group of wealthy sportsmen, he offered to meet Petersen anywhere, anytime, over any distance for a substantial purse and side-stakes. Although Jack and his backers initially showed interest in the challenge, his immediate task was to prepare for a fight against Dick Power from Risca, Monmouthshire.

Power had been adopted as Welsh heavyweight champion in April 1928, so the fight would be a further step up in class for Jack. Although it would be expensive to stage, promoters from various parts of South Wales showed interest.

The fight was eventually staged at Greyfriars Hall on 3 February 1932 as a replacement for a proposed world bantamweight title fight between Al Brown of Panama, and Luigi Quadrini on a promotion in aid of Cardiff Royal Infirmary.

Petersen and Power were contacted soon after the Brown-Quadrini fight fell through. They quickly reached agreement, and articles were signed at the offices of the *Western Mail* and *South Wales Echo* on 13 January. Power insisted on being allowed three weeks in which to prepare, whilst Petersen agreed to fight over 15 three minute rounds for the first time in his career.

The contest was such an attraction that the Welsh Area Council of the British Boxing Board of Control called a meeting at the Barry Hotel in Cardiff the following day. It was unanimously agreed that it should be recognised as being for the Welsh heavyweight title.

Although Jack had made great progress since turning professional, he was warned that Power was a dangerous opponent. He was in the class just below the best in the country. Amongst the men he had beaten were Big Jim Campbell (ko.2) at Caerphilly, and Jack Pettifer, who he beat in two rounds at the Royal Albert Hall.

It was originally planned for Petersen to have a warm-up fight against either Charlie Hickman or Dick Foley. Provided he was successful, he would meet Don Shortland in a final warm-up before facing Power. Those plans were, however, suddenly cancelled when Jack decided that nothing should interfere with his preparations to become heavyweight champion of Wales.

Jack trained at the Lynn Institute, and with chief sparring partner Selwyn Ford, most was done behind closed doors. 'We know what we are up against,' Pa Petersen told a *South Wales Echo* reporter, 'and we have a great deal at stake. If Jack wins, he will be booked for a further three contests culminating in a match with Harry Crossley for the British light-heavyweight title.'

Power, meanwhile, trained hard at the Parrott Inn at Ynysddu in the Sirhowy Valley, and took off nearly a stone in three weeks. Visitors to his camp were impressed by his form. In an interview with the *South Wales Echo*, he said, 'I have never felt so keen about a contest in my life. I believe I can beat Petersen, but if he should win then I shall shake him by the hand.'

The demand for tickets was again enormous. Ringside seats cost one guinea, while 3000 fans could watch from the galleries for two shillings and fourpence.

The contest, organised by the Welsh National Sporting Association in conjunction with the *South Wales Echo*, was a complete sell-out. Boxing was due to commence at 7pm so the doors of Greyfriars Hall opened at 5.30pm to facilitate the smooth entry of the 8000 fans. A popular musical group, *The Colney Beach Five*, were in attendance to provide pre-fight entertainment.

As he got into the ring Jack noticed that Power appeared to be rather nervous, and thought to himself, 'I think I am going to be champion of Wales in a few minutes.' It was an under-estimation because the fight ended sensationally after just 21 seconds.

After some preliminary sparring, Jack drew Power into a neutral corner, then jerked his head back with a sharp left uppercut. Dick was hurt and reeled along the ropes into his own corner. Petersen followed up with a vicious left hook to the body. As Power's guard dropped, a mighty right crashed against his jaw. The man from Risca fell like a log, his head crashing against the boards with resounding force.

Twice Dick attempted to rise but keeled over on to his side to be counted out by referee, Mr. C. B. Thomas. He remained stretched out on the floor for some while, but fortunately recovered shortly after being carried to his corner.

Greyfriars Hall was packed to capacity, and many fans had scarcely settled in their seats when the fight was all over. The swiftness of Petersen's victory seemed to take the breath away from a large majority, and some seconds elapsed before pandemonium broke out.

As a token of his victory Jack was presented with a fine silver cup donated by a London businessman who wished to remain annoymous. As he left the ring, the new champion was mobbed by excited admirers. Many in the crowd burst into song with, '*For he's a jolly good fellow.*'

Dick Power took defeat like the good sportsman he was, and for many years was one of Jack's best friends and admirers.

Within ten minutes of leaving the ring, Jack was taken by car to the Cardiff Empire Music Hall. His hands still bandaged, he received a tumultuous reception when he appeared on the stage to be introduced as the new Welsh heavyweight champion. He was then compelled to make his first public speech. 'What I said, I haven't the foggiest idea,' he said some years later. 'All I know is that the crowd gave me a wonderful reception.'

By this time, Pa Petersen had become more enthusiastic about his son's entry into the professional ranks. Although he was a hard task master in training, he gave Jack all the support he could have wanted. Whenever he tried out a new punch or move, Pa would would watch carefully and then pass appropriate comments.

'That may be alright in the gym, but try it against a man who knows the game and you'll pay a pretty price for experimenting,' he would remark. 'Only real champions can take liberties, and you're not a champion yet by a long cheek.'

Despite everything, Pa was already hatching a scheme to bring Jack right into line for a fight for the British light-heavyweight championship. His mind was always working a move or two ahead, but at the time said nothing to his son about what he was thinking.

* * *

Jack had a huge following in Wales which was growing all the time. His bouts against Bandias and Power had been sell-outs, fans having flocked from the valleys in their hundreds to see him in action. The Power fight had made a profit of £767 which was donated to the Cardiff Infirmary.

The young Welshman was well aware of the situation and within a few days of beating Power, stated that he was anxious to box in front of a real Rhondda Valley audience. Although efforts were made for him to top a promotion at the Empire, Tonypandy, no suitable opponent could be found.

Jack was still under contract to the Stadium Club who matched him with Don Shortland of Doncaster. They had been due to meet on 1 February but Jack pulled out to concentrate on his preparations to face Dick Power. Again the fight fell through and instead Jack faced George Slack of Doncaster at Holborn Stadium on 22 February.

Slack was very experienced, and in some respects the best man Jack had faced. Only five weeks earlier he had taken Len Harvey 15 rounds in London, and had also lost on points to him at Leeds in December 1930. Being very stocky with a thick neck and solid shoulders, Slack was several inches shorter than the Welshman. He looked extremely powerful, and as he climbed into the ring Jack's immediate thoughts were that he would be difficult to put away.

Petersen did not appear as composed as usual and he was not helped when the start of the fight was delayed for several minutes due to an argument over the gloves. When the contest finally got underway, he tore from his corner and attacked wildly. In his desperation to end matters quickly, the young Welshman's punches were erractic and few found their target. Slack found it easy to counter and move away from danger, and it was fortunate for Petersen that he was not punching correctly.

In round two, Slack was floored for a count of 'seven' by a wild right to the side of the head. When he rose Petersen's efforts to finish the fight were again wild and the Yorkshireman kept out of trouble for the remainder of the round. Although under severe pressure during the third and fourth, he was in no real danger of going down.

Early in round five, Jack finally found the range, and a big right hand to the chin floored Slack for a count of 'nine'. On rising a similar, perfectly timed shot knocked him clean off his feet. George crashed to the floor on all fours, and although he made a gallant attempt to rise, rolled over on to his stomach to be counted out as his cornerman threw in the towel.

After the fight, it was revealed that quite a number of people had backed Slack to halt Petersen's progress. Jack admitted that the Yorkshireman was a difficult opponent. 'Believe me, I was very glad that the fight did not go any further,' he said in an interview a few days later.

Although he eventually scored a fine victory, Jack's impetuosity was nearly his downfall. He had never been so wild and erratic, and against a more correct and damaging puncher, the outcome could have been very different.

* * *

Following the style of his victory over Dick Power, Petersen was being talked about as a champion in the not too distant future. Although comparisons were being made with Georges Carpentier, his handlers believed that he needed one more good test before challenging for major honours.

With Pa completely reconciled to his son's career as a professional, he asked him one day, 'How would you like to meet Charlie Smith over fifteen rounds? He's a clever, experienced fighter with a marvellous defence, and one of the best men in the country today. What do you say?'

Jack's response was the same as it was to all suggested opponents. 'That's up to you. If you think I'm ready, that's good enough for me!'

It was an extremely attractive contest which appealed to promoters in both Wales and London. When negotiations commenced, the Stadium Club insisted that the fight must be under their direction and in their ring. Fred Howard set things in motion with a purse offer of £200 but the club, acting on behalf of Petersen, eventually agreed to listen to offers from any promoter.

William E. Allen, acting on behalf of a prominent Welsh

businessman, eventually secured home-ground advantage for Petersen by putting up a purse of £550. Pa Petersen, however, would not agree to the fight without side-stakes. After further negotiation it was agreed that the purse would be split on a 60-40 basis to winner and loser, and each man would put up a side-stake of £150.

Petersen and Smith came face to face a week or two later when they attended the Stadium Club to sign the articles. With a genial smile on his face, Charlie went up to Jack and they shook hands. 'From that moment, I liked him,' Jack recalled years later. He did, however, have a fleeting impression that Pa was rushing him a shade too quickly because Smith looked so big and strong – a real hard man.

The fight was set for Greyfriars Hall on Easter Monday, 28 March 1932. As soon as the articles were signed, all monies were deposited with the Welsh Area Council of the British Boxing Board of Control. As a gesture of impartiality, the names of four Board of Control appointed referees were put into a hat, and that of Moss Deyong was drawn to officiate.

* * *

Charlie Smith was 27 years old and by far the most experienced man Jack had faced. He had met some of the best heavyweights in Britain and Europe. In November the previous year he had been outpointed by Reggie Meen for the vacant British title. In previous fights in 1930, however, he had twice beaten Meen, on points and inside the distance. He had also met Larry Gains twice, losing on points in December 1930, and by a ninth round knockout in March 1931.

The Petersen camp were under no illusions about the task Jack faced. Training therefore commenced as soon as terms for the fight were agreed. The recent victory over George Slack, however, made recruitment of sparring partners extremely difficult. A number of top men who were approached showed very little interest, and Jack even travelled to London specifically to try to recruit helpers. An appeal was also made to the patriotism of Welshmen, George Smith and Jerry Daley, to come to the rescue. Eventually, Jack secured the help of the giant Northerner, Don Shortland, who stood six feet, five inches tall, and weighed over fifteen stones. He moved into the Lynn Institute training quarters for the final week of preparation.

Don was a commanding figure, and after arriving at Cardiff Station, made his way on foot through St. Mary Street on route to

St. Johns Square. There was an air of menace about him, and people he passed in the street knew that the giant stranger had arrived in town as sparring partner to the new Welsh hope of heavyweight boxing.

Shortland had gone 15 rounds with Charlie Smith and also fought Reggie Meen in his own back yard in 1930. In an interview he said he had come to Cardiff determined to convince the Welsh people that Petersen was not all he was being cracked up to be. There were rumours that he was not going to pull any punches in sparring because he thought Jack was responsible for their proposed fights in recent months, being called off.

The main purpose for calling Shortland to Cardiff was for him to oppose Petersen in a 'try-out' contest a few days before the Smith fight. Although interest was enormous, there was an air of mystery about what was occurring because affairs were conducted in relative privacy. The only people admitted for the 'try-out' were six London sportsmen, a small group of Cardiff sportsmen, the promoters, and a few carefully chosen reporters. When a *South Wales Echo* reporter arrived at the Lynn, he found the doors were firmly locked. Twenty-five minutes of knocking brought no response.

There was complete silence as Petersen and Shortland faced each other over three, three minute rounds wearing 16 ounce gloves. The big Yorkshireman really put Jack through his paces, demonstrating a sharp left hand and a more than adequate defence. He was resilient and stood up well to the heavy punches the Welshman unloaded on him.

Jack's backers were delighted with the session because their man looked tremendous. He finished the session with a brisk few rounds with his regular spar-mate, Selwyn Ford.

* * *

There was an atmosphere of great excitement in Cardiff throughout the day of the fight. Charlie Smith arrived in the Welsh capital looking in peak condition after a month's hard training at The Black Bull at Whetstone. Although he was vastly the more experienced man, it was the Welshman who started as a firm odds-on favourite in the pre-fight betting. Smith's manager, Dan Sullivan, however, was so confident of his man's chances that he laid bets of £150 on him to win.

Greyfriars Hall was again packed to capacity, and several thousand fans were left outside in the surrounding streets. It seemed that every sporting man, woman and boy in South Wales was determined to see the fight, or get as close to the venue as possible.

When Petersen and his party arrived, they had great difficulty getting into the venue, but the inconvenience just served to steel Jack to the task ahead. Inside, the atmosphere was electric, with the packed, predominately Welsh crowd expecting their man to deliver.

The contrast between the two men as they stood beneath the glaring arc lights, was incredible. Petersen, giving away about a stone and a half, was tall, lean and good looking, while Smith was clearly much older. He was stocky, powerful and stern looking, and although he bore the scars of many battles gone by, he looked trained to perfection.

What was always an attractive fight between a rising young star and an experienced, seasoned professional, turned out to be one of the greatest heavyweight contests ever seen in Wales. In fact, it must rank as one of the finest in the history of British boxing.

At the opening bell, Jack leapt from his corner and launched a vicious two-fisted attack. He switched his punches from head to body, and one powerful right to the jaw rocked Smith back on his heels. The Londoner, however, was extremely durable and his defence masterful. He covered up, ducked and moved away, and Petersen soon realised that try as he did, Charlie had a counter for ever move. He was an old hand who had seen it all before.

The Welshman did have some success with single heavy shots in rounds two and three, but Smith was beginning to dictate matters with stiff left jabs to the face. He also hooked well to the body, and his persistance and accuracy had Jack confused.

Although he continued to attack furiously, Petersen could not catch his man cleanly or pin him down long enough to do serious damage. Many of his punches were taken on the arms or gloves as Charlie gradually got the measure of him. Jack's attacks were wild, and by rushing in recklessly, he was playing into the Londoner's hands.

As the fight wore on, Smith scored more freely but still took some hefty digs. He wobbled badly in round five from a right to the chin, and in the sixth was very shaky after taking a pile-driving right to the stomach. Each time, however, his immaculate skill and backward shuffles took him away from danger.

The fight settled into a pattern during the middle rounds as the Welshman was picked apart by immaculate left jabs. He was becoming exhausted, and confusion was written all over his face.

As the rounds passed, he was pounded by stiff left jabs which caused him facial damage.

Showing supreme ringcraft, Smith had assumed control of the fight and exposed the Welsh prospect as being very raw. He enticed Jack to go at him, and then countered with straight punches to the face and heavy left hooks to the body.

In sheer frustration, the young Welshman frequently lashed out wildly but invariably just hit thin air. By the end of the eighth, he was tiring badly and his legs trembled as he slumped to his stool.

'Now you've fought him all over the ring for eight rounds, what are you going to do next?' demanded Pa as he bent over and wiped Jack down with the sponge. 'Don't you think it's time to make him do some of the work?'

Jack was not clear what Pa was saying, and replied that he would continue to do his best, but his legs were like lead. 'Then take it easy this round and the next,' advised Pa. 'Skip around as you do in the gym when you are a bit stiff. That's sure to puzzle him.'

The change of tactics had exactly the effect on Smith that Pa predicted. He was bemused as Jack danced around him throughout the ninth round, throwing only the occasional left jab to the face. Unfortunately, this approach was short lived, and the Welshman's punches became wild again in the tenth, allowing Smith to regain control.

Although Jack was steadier on his feet, and showed more confidence during rounds ten, eleven and twelve, he was still taking too many punches. The crowd had become silent, and many sat disillusioned and resigned to the fact that their hero was about to taste defeat for the first time as a professional. By the twelfth, his face was a crimson mask. Cut over both eyes, his nose and mouth bleeding heavily, he looked in a sorry state. Only a knockout could prevent Smith from winning.

Both men were extremely tired, but then towards the end of round thirteen, Jack suddenly gave his fans fresh hope. A big attack caught Smith off guard, and as he retreated, the Welshman followed up with a battery of heavy punches. As Charlie's knees buckled Petersen drove a left hook to the body followed by a crashing right to the chin. The Londoner fell untidily to the floor, with one glove hanging over the bottom rope.

There was wild excitement amongst the spectators as everyone thought Smith was 'out' and the fight was over. There was so much noise that few heard the bell to end the round with the count at 'seven'.

Some people actually climbed into the ring to congratulate Petersen who was completely bemused as Pa and the other seconds dragged him to his corner. He was pushed to his stool and told that the fight was still very much on. In the opposite corner champagne was tipped over Charlie Smith's head in a desperate effort to revive him.

Petersen started the fourteenth swinging wildly, but Smith was an old ring general and clinched whenever he could. Although he was still dazed, he ducked, weaved and smothered the Welshman's attacks, and the round developed into a tame, mauling affair. As his head cleared, Charlie still managed to pump an occasional left jab into Jack's swollen face. When the bell ended the round, the Welshman looked completely spent.

It had been an absorbing and punishing fight, full of thrills, yet few people could have predicted the sensation that was still to occur. Petersen's legs were so tired that Pa had to lift him from his stool for the start of the final round. As he faced Smith in the centre of the ring, he started skipping around, desperately trying to get his legs going for one final effort. He knew only a knockout would prevent a set-back to his career.

Sensing victory, Smith came from his corner smiling, and for the first minute and a half of the round, held Petersen at bay. Suddenly, the unexpected happened as the young Welshman, his handsome face swollen and bleeding, became a fighting fury. Tired though he was, he managed to raise one last desperate effort to snatch victory.

With magnificent courage, he tore into the fray and launched a tremendous volley of punches through Smith's guard. The Londoner was driven around the ring relentlessly by an opponent he knew he could only win by a stoppage.

Somehow, Charlie managed to stay upright, but then in a last supreme effort, Jack crashed a tremendous right to the chin. With an open target in front of him, he threw a left which thudded against the Londoner's chin with tremendous power. Every ounce of strength went into those final punches.

Smith's eyes spun, his knees dipped and he crashed to the floor like a log. As he lay motionless, deprived of a spectactular victory, the whole audience took up the count. There was less than half a minute of the contest left when referee, Moss Deyong, spread his arms and called 'out'.

Jack was breathless as he looked down on his stricken opponent, but was very relieved. He had achieved what, for many rounds, had seemed an impossibility.

The scenes within Greyfriars Hall were incredible as crowds of wildly cheering fans from the back of the hall swarmed over chairs and barriers to get to the ringside. Many climbed into the ring, and it became so full that it was on the verge of collapse.

As Jack left the ring, people stood on chairs cheering and waving, and as he made his way back to the dressing room, hundreds grabbed his hands or slapped him on the shoulders.

Charlie Smith, meanwhile, was in a bad way and had to be assisted from the ring. Back in the dressing room, the doctors found that he was suffering from stomach trouble. He also bled profusely from the mouth and at first it was feared his jaw was broken. This was later confirmed not to be the case, but his general condition confirmed the power of Petersen's punching.

Battered and bruised, the young Welshman was happy to give interviews, and still managed the soft, spirited smile everyone was getting to know so well. Resting at his home at Whitchurch the following day, he said it had been the hardest fight he'd ever had.

'I learned a lot of things from Smith,' said Jack. 'It was a pity one of us had to lose.'

He admitted that as they came out for the final round, he knew his whole future depended on it.

'It was a case of do or die,' he continued. 'If I didn't put Charlie away, I'd lost it.'

There were many occasions when Jack paid tribute to Smith who he described as one of the cleanest fighters he ever met. In fact, throughout the fight, the referee rarely had occasion to speak to either man. In a subsequent newspaper article, Charlie complimented Jack on his extraordinary powers of absorbing punishment which left him sore for weeks.

The fight was in the category of some of the most remarkable duels of the past. Practically every round was packed with a succession of thrills, then reached a sensational climax in that final minute. Although Jack attacked from start to finish, he had not been able to pin Smith long enough to land his devastating right.

Yet, as punch after punch smashed into his face, he battled on gallantly and never stopped punching. His bulldog spirit was undaunting and finally earned him his reward. It was surely one of the greatest efforts ever to snatch victory from the jaws of defeat.

Jack had come through his baptism of punishment and emerged victorious. In doing so, he enhanced his reputation as a great heavyweight prospect.

4

TWO BRITISH TITLES

Although Jack was rapidly becoming an idol in South Wales, the situation placed tremendous responsibility upon his young shoulders. This became evident the night he beat Dick Power. The recognition he received from civic dignitaries typified the level of interest a top boxer could command. The fact that he represented the principal city of South Wales made that responsibility even greater.

Following the victory over Charlie Smith, Trevor Wignall of the *Daily Express* described Jack as 'without question, the greatest heavyweight of his age we have had for generations.'

Other critics, however, recognised that the young Welshman needed to put on weight and build up more muscle if he were to become a threat at world level. Physically, he was still only a light-heavyweight, but at the age of just 20, he was expected to develop into a heavier man.

Success for Petersen at championship level would have a considerable bearing on the future trade of Cardiff because top class heavyweights usually attracted massive crowds. The purse of £550 which he shared with Charlie Smith was chicken-feed compared to the amount he could earn if he became heavyweight champion.

Comparisons were already being made with current champion, Reggie Meen, from Desborough, a small village in the Midlands with about 100 cottages. Meen commanded a huge following and tens of thousands flocked to Leicester whenever he boxed. At this period in time, the Midlands bore no comparison with the South Wales coalfields should Petersen eventually assume the role of British heavyweight champion.

Although Jack was very mature for his age, the reality of the situation was daunting. To know that thousands of pounds worth of trade for Cardiff over the ensuing years could depend on his success, was a frightening prospect for a lad of such tender years.

* * *

Jack's victory over Smith brought him his first front page headline – 'PETERSEN A COMING WORLD BEATER' boldly appeared in the *South Wales Echo*. The manner of his victory had made him the most talked about fighter in Britain. After the fight, referee Moss Deyong, had remarked, 'That was the greatest heavyweight fight I have ever handled.' When he wrote his autobiography 18 years later, Deyong claimed the remark still held good.

The day after the Smith fight, Pa Petersen revealed what had been a closely guarded secret. In an interview with the *South Wales Echo*, he stated that Jack went into the fight with a damaged arm. In the try-out with Don Shortland he was caught awkwardly on the elbow, and a muscle in his right arm was torn. Jack refused to pull out of the fight but it meant he had to change tactics.

Explaining their plans for the future, Pa insisted that a fight for the British light-heavyweight title was the priority. 'I am certain Jack can beat Harry Crossley,' he remarked. 'Furthermore, he will have a go at Reggie Meen or whoever is heavyweight champion of Britain. I am confident that Jack can win the heavyweight title within a year.'

Within a few days of his dramatic victory over Charlie Smith, Jack received several lucrative offers for fights. One was for him to meet French heavyweight champion, Maurice Griselle, for a hefty, yet undisclosed sum. Francois Decamps, who managed Griselle, cabled his offer to Harry Levene in London, and he in turn contacted Pa Petersen. The Welsh camp, however, showed no interest in any offer, and within a week or so their reasons became clear.

* * *

Convinced that his son was capable of winning both the light-heavyweight and heavyweight championships of Great Britain, Pa Petersen contacted the managers of Harry Crossley and Reggie Meen. Subject to terms, agreement was reached for both men to defend their titles against Jack, and he was duly accepted by the British Boxing Board of Control as the official contender for both titles.

A fight with Meen was first discussed in early April between Pa and Cardiff newsman, Charles Barnett, who suggested it looked a good thing for Jack. In a subsequent letter, Pa told Barnett to go ahead and see if he could set it up, adding that Jack would be backed by stakes of up to £500.

Barnett immediately contacted Thomas Hatton, a Midlands book collector, with offices in London. He was anxiously trying to become involved in boxing promotion, and reached agreement with the National Sporting Club to stage the fight at Wimbledon Stadium on 28 June.

Meanwhile, offers to stage the Petersen-Crossley fight were received from promoters in Wales and London. William E. Allen and Captain W. E. Willis, proprietor of the Empire Theatre, Tonypandy, represented the promoters who staged Jack's fight with Charlie Smith, and were anxious to take the fight to Cardiff. They were, however, outbid by a London syndicate who backed a new promoter. He claimed to have Crossley's signature and planned to stage the fight at Queens Road Ice Rink at Bayswater on 23 May. Impressed by what he was told at a meeting in London, Pa agreed to the fight in principle.

When Pa returned to Cardiff, Jack was astonished when he told him of the audacious programme being lined up for him.

'Well Jack, we are getting quick action now,' he said with an air of satisfaction. 'Two five hundred pound contracts booked in one day! And I am sure, son, they mean two British championships for you within the next few weeks. Aren't you happy?'

Although Jack said he was thrilled and would do his best to justify his father's confidence, he was somewhat concerned that Pa was being a bit optimistic about his ability.

Details of the fights with Crossley and Meen were revealed at a press conference on 8 April. The news came as a great disappointment to boxing fans in South Wales who would be deprived of seeing their idol in his first championship contests. Great Western Rail, however, quickly announced that special trains would run from Cardiff to Paddington to carry fans wanting to see the fights.

Within days of the announcement being made, difficulties arose in respect of both fights. Firstly, the British Boxing Board of Control issued a confusing statement in which they stated that the fight with Meen would not be advertised as being for the British heavyweight title. Only after the contest between Petersen and Crossley would they decide whether or not to recognise Petersen against Meen as for the title.

Difficulties then arose in negotiations with the London promoters over the Crossley fight, resulting in Pa refusing to deal with them further. Eventually, Fred Howard made a very good offer on behalf of the Stadium Club which was accepted by Pa and Billy Bridgewater, the manager of Crossley. As champion, Crossley would receive £700 and Jack £500, by far his largest purse to date. Equally importantly, it meant the fight would go ahead on the agreed date of 23 May.

* * *

As Jack's popularity increased, organisers of particular promotions attempted to take advantage of it to guarantee a full house. Notices appeared in areas of South Wales declaring that he would box exhibition bouts on certain promotions being staged for charity. One stated that he would box on a show at the Palais-de-Danse, Pontypridd, on 18 April. Another announced that he would box an exhibition at the Park Club, Senghenydd on 23 April, on a show staged under the control of the Welsh Amateur Boxing Association in aid of the Aber Valley Boot Fund.

Jack had not agreed to box at either show because of his heavy training schedule for his forthcoming fights. Pa Petersen therefore contacted William E. Allen, Boxing Editor of the *South Wales Echo*, who published a statement explaining the boxer's position:

> I am asked on behalf of Jack Petersen, to point out that as much as he would like to meet the wishes of charity boxing tournaments in South Wales to box exhibition contests on their shows, this is not possible at present owing to the engagements in hand. I put this forward because many posters for charity shows have contained the statement that Jack Petersen will box exhibition contests against selected opponents. That he cannot do, but he is ever ready to help the success of any charity.

* * *

Before facing Harry Crossley, Jack agreed to have a warm-up fight against Irish heavyweight, Tommy Toner, at Crystal Palace on 2 May 1932. They had been scheduled to meet three weeks earlier but Jack pulled out due to the arm injury he sustained whilst training to meet Charlie Smith.

It was a disappointing affair which ended when Toner was disqualified in the fifth round for persistant holding.

The Irishman was floored for a count of 'seven' in the second round, and on rising hung on desperately until the bell. Despite the continual demands of referee, Mr. C. H. Douglas, to clean it up, Toner continued to clinch and maul throughout rounds three and four. Jack was given no opportunity to throw punches, and in the fifth Toner was disqualified.

* * *

As part of his preparation for the Crossley fight, Jack was invited to join British Empire heavyweight champion, Larry Gains, at his training camp at Shoeburyness. Larry was due to fight Primo Carnera the week after Petersen met Crossley, and the invitation was made as a benefit to them both.

Pa, however, considered it unadvisable to move from the Lynn Institute. Jack was on familar ground and had everything at his disposal. The Lynn was one of the finest equipped gymnasiums in Britain, with everything a fighter needed to reach peak fitness.

The latest recruit to the Lynn was British welterweight champion, Jack Hood, regarded as one of the finest ring strategists in the world. Although business commitments prevented him arriving until a week before the fight, his advice greatly improved Petersen's style. As his preparations built to a peak he showed more restraint whilst still maintaining his customary aggression.

Spectators who watched the final training session believed Jack was punching harder than ever. This was confirmed when a session on the punchball had to be halted because some terrific two-fisted punching burst the leather casing.

The Welshman's power was confirmed by his chief sparring partner, Jack Stratton, a veteran of more than 100 fights, and one of the few men to have taken him the distance. 'He is the hardest hitting man I have ever been in the ring with,' said Stratton at the end of a six rounds try-out.

The fight with Crossley was on a Monday evening show at Holborn Stadium. Jack wound up his training early in order to take things easy over the weekend. He left Cardiff on the Saturday afternoon and stayed with friends at Harrow in North West London.

Petersen was aiming to become the third man from South Wales to win the British light-heavyweight title. Gypsy Daniels (Llanelli) won the title in April 1927, and Frank Moody (Pontypridd) became champion in November the same year after Daniels vacated the title. In November 1929, Crossley took the title from Moody but had not been called upon to defend it as no suitable challenger was available.

Crossley was born at Swinton in Yorkshire but brought up at Mexborough. A former pit-boy, he was recognised as one of the cleverest defensive boxers in Britain. He was vastly more experienced than Petersen, having had almost seventy professional contests. At 12 stones 6, he was half a pound heavier than Jack, but at least two inches shorter.

Both men received rousing receptions when introduced to the packed house. Jack was thrilled to be boxing at Holborn Stadium again because not only did he feel at home there, he also knew he would be fighting under the most encouraging conditions.

'A fight may be a fight anywhere but there is an inspiring feeling of confidence performing in front of people you know, who are interested in you, and would like to see you win,' he remarked years later when reminiscing about the Stadium Club.

Although Jack opened the fight with his customary vicious attack, he soon realised he was up against a good champion. Apart from being very strong and well trained, Crossley's defensive skills quickly became evident. In round two, Harry made the challenger miss badly on several occasions, whilst countering with his own hard right to the jaw which made Jack hang on.

Petersen became unusually subdued as the champion whipped in hurtful punches to the ribs and head, and by round four, he was clearly behind. During this round Jack injured a knuckle on his right hand which would give him intense pain for the remainder of the fight.

As he returned to his corner at the end of that round, he began thinking that if there were better men in the ring than Crossley and Charlie Smith, his path to the titles was not going to be an easy one.

Pa worked wonders on Jack during the interval, and he came out for the fifth with renewed spirit. After taking three rights to the face in quick succession, he was stung into action. Ignoring the pain from his hand, he landed five right hooks to the head without reply.

Suddenly, the audience were screaming with excitement. 'Ten to one on Petersen,' yelled one spectator as Jack punished the champion with heavy punches to the face, drawing blood from his nose and mouth. It was a dramatic turn-around, but the Yorkshireman was a tough proposition and showed he could take it.

The sixth was quieter but Jack was on top again in round seven, staggering the champion several times with hard rights to the head. At this stage the fight was probably level, with both men showing signs of punishment. Petersen was bleeding from the mouth and had a swelling over his right eye, while Crossley's lips were cut and swollen.

With half a minute to go in the eighth, two terrific rights from the Welshman had Crossley in trouble. His knees buckled and he staggered across the ring wide open to further attack. Instead of biding his time, Jack became wild, and once again his impulsiveness was his failing. Crossley was allowed to recover, and using his excellent defensive skills, survived the round.

Although Crossley started the ninth strongly, the passion and stamina were on the side of his young challenger. Yet, try as he did, Jack could not find an opening to land a finishing punch. As Crossley's skill kept him out of trouble, the Welshman was content to plod forward using his left jab.

The champion was repeatedly cautioned in round eleven for holding, and Jack could sense he was tiring badly. He decided it was time to step up the pressure.

Round thirteen began in explosive fashion as Petersen leapt from his stool and hurled himself across the ring at Crossley. A right crashed against the Yorkshireman's jaw sending him heavily to the floor. He gallantly rose at 'eight' but was in serious trouble. Another heavy shot to the head put him down for a further count of 'eight.'

This was the real Petersen, but in Crossley he faced a man of immense courage. As he climbed from the floor he walked into a battery of punches. A heavy right sent him reeling across the ring as the bell ended the round. One more shot would surely have ended the fight.

Jack was extremely tired and although well on top, he was unable to land a telling blow during the fourteenth. Crossley was as tough as steel and skilfully moved around the ring boxing on the retreat.

In the final round, Petersen fought viciously just as he did against Charlie Smith. Head down, he bored into the champion, swinging punches from all angles. Crossley was driven across the ring, and only the ropes held him up. When the final bell sounded, he had nothing left, and wobbled badly as he returned to his corner.

Petersen got the decision and leapt into the air with joy as referee Percy Moss raised his arm. After shaking hands with Crossley, he skipped back to his corner with the agility of a ballet dancer. Although he was very excited, Jack knew he had been in a dour battle. Both his eyes were swollen, his nose bruised and bloodied, and his lips cut. He had fought eleven rounds with a badly damaged hand and had been in agony every time he used it.

Instead of receiving the National Sporting Club championship challenge belt in recognition of his victory, Jack was presented with a silver cup. The fact that the contest had not been staged under the auspices of the N.S.C. was undoubtedly the reason.

In making the presentation, Lord Lonsdale, the President of the

Jack Petersen as an 18 year old amateur.

Jack Petersen (far right), and members of the Welsh amateur boxing team for the 1930 tour of Denmark.

Jack Petersen has tea aboard a train from Paddington to Cardiff in November 1932.

Harry Crossley (on the scales), and Petersen weigh-in for their British light-heavyweight title fight at The Stadium Club on 23 May 1932.

Reggie Meen crashes to the floor at Wimbledon Stadium on 12 July 1932 as Jack Petersen captures the British heavyweight title.

Petersen with his father and step-mother at his hotel the morning after winning the British heavyweight title from Reggie Meen.

Jack Pettifer (left) is under pressure from Petersen in their fight at Olympia on 26 January 1933.

Petersen (right), shakes hands with Jack Doyle after signing contracts for their contest in July 1933. Centre is promoter Jeff Dickson.

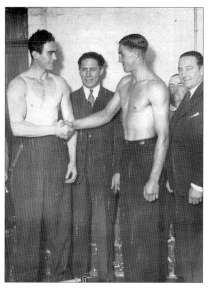

Jack Doyle (left) and Petersen weigh-in for their fight at White City on 12 July 1933. Promoter Jeff Dickson (centre) and Pa Petersen (right) look on.

Petersen (left) staggers Jack Doyle with a left hook at White City on 12 July 1933.

Referee, Mr C. H. Douglas, attempts to halt the action between Petersen (left) and Jack Doyle at White City on 12 July 1933.

Jack and Pa Petersen surrounded by adoring fans at Cardiff Station in 1934.

Jack (left) and Pa Petersen engage in a bout of wrestling whilst training at the Lynn Institute, Cardiff.

Petersen (left) shakes hands with Len Harvey at the office of promoter Jeff Dickson (centre) after signing contracts for their fight on 4 June 1934.

Ben Foord (right) attacks Jack Petersen in their fight at the Royal Albert Hall on 8 March 1934.

Petersen floors Ben Foord at the Royal Albert Hall on 8 March 1934.

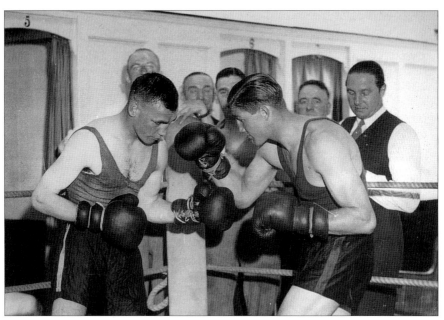

Jack Petersen (right) sparring with Charlie Bundy at the Lynn Institute for his contest with Len Harvey at White City on 4 June 1934.

Jack Petersen pounds the heavy sand-bag whilst training at the Lynn Institute in 1934.

Jack Petersen and Larry Gains weigh-in for their fight at White City on 10 September 1934. Watching are (from the left), Pa Petersen, Billy Diamond, Jeff Dickson, Snowy Buckingham and George West (heavyweight boxer).

National Sporting Club, spoke for everyone present when he said, 'It has been a real pleasure to watch two young men fight such a clean and game contest.'

Back in the dressing room, Jack's right glove had to be cut from his hand because the fist was badly swollen and discoloured. An x-ray later confirmed a cracked knuckle. Whilst speed and stamina were features of his victory, it was a testimony of the young Welshman's courage that he cleverly and bravely disguised the injury without which he must surely have won much earlier. After the fight he was extremely sick, and later admitted it had been more gruelling than the affair with Charlie Smith.

Crossley accepted defeat like the true sportsman he was, and within a few minutes of leaving the ring, went to Petersen's dressing room. 'I wish you all the luck going Jack,' he said shaking the new champion by his uninjured hand. The Welshman smiled broadly and thanked him.

Arriving back in Cardiff the following morning Jack went straight to the Lynn Institute and got into a hot bath. Interviewed by William E. Allen he beamed with joy as he explained what it meant to him at becoming British champion at the first attempt. 'I'm more than delighted with my success,' he remarked. 'No words can express my happiness at this moment.'

Jack had achieved exactly what he set out to do. Pa had strongly advised him against becoming a professional fighter unless he was determined to become a champion. Jack vowed to do everything in his power not to let his father down. 'Well, I justified myself last night,' he told William E. Allen.

He was also quick to praise his opponent. 'Crossley was a very hard and difficult man,' he explained. 'Next to Smith, it was the best I have fought in my life.'

The Stewards of the Board of Control were quick to reward Jack for his success, and at a meeting the following day, agreed to recognise his fight with Reggie Meen as for the British heavyweight title.

* * *

The fights against Smith and Crossley took a lot out of Jack so he set off on a sea cruise to re-build his strength. When he returned two weeks later, he looked a picture of health. The cracked knuckle had healed well and his weight had gone up to about thirteen stones. To continue the benefit of sea air, he moved temporarily to Porthcawl to commence light training for his fight with Reggie Meen.

When Jack returned to the Lynn Institute for heavy training he had difficulty getting sparring partners. It had been planned to use Leo Bandias and Eddie Phillips, but they were too small. Jack Stratton, who was built on similar lines to Meen, was eventually recruited along with Phil Barnes from Malvern who stood six feet two inches tall and weighed over fourteen stones. There was also speculation that Jack Hood would again travel to Cardiff, but he discounted this saying, 'Let the boy fight his natural way is the only advice I can give him.'

Jack's popularity was increasing tremendously, and while he was training to meet Meen, crowds flocked to the Lynn Institute every day. There were all nationalities – Chinese, Sudanese, Arabs, many of whom were seamen or residents from the docks area.

One day an Indian man with a reputation amongst his fellows of being a prophet of parts, offered to trace Jack's horoscope. Not knowing what to expect, the Welshman smilingly consented. When the man returned a few days later he told Jack, 'Before you finish with boxing you will be champion of the world.'

The fight with Meen was officially set for 28 June 1932, but due to the injury to Petersen's knuckle it was put back to 5 July. Ticket sales started well, but suddenly Jeff Dickson, the leading promoter in London at the time, announced he was staging a world middleweight title fight at the White City on 4 July between Len Harvey and Marcel Thil of France.

Sales for the Wimbledon promotion dropped off dramatically, which is exactly what Dickson had hoped. He was annoyed at Thomas Hatton's intrusion into boxing promotion in the capital, especially as he had succeeded in signing up a fight as attractive as Petersen-Meen.

Hatton, who made a name for himself promoting at Leicester, had secured Meen's signature. Although he worked hard to make the show a success, luck was not with him and it became a financial disaster.

On the day of the fight, a torrential thunderstorm blew up in the early hours, and it continued to rain throughout the day. Wimbledon greyhound track became so flooded it resembled a huge lake. Venturesome people trying to reach the ring could only do so by wearing wellington boots or waders.

At 6pm, Matt Wells, a Board of Control inspector, pronounced the ring unsafe for boxing. It had been left uncovered during the downpour and became soaked with water. 'A man could scarcely stand up on it yet alone fight,' declared Wells in advising that the show must be postponed despite the weather having improved.

When the official announcement was made there was an angry demonstration, and mounted police had to be called to prevent fans from breaking into the stadium. Thousands were in the surrounding streets awaiting admission, including several train loads of Welshmen who had travelled to London specially for the fight.

By this time, large numbers of police, stewards, programme sellers, and members of the Veterans Corps had reported for duty, and most of the boxers had arrived as well. The promoter did his best to warn the public of the decision which was printed in the late editions of the evening papers. Yet earlier in the day, despite the weather being suspect, he had said that wet or fine, the fight would take place.

In a press statement, Hatton said he was reluctant to postpone the show because advance bookings assured him of success. The Board of Control, however, insisted on the postponement in the interests of safety.

'I am most grieved to know that after my strenuous efforts to bring to London, all the provincial supporters of Meen and Petersen, they should have had a fruitless journey.'

He stated that all tickets would be valid for the new date of 12 July, or money would be refunded. This was little consolation for the hundreds of Welshmen who had paid to travel to London. Many couldn't afford to make the trip again.

By the new date, a lot of the emphasis had gone and the attendance was poor. It resulted in heavy losses for the promoter, and as a result Jack got less than half the expected £500 purse. The amount he received did little more than cover training and travelling costs.

*   *   *

Reggie Meen was born at Leamington Spa in 1907, and turned professional at the age of 20. Now boxing out of Desborough, he was far more experienced than Petersen, having engaged in more than 60 contests. A known puncher he had stopped over 30 opponents, but had suffered his share of defeats. Amongst the men who had beaten him were Charlie Smith (twice), Primo Carnera, Harry Crossley, Eddie Steele and George Cook.

Boxing historian, Gilbert Odd, gave a perfect assessment of Meen when he once wrote; 'He was beautifully built and looked every inch a fighting man. The trouble was that no one had taught him defence.'

Meen had a tremendous following in the Midlands, and

whenever he fought at the Granby Halls, Leicester, a sell-out crowd of 10,000 was guaranteed. It was there that he won the title in November 1931, outpointing Charlie Smith after an epic battle.

Although he went into the fight with Petersen on the back of defeats by Heine Muller and George Cook, Reggie was still the bookies favourite. At 14 stones 11½ lbs, he had a weight advantage of over two stones. Many critics believed that the longer the fight went, the more it would favour him. 'PETERSEN MUST WIN QUICKLY' was the bold headline across the front page of the *South Wales Echo.*

Petersen knew what he had to do, and scored a spectacular knockout in the second round. It was as good a display as any seen in a British ring for a very long time. He accomplished victory in a way that astonished even his most ardent supporters. Not only did he display boxing ability which made Meen look like a third rate opponent, but he also showed that despite weighing only 12 stones 9 lbs, he possessed by far the harder punch.

Recognising that the champion was very nervous, Petersen didn't waste a second with preliminary sparring. Rushing from his corner at the opening bell, he drove left after left into Meen's face. Reggie was taken completely by surprise and had no defence to the onslaught. A desperate left hook did catch the Welshman flush on the nose causing blood to flow, but only served to stir him into a greater attack. Throughout the final minute of the round he smashed punch after punch to the champions face and body.

As Meen reeled against the ropes he looked completely out of it. Sensing his chance, Petersen stepped back and let go a thunderous right to the chin. The champion crashed to the floor and was still there when the bell ended the round with the count at 'six'.

It was obvious that Meen had not recovered as they came out for round two. Sensing the title was his for the taking, Petersen smashed three lefts to the face which shook Reggie to his boots. As he tottered backwards, a perfectly timed right crashed against his chin. He was already heading to the floor as a stiff upper-cut completed the job.

It was the complete knockout in every sense, and it was more than five minutes before Meen could be raised to a sitting positiion. He had been completely unconscious, and still required attention for some while in his corner.

Once he realised that Reggie had recovered, Jack danced uncharacteristically around the ring, his hands clasped above his head. It was so unlike him, but he was overjoyed at his success.

Victory not only gave him the British heavyweight title but also the National Sporting Club challenge belt which had been donated by Lord Lonsdale. The belt, which had not been contested at heavyweight since 1923 when Joe Beckett beat Dick Smith, was presented to Jack in the ring by Lord Tweedmouth.

The scenes which followed the Welshman's victory were incredible. The stadium rang with cheering for the new champion, hats and sticks were thrown into the air and an attempt was made to storm the ring. Fortunately, this was averted by the stewards.

In less than twelve months as a professional, Jack had won three titles and was not yet 21. It was an incredible achievement, unparalleled in the history of British boxing. Back in his dressing room he was besieged by pressmen, but as usual it was Pa who addressed them: 'Jack chose to fight rather than study medicine. It was his desire to become a boxing champion and I did not attempt to influence him either way. Having decided to fight, I resolved that he should have proper training. Scientific training has resulted in a champion England has never before possessed.'

'I, as you know, am a physical culture expert,' continued Pa. 'Jack, like such famous boxers as Jimmy Wilde, Jim Driscoll and Billy Wells, has had the full benefit of what I might have acquired during my twenty years study of the mind and anatomy.'

Looking respectfully at his father, Jack remarked; 'He is right of course. Dad is right in most things he does and says. My training? Well, Dad has told you all about that. I really do nothing until I am in the ring.'

Expressing his delight at becoming champion, Jack was surprised that victory came so easily. 'I meant to do the job quickly,' he said,' but I expected Meen to give me a stiffer task.'

Behind the scenes, Jack was sure he had the beating of Meen from the day the fight was made. He was much more certain of victory than he had been about Crossley. It was not cockiness, just simple psychology.

Interviewed as a doctor examined him, Reggie Meen was very distressed, and would only express his disappointment. 'I do not grumble, and I make no excuses for my defeat,' he said sportingly. 'Petersen is a fine fighter, and I wish him well as champion.'

* * *

The manner of Petersen's victory thrilled the sports writers of almost every national newspaper in Britain. Their feelings were highlighted by W. F. Sanderson in the *Daily Mail* who, the morning after the fight, wrote:

51

Twenty years of age, only a boy, but we have found a Carpentier. We have found a fighter, a lad who hits back when he is hurt, and who will drop any man in the world who is unlucky enough to meet that appalling right hand punch....

A huge crowd was at Cardiff railway station to greet the new champion when he returned home the day after the fight. The occasion was particularly special because Jack was the first Cardiff born boxer to win a British title since Jim Driscoll in 1907.

A car was waiting to take Jack and Pa straight to City Hall for a reception to celebrate the occasion. Huge crowds of men, women and children lined the route, and, outside City Hall, an excited crowd of 2,000 cheered loudly as they arrived.

Jack was greeted at the main entrance by the Lord Mayor, Alderman C. W. Mellish and members of the City Council. After warm hand-shakes, the mayor and champion examined each others laurels – the chain of honour and National Sporting Club belt.

After moving inside to the mayor's parlour, Jack signed the visitors book. At the reception which followed, the mayor proposed a toast to the new champion. 'I am no judge of pugilistic matters,' he remarked, 'but at the same time I am always proud to receive anyone who has brought distinction to the City of Cardiff.'

The speeches which followed embarrassed Jack. He was told about Jim Driscoll and Jimmy Wilde who had brought championships to Cardiff in the past, but this was different. He had won the British heavyweight championship, and no Welshman had ever achieved that before.

His response was typically brief and modest. 'I thank you for this great reception and all the kind things you have said about me,' he remarked. 'I will go on trying to win my fights for Cardiff, and of course myself.'

As Jack left the Civic Hall his attention was drawn to a disabled lad who had been taken into the building to get a glimpse of the champion. With typical caring, Jack went over to the boy, thirteen years old James Evans from Cathes, and shook hands with him. Stooping down, he placed the championship belt around his waist and handed him an autographed photograph. His kindness brought loud cheers from onlookers still gathered around the Civic Hall.

* * *

Within a few days, Pa Petersen had his first major difference of opinion with members of the syndicate backing Jack. They knew, that as British heavyweight champion, he must be more than just a boxer. He would be expected to be a man of the world with a sense of social balance. In reality, they wanted to turn him into a kind of British Gene Tunney.

The problem facing the syndicate, however, was that Jack did not like London and its fast life. He was uncomfortable among crowds in fashionable restaurants, preferring instead the quietness of Wales. One fight at a time and retention of the simple life was what Pa insisted upon, resisting offers on the social side which would have cost them nothing. They were willing to train, fight and earn money, but he was not prepared to allow Jack to spend a few days in London every so often in order that he could be seen in fashionable places mixing with society folk.

* * *

As Jack relaxed at his home in Barry overlooking the Bristol Channel, he received numerous offers of fights. Eddie Phillips issued a challenge for the light-heavyweight title; George Cook wanted to meet him in an eliminator for the Empire heavyweight title held by Larry Gains; from America came an offer to face new sensation, Steve Hamas, a star basketball player who, in January, had caused a major upset when he knocked out former world light-heavyweight champion, Tommy Loughran in two rounds. There was also an invitation to travel to America to meet Maxie Rosenbloom who won the world light-heavyweight title two days after Jack beat Meen. Len Harvey and Don McCorkindale also issued challenges.

As speculation grew about who Jack would fight, Pa Petersen revealed that no offer would be considered for some months. In an exclusive interview with the *South Wales Echo*, he said, 'We can entertain no matches with Harvey, Cook, McCorkindale or anyone else. And Jack will certainly not go to America to fight. If the Americans are anxious to fight him, they will have to come to England.'

Jack's advisors, Harry Jones and Fred Howard, agreed with Pa that the young champion badly needed a rest. They also made it clear that they were not interested in a fight with Larry Gains for the British Empire title. Despite Petersen's tremendous talent, they knew it would be suicidal to throw him in with one of the masters of the heavyweight division at this stage of his career.

His success brought Jack many tributes, not only in the press, but also at public and private functions. Yet despite the attention being heaped upon him, the youngster remained unspoiled. Rather than live it up at lavish celebrations, he was happier amongst people he knew. In particular, he preferred the company of folk of the Welsh hills and valleys. He had little time for the loud sporting set who wanted to tag on to him because he was the heavyweight champion of Great Britain.

Although he neither smoked nor drank, Jack spent many hours yarning with miners in villages near his home as they sat over their pots of ale. He was content and at ease in the company of people who did not point or stare, but accepted him as an ordinary man. There were many occasions when he cleverly drew caricatures of himself. These were treasured by recipients, and many years later they could often still be found pinned on a wall of a little Welsh Inn or Working Mens Club.

A typical caricature which Jack Petersen drew of himself and gave to his fans.

Despite his rugged profession, Jack was quite shy and sometimes became embarrassed. One day, shortly after becoming heavyweight champion, he was on a tour of mining villages in the Rhondda. Being a tall and extremely handsome young man, he naturally attracted the attention of many young ladies. When this was pointed out to him he became extremely embarrassed and blushed like a schoolboy. He did admit, however, that the girls, most of whom were miners daughters, were amongst some of the prettiest he had ever seen.

* * *

Towards the end of July 1932, Petersen became one of the leading members of a movement formed to raise funds for the dependants of former boxer Billy Beynon of Taibach. Earlier in the month, he had been killed under a fall of stone at the Brwn Navigation Colliery near Maesteg.

In a professional career between 1909 and 1931, Beynon was the hero of 192 fights, and was never knocked out. He won the British bantamweight title and championship belt in 1913 by beating Digger Stanley, and was claimant to the European title the same year. He boxed many exhibitions for charity, and after retiring from boxing at the age of 41, became a referee.

There was tremendous public feeling for Jack Petersen when he led a group of delegates from the British Boxing Board of Control at Beynon's funeral at Port Talbot. Jack recognised the plight of the family, and people knew he had already made a generous contribution to help the former boxer's thirteen children, one of whom was only six weeks old.

Realising the value of a good start in life, Jack was determined to do whatever he could to help the children get a good education. He was spurred on even more when he learned that one of Beynon's sons had won a scholarship to Maesteg Secondary School, but following his his father's death, this was in jeopardy.

The first public event to aid the Beynon Fund took place at the Mayfair Cafe, Queen Street, Cardiff, on 28 July. Petersen was the star attraction and his presence ensured a large gathering. In recognition of his achievements in the ring he was presented with a silver statuette by Mr. Griffin J. Llewellyn, President of the Welsh Area of the British Boxing Board of Control, on behalf of the sportsmen of Wales.

Later that week, Jack attended a gathering in his honour at the Rhiwbini Scout Hall, and was presented with an engraved staff and roll bearing signatures of members of the Rhiwbini Troop. An oak cigarette case was presented to Pa.

Jack's tremendous success was recognised by many business and sporting bodies, and a number of other presentations followed. It was generally thought that his achievements would never be repeated by a man of such tender years.

5

REFRESHED

As British heavyweight champion, it followed that Jack would have to continually face bigger men. At the time, there was great excitement about the progress of a young Irishman named Jack Doyle. He was a handsome fellow who stood about six feet five inches tall and weighed over 15 stones. He had been bought out of the Army by Dan Sullivan, and was being talked about as a potential world beater.

Doyle had boxed on the shows when Petersen won the light-heavy and heavyweight titles, beating Bill Partridge (rsf.1) and Guardsman Gater (rsf.2). Comparisons were already being made with the Welshman, and as the months passed by, Doyle was talked about as a possible challenger for the heavyweight title.

Pa Petersen went to see Doyle fight on a number of occasions, and was particularly impressed by his display against George Slack who he knocked out in two rounds at Swansea on 13 August. Yet whatever opinion he had of the big Irishman, he kept it to himself. All he said to Jack was, 'We'll get Doyle when the time is right.'

Before fighting again, Pa was keen for Jack to have another long trip to sea. It had been a demanding year and they agreed that the sea breezes were essential to re-vitalise his system. So rather than stay at home and bask in the glory of being champion, he packed his suitcases and boarded the modern ocean tramp steamer '*Queensbury*' at Cardiff Docks, and headed for the Azores and Rio.

The weather on the trip was glorious, and the experience a wonderful contrast to the months of hard training. Jack did just as he pleased on board. If he felt like work, he heaved coal and sacks of wheat, clipped the iron, spliced the ropes and scrubbed the decks. He worked as the ships carpenter and also took a turn at the wheel. He was accepted as a crew member, not a double British

56

boxing champion, which suited him far better than the constant attention he would have received back home.

Intending to keep himself in trim, Jack took a punchball to sea with him, but after installing it on deck, a strong gust of wind blew it over the side. Instead, he resorted to weight-lifting using bags of linseed meal.

The amount of food Jack ate on the trip was phenomenal, but he didn't put on any weight as had been hoped. Whilst the hard work strengthened him and hardened his frame, he returned home weighing more or less the same as when he went away.

The cruise lasted about three months, and the young man with simple tastes loved every minute of it. 'They are great fellows, my pals the sailors,' he said jovially when he returned to Cardiff docks in November.

Soon after returning to Cardiff, Jack paid a visit to his old school, St. Illtyds. Although it was an informal visit, it coincided with that of the college governors, allowing him the pleasure of meeting the Archbishop of Cardiff and renewing his acquaintance with those he knew as a pupil.

After posing for photographs with the governors, Jack was taken on a tour of the school. Tremendous interest was shown in his career, and it was obvious that he was the idol of every Illtydian. Loud applause greeted him as he visited every classroom, and he enjoyed discussing his achievements over cups of tea in the staff room.

The most amusing moment of the day came when a class prefect asked Jack if he could arrange for homework to be relaxed for the day. For a moment the champion was speechless, but rising to the occasion suggested that if the prefect could stand up to him for three rounds, the class should have no homework. The offer was politely declined.

* * *

Whilst Jack was away on his cruise, Pa was busy finalising a defence of the heavyweight title against Jack Pettifer at Olympia on 26 January 1933. Welsh fans were longing to see the new champion in action, so as a warm-up it was arranged for him to meet tough German heavyweight, Hans Schonrath, at Greyfriars Hall, on 2 January.

Jack was raring to get back into the ring. He felt fitter than at any time in his life, and the six weeks he had to prepare for the fight was more than adequate.

On 12 December, Len Harvey successfully defended his British middleweight title against Jack Casey at Newcastle. It was his sixth defence, and afterwards stated he considered himself a logical contender for Petersen's light-heavyweight title.

In reviewing the situation, the Board of Control wrote to Jack asking if he intended defending the title. Although they wanted time to consider all options Jack and Pa knew that by staying with the heavyweights, they could command far larger purses.

* * *

Hans Schonrath arrived at Cardiff in plenty of time to complete his preparations. In the days leading up to the fight, Mr. Alec Matthews, the German Consul at Cardiff, acted as his interpreter. In a pre-fight interview the German said, 'I have read all about Jack Petersen. I know about his speed and punching power, but I am out to do my best to win. Success over your brilliant young champion will mean everything to me.'

On the morning of the fight, the two boxers passed the time in contrasting ways. After a breakfast of porridge, eggs and bacon, toast, marmalade, and weak tea, Schonrath went on a shopping expedition. 'I must get my wife a vanity bag, and a toy for my ten months old son,' he told interested reporters. Petersen, meanwhile, drove to the Lynn Institute where he was given a thorough massage.

The fight broke every record for an indoor contest. Had Greyfriars Hall been twice as big, it would still not have accommodated the immense throng of people who converged on Cardiff from all parts of Wales and the West of England. The promoters anticipated a big turnout but were astonished at the chaos outside the hall.

As the crowds built up the scenes were frightening. Between eight and nine thousand people fought and struggled around the narrow entrances into Greyfriars Hall, waving tickets and screaming for admission. Many hundreds failed to get near the doors.

The problem arose because doors to the hall were not opened early as on previous occasions when Jack boxed there. Hundreds of police on duty did their best to control the multitude, but were powerless. The scenes were described as being worse than anything which had ever occurred in the history of sporting events in Cardiff.

By the time the boxing programme began, the crowd had grown even larger and the situation was terrifying. Greyfriars Hall became more packed than at anytime in its history. In the surrounding streets, a number of women fainted in the crush. One man collapsed and was found to be dead on arrival at Cardiff Royal Infirmary. An elderly man who had travelled from Liverpool for the fight, got mixed up in a mob near the Park Hotel entrance. He remembered nothing more until he found himself in a reporters seat at ringside.

A London press man was so frightened that he was convinced he was going to be crushed to death. He had suffered from rheumatism for a week or two, and one of his legs was so painful that he could scarcely bear to put weight on it. As he got swallowed up in the melee, he crooked his bad limb, put his arms round the necks of two burly miners from Treherbert, and implored them to 'save his life'. They not only did so, but managed to get him to his reserved seat.

Many ticket holders waited for hours trying to get in. Some gave up and went home. Others meanwhile became more adventurous and climbed on the roof of Greyfriars Hall and managed to watch the boxing through skylights and side windows. The situation was so chaotic that fans were still being admitted after 9 pm having spent hours outside.

Two supporting contests had ended before police, forming a human barrier, finally succeeded in getting the battling crowds in some sort of orderly queue. Luckily, everyone was inside by the time Petersen and Schonrath entered the ring. The fight certainly concentrated the minds of everyone because it developed into one of the most gruelling ever seen in Cardiff.

Conceding almost two stones, Petersen fought with all his customary fire. Stocky and broad shouldered, Schonrath took tremendous punishment throughout the fight. He was a man of iron, and stuck to his task magnificently until forced to retire after eight rounds with an ugly gash above his left eye.

The German was under heavy pressure throughout the first two rounds, but although badly shaken on several occasions, he was always willing to stand his ground and evade punches. Midway through the second, Schonrath emerged from a fierce exchange with blood streaming from a nasty cut over his left eye.

In another toe-to-toe slog, Petersen scored heavily with several right uppercuts, but the German responded with three crisp shots to the chin. Although he was hurt and reeling against the ropes, Petersen's response was immediate, hitting back viciously as the bell ended the round.

Schonrath was proving to be a difficult opponent, and round

three was a gruelling affair. Having felt the power of his opponents punches, the Welshman became very cautious whenever they got to close quarters. He was badly shaken by a left to the chin, but responded well with a heavy right to the head. Then as the German slowed towards the end of the round, Jack had him reeling from another powerful right to the chin.

The fourth and fifth were close, hard fought rounds. The German scored well at close quarters, but Jack countered with good uppercuts and left jabs. There were some thrilling moments in round six as the Welshman rammed three sharp lefts to the face. As Schonrath reeled backwards, he was caught by a heavy right to the chin.

With blood streaming from his damaged eye, the gallant German rocked and swayed, but somehow managed to stay upright. He fought desperately to avoid defeat, and in the final half minute of the sixth, caught the British champion with a tremendous left hook to the jaw. Although Petersen was badly shaken, Schonrath did not have the strength to finish him. It was an extremely punishing round and both men were unsteady on their feet at the bell.

In the seventh, both landed heavy punches as they fought savagely at close quarters for all of a minute without let-up. The German showed good defensive skills to Petersen's dangerous right hand, and three solid lefts had the Welshman defending for all he was worth. Typically, however, Jack responded in the only way he knew when he was in trouble. He hit back viciously, driving three fierce uppercuts through Schonrath's guard. It was another gruelling round in which both men were badly hurt.

Schonrath showed tremendous courage again in round eight as Petersen smashed several hard rights to the head. Attack after attack virtually reduced the bloodied German to a punchbag, and he appeared about to fall on a number of occasions.

In a last desperate effort to turn the fight around, Schonrath suddenly hit back with a vicious left hook to the stomach. Petersen, however, took it well, and, sensing victory, put every ounce of power into four hard rights to the head. Amazingly, the tough German stayed on his feet until the bell ended the round, but looked very weak as he trudged to his corner. Blood streamed from the cut above his left eye, and his right was almost closed. There was a brief discussion between Schonrath and his manager, after which referee, Mr. C. B. Thomas, was called to the corner.

'Hans cannot fight any longer,' said the manager pointing to the boxers closed right eye. 'He cannot see his opponent.'

'If he's had enough, then throw in the towel,' replied Mr. Thomas.

'Not me, no surrender,' said the manager stubbornly refusing the referee's suggestion.

Mr. Thomas briefly examined Schonrath's injuries, then surprisingly ordered him to continue. When the bell sounded for round nine, however, the German remained on his stool. His manager stood in the corner holding the towel aloft to signal his retirement. Only then did Mr. Thomas call a halt and award the fight to Petersen.

After the contest, Mr. Thomas explained his peculiar action. He said that Schonrath's chief second called him to the corner and pointed to the boxers left eye saying that he was unable to continue. 'He asked me to stop the fight,' said Mr. Thomas. 'I made a careful inspection of the eye, and whilst he certainly suffered injury, I formed the opinion that it was not bad enough for me to stop the fight.'

The referee explained that the German seconds protested vigorously at his decision. 'But I waved aside their objections,' he continued, 'and prepared for the contest to go on. Schonrath did not get off his stool for round nine, although I believed he was physically strong enough to do so.'

Mr. Thomas went to great lengths to explain to reporters that he would never stop a fight while a contestant was, in his opinion, still in a condition to continue. He knew that after Schonrath had been stopped in seven rounds by Walter Neusel in 1932, he later claimed he had been harshly treated. Mr. Thomas was therefore not prepared to give him the opportunity to leave Wales claiming an injustice.

Schonrath made no complaint after retiring against Petersen. He was in a bad way and had to be assisted to his dressing room. Later, he described Jack as the hardest punching heavyweight he had ever faced.

Petersen did not come out of the fight unscathed. His left eye was almost closed as he left the ring, evidence of Schonrath's powerful, short-arm punches. In his dressing room, Jack told reporters that he had never been in a more gruelling fight. 'Schonrath is a man of iron,' he said. 'I hit him as hard as I knew how, but could not get him down.'

At a press conference the following morning, Jack admitted that throughout the fight he had tried desperately to knock out the German. Without detracting from Schonrath's immensely courageous performance, Jack said he felt he had not been at his best because for the first time in his life he had gone into the ring weighing nearly thirteen stones.

A couple of years later, an amazing story emerged concerning the ending of the fight. John MacAdam, a prominent sports writer, was in Paris with London promoter Jeff Dickson and Charlie Henry, manager of world rated American heavyweight Steve Hamas. It was claimed that at the end of the eighth round Schonrath asked his cornerman what the time was. When told, he pleaded with them to throw the towel in.

The explanation given to MacAdam was that the German's wife was having a baby within a day or two, and he had promised to be at home when the time came. To do so he had to catch a particular train from Cardiff that night. When he realised the fight was likely to go the full distance, he knew he would miss the train, so he quit.

* * *

When Jack eventually heard about the extent of the crowd trouble outside Greyfriars Hall before the fight, it made him realise the responsibility he carried. It caused him great personal concern because the last thing he wanted was for people to be hurt and Cardiff subjected to adverse criticism.

A full enquiry was subsequently conducted by the Cardiff Watch Committee and presided over by the Lord Mayor. It was agreed that the police were powerless to contain the trouble because there were insufficient numbers on duty.

It was revealed that the chief constable was asked to provide only 23 constables, although he personally had insisted on 31 being on duty. As the trouble escalated, reinforcements had to be called, and eventually a total of 125 officers were drafted into the vicinity of Greyfriars Hall.

The enquiry concluded that the promoters were responsible for what occurred, and therefore ordered them to pay the full cost of services rendered by the police.

* * *

Meanwhile, on 13 January 1933, Jack Petersen was guest of honour at a boxing tournament organised by Cardiff City Boxing Club at St. Saviours Hall, Splott Road. It was the first show to be staged at the venue, and tremendous interest was shown once it was announced that Jack would attend and present the prizes.

On the night, hundreds of people were turned away. There was so much excitement that, in the interests of safety, the British champion was quietly ushered into the building by the stage door entrance. Once inside, he stood in the wings, unnoticed for some minutes. Once the crowd saw him, however, they went wild with excitement. A six rounds contest was in progress, and during the interval between rounds four and five, there was a shout of, 'three cheers for Jack Petersen.' The response was deafening.

* * *

Jack was already in strict training for his fight with Jack Pettifer, and plans were also being made to match him with some big names, including Young Stribling, during the summer.

Meanwhile, Jack Doyle arrived in London from Cork where he had spent Christmas. He told newsmen that he intended making a strong protest against Pettifer being nominated to face Petersen for the heavyweight title. Doyle insisted that having beaten Pettifer in two rounds at Crystal Palace three months earlier, he was the logical challenger.

'What has Petersen done in winning his fights?' enquired Doyle. 'He has not met a man with a punch.' The Irishman boasted that if he could get Petersen into the ring, he would knock him out inside three or four rounds.

At a meeting at Cardiff between the Petersen's and their associates, it was agreed that Jack should relinquish the British light-heavyweight title. This decision was conveyed to the British Boxing Board of Control by letter.

At a press conference at the Lynn Institute, Pa made no secret of the fact that money was the deciding factor. 'Purse money amongst the heavyweights is considerably greater than in the lower division,' he insisted.

Pa did, however, disclose that they still had an attractive offer for Jack to box in America as a light-heavyweight. 'If there is the possibility of meeting Maxie Rosenbloom for the world title,' he remarked, 'we will give it serious consideration.'

Pa added that, in his opinion, it was not a wise policy to keep Jack down at the light-heavyweight limit. More knowledgeable critics found this to be a somewhat confusing statement because it was well known that Jack rarely went into the ring weighing much above twelve and a half stones.

* * *

For the Pettifer fight, Jack put himself under the direction of Danny Davies, but training did not go according to plan. Not for the first

63

time, there was great difficulty in finding suitable sparring partners. Pa Petersen even put advertisements in national newspapers in an attempt to recruit some good men into the camp. The response was incredible, and they were inundated with offers from all parts of the country. Pa had the task of sifting through the masses of letters which arrived at the Lynn Institute almost hourly. Unfortunately, most came from young inexperienced boxers who were unsuitable.

A number of letters were received from unemployed men saying they were willing to be knocked about daily just for the chance to earn something to eat. It was a sign of the difficult times. One letter read:

> I am willing to take a hiding every night for the sake of boxing with Jack, but of course I shall expect some dough. I've not put a stamp on the envelope because I am hard up.

Another individual wrote saying:

> 'I'm an undiscovered heavyweight champion. If you don't answer me, I will worry all the boxing managers in London.'

'We have searched the country but with not the slightest result,' Pa told the *South Wales Echo*. 'Now we must do something big.'

He said they were prepared to pay Larry Gains, Walter Neusel, Reggie Meen, George Cook or Charlie Smith £100 plus free board and lodging for one of them to travel to Cardiff to box three rounds with Jack every night for a week. 'This offer is made seriously,' insisted Pa, 'and I hope the response will be a quick one.'

Neusel was the only man to show any interest. He was training to meet George Cook at the Royal Albert Hall, and in a telephone call to the promoter, Jeff Dickson, said he was prepared to pay Petersen £200, plus travelling expenses for three people, if he would go to Berlin and spar with him.

Neusel pointed out that it would be in both their interests because their fights were within a couple of days of each other. On being contacted by Dickson, Pa declined the offer on the grounds that travelling to Berlin and back within a short space of time could unsettle Jack.

The determined young Welshman did not allow the lack of sparring partners to discourage him from making every effort to attain the peak of fitness. He spent a great deal of time working on a huge punch bag which was suspended from the ceiling of the gym at a level corresponding to Pettifer's height. On it was painted a lifesize reproduction of the Londoner's face, which Jack pounded mercilessly on a daily basis.

The only serious sparring Jack got was just three days with Jack Stratton and Phil Barnes who had helped him prepare for his fight with Reggie Meen. In a final try-out, the champion pulled no punches, and flattened Stratton in less than a minute with a perfect right to the chin. The Londoner was left flat on his face and took some time to recover. After a break, he agreed to try again, but Petersen knocked him to the floor again within 30 seconds with a vicious left hook.

Although Barnes lasted two rounds, he also took heavy punishment. Onlookers priviledged to be at the try-out soon realised why the British champion had such difficulty getting sparring partners.

'I'm fit for anything now,' Jack told William E. Allen. 'As in every other contest, I'm going out to win as quickly as I can.'

After a few days keeping loose by doing light exercises, Jack travelled to London the day before the fight and stayed with friends at Harrow.

* * *

The man behind the promotion was Arthur Cyril Jefferson Peake, a well-known figure in Brighton, who intended using the fight to show himself as a generous patron of the sport. Described as being a man with society connections, he had been an actor, film producer and financier, and was not the kind of individual normally involved in the world of professional boxing.

Preferring to hide his true identity under the pseudonym of 'Mr. Arthur', it was Peake's first venture into boxing promotion. He was not a licensed promoter so in a technical sense did not promote the fight. This was done on his behalf by Jack Callaghan, but Peake gave the orders whilst preferring to remain as a modest sportsman.

Being unknown within boxing circles, Peake knew it was essential to draw attention to himself if he was to become a success. He therefore invited many national newspaper representatives to a prestigious luncheon at Olympia on 7 December 1932 for the signing of the contracts.

In a speech, Peake announced that he was going to present a gold cup of great value to the winner of the fight. He also intended introducing a number of other lavish extras which would make the fight different from anything which had ever occurred before.

Each boxer would be presented with a silk dressing gown, and flowers would be displayed in their corners. Petersen would be led

BOOK NOW For the Fight of the Century!

OLYMPIA CIRCUS, LONDON

THURSDAY, JAN. 26, 1933, at 8 p.m.

Under the personal supervision of Mr. JACK CALLAGHAN.

HEAVY-WEIGHT CHAMPIONSHIP OF GREAT BRITAIN
and Lord Lonsdale Championship Challenge Belt.

15 (3-min.) Rounds.

JACK PETERSEN

(CARDIFF), HOLDER, versus

JACK PETTIFER

(LONDON), CHALLENGER

Men in the Ring 9.30 Sharp   Referee appointed by B.B.B. of C.

Supporting Bouts—6 (3-min.) Rounds

BOB CARVILL *(Bridlington)*	v.	JACK STANLEY *(Deptford)*
JACK DANE *(Canada)*	v.	DAVE FORBES *(Glasgow)*
GUNNER BENNETT *(Windsor)*	v.	GEORGE SLACK *(Doncaster)*
FRED ROWLANDS *(Exeter)*	v.	IVOR MALCOLM *(Leigh-on-Sea)*
P.O. STUBBS *(Plymouth)*	v.	JEFF WILSON *(Windsor)*
GEORGE BENNETT *(Manchester)*	v.	EX-MARINE SMITH *(Deptford)*
ARTHUR CANDY EVANS *(Halifax)*	v.	NORMAN BAINES *(Liverpool)*
TED MASON *(Maidstone)*	v.	JACK STRATTON *(Highbury)*
EX-GDSMN. LEAKE *(Windsor)*	v.	TERRY MANTON *(Herne Bay)*

ALL ACTION—ALL THRILLS

Doors Open 7 o'clock.   Commence 8 o'clock Sharp

Prices of Admission:

6/-, 12/-, £1/4/-, £2/8/-, £3/6/- (INC. TAX)

SEATS CAN BE BOOKED and Tickets obtained from The Queen's Hotel, Leicester Square, London, W. 'Phones: Gerrard 6853-4-5. Messrs. Keith Prowse, Alfred Hays, Webster & Waddington, Ltd., OLYMPIA, and other Agencies.

Poster advertising British heavyweight championship contest between Petersen and Jack Pettifer.

66

to the ring preceded by a Union Jack bearing daffodils, and Pettifer would follow behind the flag emblazoned with roses. Coloured souvenir brochures would be on sale, and the handsome gold cup would be presented to the winner in the ring at the conclusion of the contest.

Invitations were extended to a number of prominent people including the Prince of Wales and Lord Lonsdale. It was hoped to fix coloured cloth to the base of all the seats, so that when the Prince of Wales arrived and people stood up, the seats would swing up and present an enormous Union Jack. That bizarre plan, however, eventually fell through.

The promoters fancy ideas were given massive coverage by the media causing great irritation to Jeff Dickson. He resented the fact that another newcomer into boxing had succeeded in staging a fight involving Petersen and the British heavyweight title. On 12 January 1933, solicitors acting on his behalf made application before Mr. Justice Hawke in the High Court, for an injunction to restrain Pettifer from fighting Petersen. The case was adjourned until 17 January when it was heard by a Judge in Chambers who refused Dickson's application.

The promotion cost Peake a great deal of money, and he made the mistake of charging too much for seats. Consequently, despite about 3,000 Welshmen making the trip to Olympia, the show was not the financial success he had hoped for.

* * *

Jack Pettifer had his first professional contest in October 1930. When he faced Petersen he had lost just one of his 19 contests, eleven of his victories coming inside the distance. His only defeat was in October 1932 when he was knocked out in the second round by Jack Doyle. Since then he had outpointed Charlie Smith over ten rounds at the Royal Albert Hall. That performance alone made the contest with Petersen an intriguing one.

The weigh-in was at the Stadium Club at 2pm on the day of the fight. Pettifer, who stood six feet seven inches tall, scaled 16 stones 10 lbs, whilst Petersen's weight was called at 13 stones. Although many critics believed the challengers physical advantages would be too much for the Welshman, the betting boys disagreed. Petersen was made a firm favourite at 6-4 on.

The fight opened in sensational fashion as Petersen scored with a solid left to the body followed by a vicious two-fisted attack. Pettifer was driven across the ring, and a left and right to the jaw sent him heavily to the floor. Amid pandemonium, he rose at the count of 'three' and immediately caught the champion with a left and right to the head.

Although badly shaken, the Welshman attacked again. Pettifer ducked beneath a vicious left and countered with a right to the head. Again Petersen hit back with a good right flush on the chin. The Londoner took it well and replied with a left and right to the champions head. It was hard, exciting stuff as both men looked for a quick finish, and the round ended to rapturous applause.

Pettifer kept the champion at bay with long left jabs in the second, and despite taking a heavy left hook to the jaw, fought as never before. He smashed into Petersen with both hands and had him reeling on the ropes. Although the Welshman jabbed his way out of trouble, he took a stiff left to the face which brought blood dripping from his nose as the round ended.

Making good use of his long left, the massive Londoner had the better of rounds three and four, and Petersen was badly marked about the face. He found it difficult to get to close quarters as Pettifer moved remarkably quickly for a man of his size.

Changing tactics, the champion boxed better in the fifth. Waiting in the centre of the ring, he let Pettifer do the chasing, and then picked him off with good lefts to the face without reply. As the big man slowed, Petersen picked up the pace and scored heavily.

It was a dramatic turnaround and the crowd yelled with excitement as the challenger rocked back on his heels from a two fisted attack. Pettifer was very groggy when he returned to his corner, and his anxious seconds splashed Eau-de-Cologne on his chest during the interval to help revive him.

In the sixth, the Welshman continued his onslaught, but Pettifer was still strong and hit back with hurtful punches. Despite being the much lighter man, however, Petersen's punches carried the power, and at the bell the huge Londoner was reeling under another bombardment.

There were further heavy exchanges in the seventh which was an even round. In the eighth, Petersen was marked under the left eye by the accuracy of Pettifer's jab, and was covered in blood from his damaged nose. Both men had been badly shaken, and by this stage neither seemed prepared to take any chances.

Petersen suddenly changed tactics in this round and did most of the scoring with his left jab. He was amazingly agile, and at one stage landed five punches to the face in quick succession without reply.

Pettifer's performance amazed those fans who saw him beaten

by Jack Doyle, but by round nine he had slowed considerably. The energy used in the early rounds had taken their toll, and the lighter, quicker Welshman was up on his toes ramming his left through the Londoner's guard and punishing him heavily.

The champion shot from his corner at the start of round ten and rocked Pettifer with a right to the jaw. The Londoner hung on grimly, but was badly shaken by another heavy right. He tried to fight back but Petersen defended well, and by this stage was dictating the fight. Three sharp lefts in quick succession jolted Pettifer's head back, and all he could do was cover up.

The challenger showed great courage in round eleven as he threw big punches in an attempt to turn the fight around. In doing so, however, he took several heavy punches to the chin. He appeared to have nothing left and Petersen took complete control with a stream of solid lefts to the face.

The twelfth started in dramatic fashion. Petersen crashed a left to the jaw and as Pettifer straightened, smashed a left hook to the body followed by a right to the chin. The Londoner stood up magnificently and fought back strongly, his onslaught forcing the champion to cover up. To tremendous cheering, the two men then stood up to one another and traded blows. It was a fight to a finish as both scored heavily to the head. Although many shots missed, the end was spectacular.

Petersen skilfully manoeuvred the challenger into a corner and swiftly crashed a left to the jaw. It was the best punch of the fight, and a decisive one. Pettifer's knees dipped, his guard dropped, and like a flash the champion threw two vicious rights to the jaw. The big Londoner crashed onto his back, and lay spreadeagled on the ring floor to be counted out.

It had been a tremendous performance by the young champion. As soon as the count was completed, an excited, yet relieved Pa Petersen, jumped into the ring and kissed his son's badly bloodied face.

Although many critics had derided Jack's skill, he was a revelation whether he chose to box or fight. His left jab had matched that of his much bigger challenger, and although he was occasionally rocked, he invariably hit back with interest.

'Jack and I thoroughly enjoyed the fight because it was a good clean one throughout,' Pa told a *South Wales Echo* reporter who called to see them. 'There was not one thing done by either man to which exception could be taken.'

Apart from a badly swollen and discoloured left eye, the champion showed no signs of the gruelling contest. He laughed at his reflection in a mirror, and dabbing gingerly at his injured eye, said, 'When I fought Schonrath, I had two black eyes. This time I have escaped with one.'

Paying tribute to his opponent, Jack said, 'What father says is quite right. I think Pettifer is a very fine fighter, and fought cleanly in a very sporting and manly fashion. I for one never expected the easy victory which apparently so many people did.'

Battered and bruised, the gallant Pettifer was quick to pay tribute to his conqueror. 'He is a really great boy,' he said sportingly. 'My, how he can hit. He is a real champion, and good luck to him.'

One spectator with particular interest in Petersen, was Dan Sullivan who had close connections with Jack Doyle. 'What do you think of the Welsh boy now?' he was asked by William E. Allen immediately after the fight.

'His form was a revelation,' replied Sullivan, 'but I still think my lad can whip him.'

A film of the fight was shown at a private viewing at the Queens cinema in Cardiff the following evening. Interest was so great in South Wales that it was then screened to the public at the Queens and Pavillion cinemas throughout the week. Every showing drew virtually a full house. The film was said to be one of the best involving a fight ever produced, the dramatic ending being particularly well covered.

* * *

On the night of the fight, Jeffersen Peake was ill in bed at his home at Brighton suffering from pleurisy. Telephone calls were made to him minute by minute advising him of the progress of the promotion. The only sour note of the evening was that Petersen did not receive the gold cup which Peake had said would be presented to the winner.

According to Pettifer, the Brighton impresario had bought it for him because he was training for the fight on Brighton pier and was a great local hero. He believed that win, lose or draw against Petersen, he would receive the cup. When he later asked for it, Peake rejected him.

The cup appeared to have gone missing, but as Jack was the winner, Pa was determined he should get it. Intent on resolving the matter, he travelled to Brighton and confronted Peake who evaded the issue and gave no explanation as to why he did not hand over the cup. He went into a long, rambling and disjointed statement in which he accused practically every boxer, promoter and fight fan of being engaged in a conspiracy to defraud him. He said he had been badly let down by everyone, and lost a lot of money on the promotion.

Peake also complained that the dressing gown Jack wore into the ring, and which was to have been auctioned after the contest, was taken away. Pa explained that it was a genuine mistake and promised to return it.

During the course of subsequent correspondence between the parties, Peake maintained that the cup was always intended for Pettifer. He had, however, changed his mind about that because the London boxer had not treated him properly.

Peake eventually told Pa he wanted to present the cup to Jack. Believing it to be a genuine offer, Pa assured him that the people of Cardiff would give him a rousing welcome in appreciation of his sportsmanship in connection with the fight. Despite Pa's patience, however, the cup was not forthcoming.

Determined to get justice for his son, Pa Petersen served a writ on Peake claiming the trophy and damages for its retention. It then became clear that all was not well with the man from Brighton who was arrested outside a solicitors office in the City of London for breach of the peace. He appeared at the Lord Mayors court and was remanded to Brixton prison for evidence of his state of mind. At a subsequent hearing, Peake was bound over to be of good behaviour and keep out of London for a period of twelve months.

In November 1933, Peake was adjudged bankrupt, and during the course of proceedings, claimed his entry into boxing caused his financial downfall. He lost £4,000 over the Petersen–Pettifer fight which was his only promotion. Pa raised the situation of the cup with the Trustee in Bankruptcy who said it was not relevant to Peake's affairs.

The claim for damages against Peake came before Mr. Justice Charles and a common jury in the Kings Bench Division of the High Court on 14 February 1934. The action was defended, with Peake claiming Jack had no right to receive the cup.

Counsel representing the Petersens' described Peake as 'a man who became bitten with the ambition to figure as a patron of sport.' The court was told that on 12 December 1932, he purchased an ordinary silver gilt cup on a pedestal costing about £50. A pair of flagstaffs with an enamel Union Jack were added to the lid, and a pair of fighting cocks in boxing gloves to the handles.

After the cup was delivered to him, Peake began using it for legitimate purposes of advertising. 'He seems to have been a man of great resource intent on introducing novelties into boxing contests,' remarked Counsel.

Referring to Peake's comment to Pa that he originally intended giving the cup to Pettifer, Counsel said, 'It may be that he put his money on Pettifer. He may have thought Pettifer would win, but when he lost he did not feel as generously disposed as he otherwise would have.'

The court was told that at one stage Peake claimed the cup had been stolen from a hotel at Leicester Square where it had been taken for a luncheon.

'Did one of the journalists take it?' asked Mr. Justice Charles.

'No,' replied Counsel, 'we suspect the defendant put this rumour around for the sake of publicity. It was never stolen.'

Counsel said that Jack was prepared to pay for the trophy. 'It is of great value to him even though it might be an encumbrance to everyone else.'

There was great laughter when the judge remarked, 'What the plaintiff can do with it, I don't know. He can't have a drink from it with all its poles, flags and gloves on.'

After legal submissions, the case was stood over in order that Jack could amend his claim. Although the judge directed that the case came before the court again on the earliest possible day, settlement was reached out of court. Although no public announcement was ever made, it was generally known that Jack obtained possession of the cup. Some sources claimed he actually paid Peake for it. All Jack would say was, 'the lawyers have made much more than its value in fees.

* * *

Jefferson Peake appeared at Lewes Assizes on 8 December 1936, accused of murdering his chauffeur, Arthur George Noyce, aged 22 years, by strangulation at a flat in Hove two months earlier. The court heard that after committing the atrocity, Peake attempted to take his own life by swallowing eight tablets, cutting his throat and wrists with a razor blade and trying to gas himself.

After a trial lasting two days, he was found guilty of murder, and sentenced to death. In February the following year, however, Peake successfully appealed against the sentence, and an order was made under the Mental Health Act and he was committed to Broadmoor Hospital.

* * *

The morning after the Pettifer fight, Jack Callaghan contacted Pa Petersen seeking a return. He wanted to stage it within six weeks at a venue where seats could be priced more cheaply. Although Pa was interested, he made it clear that he would only consider a return if agreement was reached for it to be staged at Cardiff where substantial ticket sales would be guaranteed.

Pettifer's manager, George McDonald, liked the idea and had talks with London promoter, Sydney Hulls, who had an option on his boxers services. Hulls agreed to postpone the option provided a return fight with Petersen could be arranged.

The Welshman, however, was in great demand. Reggie Meen, unhappy at losing his title to Jack six months earlier, had already challenged him to a return with side-stakes of £200. A number of other promoters were offering good money for his services. Among them were Jeff Dickson, who promoted in London and Paris, and Jerry Walsh, acting on behalf of prominent Welsh sportsman, Jimmy Jones.

At a meeting with Pa, Walsh made an offer of £6,000 for Jack to take part in three contests. After hard negotiation, agreement was reached for contests to be staged on 8 May, 26 June and in August at venues in South Wales to be agreed. It was stipulated that each contest would be over 15 rounds, and Jack must remain undefeated for the agreement to stand.

Meanwhile, a number of opponents were considered for Jack's next fight. Harry Levene, manager of British Empire champion, Larry Gains, wrote to William E. Allen, stating that his man was willing to defend his title against Petersen. 'I merly await a challenge,' said Levene, 'and a match can be ratified immediately.' Levene also suggested French champion, Maurice Griselle, for whom he acted as British agent.

Allen was very prominent in Welsh boxing circles, and as Boxing Editor for the *South Wales Echo*, was well connected and highly respected. He agreed to put Levene's proposals to Petersen's people.

Another challenge came from Len Harvey. His manager Charlie Rose, offered to put up £500 to secure a contest, with a similar amount as a side-stake.

'I am authorised by Len Harvey to state that he is so confident of being able to outbox Petersen, that £250 of the side-stake will be his own money,' declared Rose.

Although Jack had tremendous respect for Harvey, Pa did not take the challenge seriously. By this time, they already had a number of fights lined up, but through the *South Wales Echo*, Pa stated that as soon as Jack was free, he would willingly defend his title against Len. He said they were willing to raise the side-stakes to £1,000, but insisted the fight must be on a winner-take-all basis.

Harvey was annoyed at Pa's response, and in a letter to William E. Allen, he said:

> Mr. Petersen said my challenge is all nonsense, but I will prove it is not. I'd like him to know that I am quite serious, and I resent his attitude.
>
> Does Mr. Petersen forget that when Meen held the title, his son's challenge was accepted? Jack then weighed twelve stones, seven pounds, and Meen fifteen stones. So I cannot see that any disparity in my own and Petersen's weights is an excuse to refuse to meet me.
>
> Petersen says I may get a match after August, and that there must be a winner-take-all basis. Very well, I'll accept, and I'll wager £500 on the result, but I don't want to wait six months. Petersen, it seems, is being fixed up with fights until August. He can very well take me as one of those opponents on the conditions named by his father.

Despite the firmness of Len's challenge, it was ignored. Instead, agreement was reached for Jack to meet Ernst Guehring of Germany at the Royal Albert Hall on 23 February. The German was considered a good opponent for Jack because amongst the men he had beaten were Hans Schonrath and Maurice Griselle.

The day after the fight was announced, however, the German pulled out. Having won a fight in Paris a few days earlier, he put a price on his head and refused to box on the terms originally agreed. Dickson attempted to negotiate with him but to no avail.

Anxious to save the show, the promoter contacted Moutzi Spakow, described as the heavyweight champion of Romania. He agreed to fly to London and train at The Dolphin at Slough. Two days later, Dickson announced that Spakow had pulled out because he was too interested in the political situation in his home country. The fact was, the Rumanian had not performed well on the continent. Dickson became concerned about public opinion of Spakow as an opponent for Petersen, so he changed his mind.

The promoter then had a further meeting with Guehring in Paris where he was sparring with Spakow. The German eventually agreed to meet the British champion on the original terms, and flew to London with Dickson the following morning. He amused waiting newsmen when he remarked; 'You can take it from me that Petersen could not give me as rough a time as I had on the trip across here this morning.'

* * *

Poster advertising the contest between Jack Petersen and Ernst Guehring of Germany.

Jack Petersen continued to involve himself with events for charity. He autographed a pair of boxing gloves to be auctioned at a big boxing event at Merthyr Stadium on 20 February in aid of funds for the Merthyr War Memorial. The gloves were forwarded to him by the Welsh Area of the British Boxing Board of Control on behalf of the Merthyr branch of the British Legion.

Jack also donated a fine signed photograph of himself wearing the National Sporting Club belt. Although a clashing engagement prevented him from accepting an invitation to attend the Merthyr event, he insisted that he and his father were always delighted to assit any good cause.

* * *

Ernst Guehring was rated the third best heavyweight in Germany behind Max Schmeling and Walter Neusel. He had never been knocked out, and it was claimed that he had only been floored on one occasion. He put up a good performance against Primo Carnera in February 1932, and had beaten Hans Schonrath and former European champion, Heine Muller. Standing six feet three inches, Guehring scaled 15 stones at the weigh-in at Jeff Dickson's office in the west end of London.

Petersen's weight was called as being 13 stones 13 lbs, his heaviest ever. Although Jack went to the scales fully clothed, there was considerable doubt about the accuracy of the weight.

In his first appearance at the Royal Albert Hall since winning the A.B.A. title, Jack was anxious to make a good impression. Yet, whilst being entertaining and competitive, the fight was a disappointment to many in the 4,000 crowd. Guehring proved to be a rugged, awkward fighter who showed he could absorb a good punch and still throw plenty back. Despite being pounded heavily, he extended the British champion who had to be content with a points victory.

Both men took a great deal of punishment during the twelve rounds, but Petersen was unable to produce the fireworks of previous contests. In the main he dictated matters with his left jab, and his speed and alertness to seize an opening were impressive. At the end he was still boxing at top speed, proving beyond doubt to be one of the fittest heavyweights seen at the Albert Hall for many years.

Although Jack rarely looked like winning inside the distance, his best moments came in rounds eight and ten when the pace of the contest was amazing. In the eighth, he staggered Guehring with two vicious punches to the head but the German's powers of resistance were incredible. He just shook his head, mauled, and survived.

The tenth was the most exciting round of the fight and proved a severe test for the young Welshman. He caught Guehring with a stinging left jab and a glancing right to the chin, and before the German could recover, two more hard rights slammed against his chin. The end finally seemed in sight but Guehring clung on tightly. Petersen shook himself free, threw punch after punch at the German who sagged, reeled and shook his head sadly. Jack, however, showed no restraint, and his inexperience and impetuosity cost him a glorious opportunity to end the contest.

It was just one of a number of occasions during the twelve rounds when he showed all the defects of youth – carelessness, rashness and a tendency towards wildness when he was stung. It was these areas that the critics seized upon in the newspapers the following day. The *South Wales Argus* boxing correspondent wrote:

> After last night's display, I have grave doubts as to whether Petersen has the physique and stamina to carry him to his goal of the world championship.

Although Guehring was by no means a world class fighter, he remained strong throughout the contest, and received a tremendous ovation as he left the ring. 'Petersen is very quick, but sometimes I felt I had him going,' he told reporters. 'He is a great sportsman and I enjoyed every moment of the fight.'

Jack was unmarked when he returned to his dressing room to face the press. 'A very tough fellow indeed,' he told them, 'but I do think I won every round. I had many opportunities during the fight to knock him out, but he was very strong and always came back.'

In the days following the fight, the British champion was subjected to a great deal of criticism. Fans and critics alike felt he had been exposed and did not possess the punching power to be successful at the top level. At that stage, however, it had not been disclosed that Jack had boxed twelve rounds under the tremendous handicap of damage to his right hand.

In an exclusive front page story in the *South Wales Echo* on 28 February 1933, it was revealed that the British champion only went into the ring to keep faith with promoter, Jeff Dickson, for whom he was boxing for the first time. He did so against the express advice of his doctor.

William E. Allen described having seen an x-ray of Jack's right hand on the Friday before the fight. It clearly revealed a fracture of the metacarpal bone, and a considerable thickness of fluid covering the knuckles.

Pa Petersen told Allen that they were actually inside the Royal Albert Hall before Jack finally made the decision to fight. According to Pa, Jack said, 'Well Dad, since we are here, I might as well fight as be idle. This is our first fight for Mr. Dickson and I'd hate to let him down, although this is a big risk.'

Pa insisted that Jack would require specialist treatment and would not box again until May. A number of lucrative engagements would have to be cancelled, including a fight with Maurice Griselle set for Leicester in March.

Meanwhile, Larry Gains, who had been at ringside for the fight with Ernst Guehring, offered to back himself heavily against Petersen in a defence of his British Empire title. Pa responded angrily to a suggestion by Gains that he would be glad 'to teach Jack some of the principles of boxing.'

'We offered Gains £100 to come down to Cardiff before the Pettifer contest,' he growled. 'I leave it at that.'

Although Jack would be out of action for some while, negotiations proceeded for him to meet world light-heavyweight champion, Maxie Rosenbloom. A Welshman living in New York, approached William E. Allen on behalf of the American's manager, with a view to a fight being staged in Cardiff.

Jack was delighted when told, because despite what had been said to the contrary, he could still easily make the 12 stones 7 lbs limit. He was, however, adamant on one point; that such a fight must be for the world title. The stumbling block appeared to be a comment contained in a letter from Rosenbloom's manager in which he said his man would not be prepared to risk his title. He was, however, prepared to meet Petersen anywhere at catch-weights.

William E. Allen was very close to the situation, and although negotiations continued, he expressed doubts about whether the contest would ever take place.

6

CHAMPION IN DEMAND

Although the hand injury prevented Jack from training, he continued to involve himself with charity work. During March 1933, he assisted in a scheme devised to raise money for the unemployed of Taff's Well, one of the most poverty stricken areas of the British Isles. More than 88 per cent of people were unemployed and there was a desperate need for boots for over 400 children in the area. At least £100 needed to be raised to enable the local boot fund to reach it's goal.

Jack Petersen's desire to become involved in helping these poor and needy people, earned him the title of the 'Philanthropic Champion of South Wales.' In an interview, he stated that his prize for helping to raise the required amount of money, would be the satisfaction of knowing that he had done something for the unemployed.

Always a practical man with plenty of good ideas, he was the perfect individual to be at the helm of any fund raising cause. He enthusiastically agreed to appear at an amateur boxing show, one of a number of events staged to raise money for the fund. His presence alone ensured that most of the required £100 was raised by admission fees. People loved and respected Jack, and they flocked to the event just to see him. His support was greatly appreciated, and members of the local committee expressed gratitude that he had not forgotten them in their time of need.

Meanwhile, negotiations for the three fights in South Wales, were taking shape. Agreement was reached for Jack to meet German heavyweight champion, Heine Muller, over fifteen rounds at Ninian Park, Cardiff, on 15 May 1933. The Welshman's hand injury responded well to treatment, and as news spread of his return to fitness so further challenges were received.

Over a period of a few days at the end of March, William E.

Allen again became involved on the British champion's behalf, and had a series of discussions regarding possible fights. He first met with a leading sportsman regarding a proposal from London promoter, Jeff Dickson, for Petersen to meet Jack Doyle. Dickson wanted to stage the fight at London's White City on the eve of the Derby, (29 May), and offered a purse of £5,000 to be split on a 60-40 per cent basis.

Allen put the proposal to Pa Petersen who angrily rejected it. 'Jack will not fight Doyle for less than £5,000, win, lose or draw,' he said. Pa was convinced that a crowd of 100,000 would pay to see a fight with Doyle in the open air at Cardiff. 'So, as far as we are concerned,' he insisted, 'it's £5,000 or no fight.'

Later the same afternoon, Allen received a further offer from Dickson, for Petersen to meet the winner of a fight between Young Stribling and Don McCorkindale. Acting as the go-between, the journalist was told by Pa that the same terms applied. 'Jack is the champion now,' said Pa firmly, 'and we are going to dictate our own terms.'

The following day, a remarkable challenge was made on behalf of Larry Gains. His manager, Harry Levene, said he was prepared to match Petersen with Gains for the British Empire title, and wager a heavy sum on the result. 'I will forfeit £1,000 if Gains fails to knock Petersen out inside six rounds, said Levene.

Pa Petersen smiled broadly when Allen told him of the proposal. 'You just tell Gains through the *South Wales Echo*, that just at the moment we are too busy to concern ourselves with his challenge,' retorted Pa.' 'Perhaps a little later we might give it some consideration."

The same day, the Welsh Camp received an increased offer to meet Jack Doyle. Jeff Dickson offered Jack £4,000, but Pa remained adamant. 'Our price is £5,000 or nothing.'

Despite all those challenges being made, it had to be remembered that Petersen was under contract for three contests at Cardiff. The articles laid down that he could only have one other fight between 15 May and 26 August.

Anxious to secure the British champion's services, Jeff Dickson eventually agreed to pay Jack the purse of £5,000 to meet the winner of Stribling and McCorkindale. The promoter wanted to stage the contest in London on 29 May, over fifteen rounds, with the referee to be appointed by the British Boxing Board of Control once both men were in the ring. Dickson also proposed that both men wore foul-proof cups, and that Petersen and his backers put up side-stakes of £2,500. Both Stribling and McCorkindale had agreed to accept the fight on five per cent of the gate, but had insisted on the side-stake.

'I am astonished at this condition that, if the contest is accepted, Jack must wear his shield,' remarked Pa Petersen angrily when William E. Allen told him of Dickson's proposals. 'It would appear that he is desirous of introducing all-in fighting with fouling allowed.'

Pa was convinced that neither the public nor the Board of Control would stand for such a situation. 'I would certainly not allow Jack to fight anybody under such conditions,' continued Pa. 'British rules for me, and British rules only.'

Pa told Allen that they were not in the least concerned who won between Stribling and McCorkindale. The only man they were prepared to seriously discuss at this stage was Jack Doyle. He argued that his original offer of a large side-stake was directed at Doyle, not Stribling or McCorkindale.

In a letter to Jeff Dickson, Pa said, 'You asked my price to fight Doyle in London on 29 May. I confirm what I told you, namely £5,000 win, lose or draw, over fifteen three minute rounds for the British championship. We would not fight anyone else under those terms.'

Dickson hit out dramatically at the demands of Petersen and his backers. 'Their demand is simply crazy,' he said. 'I will not pay such a sum as a guarantee to any boxer in the world.'

Speaking to the *South Wales Echo*, Dickson said that four years earlier he had decided to put all his boxers on a percentage of the gate to prove who were the drawing cards, and what each man was actually worth to him as a promoter. 'It took me six years to get boxers to agree to go on the gate,' continued the promoter, 'and I am certainly not going to spoil six years work by giving Jack Petersen £5,000 now.' Dickson insisted that if Jack's advisers stuck to their demands, he would match Doyle with another opponent for his White City promotion.

Through William E. Allen and the *South Wales Echo*, Pa Petersen suddenly, and somewhat surprisingly, stated that Jack was prepared to meet Larry Gains for the British Empire title, on the terms put forward by Harry Levene.

'We must point out, however, that Jack is booked up until the end of August,' insisted Pa, 'although opponents for his second and third fights have not been found.'

He suggested that Levene got in direct contact with the promoter of Jack's three contests in Wales, adding that Jack was also agreeable to side-stakes of £500 with the purse on a winner-take-all basis.

The reason for Pa's sudden change of heart came as a result of the on-going situation with Jeff Dickson. In response to the London promoter's comments, Pa said. 'I am sick of the whole business. I want Mr. Dickson to know that not for even £5,000, will I let Jack box Doyle now. But he can have the match if he pays Jack £6,000, and Doyle has a side-stake of £1,000 on the result.'

Pa stated that a fight between Petersen and the Irishman would probably draw the biggest crowd ever seen at a boxing match in Britain, but added that it would also bring a handsome profit to the promoter.

'I intend to keep the offer open for a week,' continued Pa. 'If Doyle is worth £5,000 as he demands, then Jack is worth £6,000. It does not matter about the drawing power of the Irishman. The fact remains, our man is the champion, and demands his price.'

A fight between Petersen and Doyle was undoubtedly the greatest attraction around, and until they were finally matched there would be all manner of speculation.

In early May, a story appeared in a London newspaper stating that the fight was definitely signed. Jeff Dickson confirmed that he had offered Petersen 25 per cent of the gate, but like his previous offers, this one had also rejected. The story was therefore premature.

As Dickson appeared to be making little headway with the Petersens, Welsh promoter Jimmy Jones, a Newport businessman and racehorse owner, announced that he was prepared to put up a purse of £7,000 to stage the fight in Cardiff. Pa Petersen was extremely interested and stated that he hoped the fight could be staged for the people of Wales.

The sudden interest of Jones put pressure on Dickson who promptly matched Doyle with veteran Belgian heavyweight, Jack Humbeeck, to take place at Olympia two days after Petersen met Heine Muller. The London syndicate behind Doyle were anxious to raise public interest even further, and show the Irishman as an outstanding contender for the British heavywieght title.

* * *

The whole of Wales was gripped with fight fever. When Heine Muller arrived in Cardiff, he was given a wonderful reception by a crowd of about 5,000. He was a mild mannered man, and said he was full of confidence. 'I have no fear of the outcome of the fight,' he remarked quietly. 'I have beaten men in England, America and on the continent with bigger reputations than Petersen.'

Muller was 26 years old, stood six feet three, and was former European heavyweight champion. He won the title in August 1931 by beating Pierre Charles of Belgium on points in Berlin. In a return in Brussels the following May, Charles regained the title on points.

Amongst the men Muller had beaten were Walter Neusel, Maurice Griselle, Hans Schonrath, Gypsy Daniels and Reggie Meen, who he stopped in four rounds. Apart from Charles, the only other men to have beaten him were Larry Gains and Don McCorkindale. He had boxed at every weight from light to heavyweight, and won a number of German national titles.

Welsh boxing referee, Mr. C. B. Thomas, had seen the German box on many occasions. In an interview with the *South Wales Echo*, he said he regarded him as the cleverest European heavyweight to fight in Britain since Georges Carpentier.

The demands for tickets for the fight was tremendous, and it was anticipated that the crowd could be in the region of international football match proportions. During the build-up, the contest was advertised as 'the greatest boxing carnival ever staged in Wales.'

The Phoenix Film Service Company arranged to make a film of the contest, and William E. Allen was invited to do the commentary. The promoter asked newspapers one week in advance, to advise fans to get to the venue early to assist traffic arrangements to operate smoothly. Jones was determined to make Ninian Park the centre of boxing in Wales. His ambition was to make Cardiff a serious rival to London and Manchester.

In the days leading up to the fight, the home of Cardiff City Football Club was completely transformed. Elaborate arrangements were made to accommodate huge numbers of spectators, and no expense was spared. Fans paying one shilling and sixpence would get a view almost as good as those paying fifteen shillings.

The promoter also went to great lengths to ensure that wherever fans sat, the atmosphere would be as intimate as within a closed building. Microphones were installed at ringside, and would carry sounds from the ring through loudspeakers erected in all parts of the ground.

The football pitch was hidden beneath a forest of seats and benches. Lines of barbed wire were erected around the sides of the pitch to prevent anyone moving from the stands to the seats on the field.

* * *

Petersen trained hard for the fight, and with just ten days to go, was joined at the Lynn Institute by Gypsy Daniels, who was paid £30 plus expenses. With the help of William E. Allen, ex-seaman, Ivor Powell, of Newport also joined the camp. He was a tough man and a hard hitter. Although he had been out of the ring for some time, he was in splendid condition.

In his final try-out, Jack did an impressive hour of strenuous exercises followed by three gruelling rounds with Daniels. Both men put everything into the session and it was fortunate for Gypsy that they were wearing 20 ounce gloves. Petersen also did three fast rounds with London heavyweight, Tony Arpino, and finished the session as fresh as when he started.

Petersen's popularity was incredible, and throughout the day of the fight, special steamer excursions from Bristol channel ports, brought thousands of fans to Cardiff. Special trains ran from destinations within an 80 mile radius right into Ninian Park Station. Special bus services were also in place, and motor coach proprietors were inundated with reservations for return trips to all parts of South Wales. The Directors of Cardiff Arms Park Greyhound track decided to bring a scheduled evening meeting forward to the afternoon because of crowd trouble on a previous occasion when Petersen had boxed.

The weigh-in took place at 2 pm on the day of the fight, at the offices of the *South Wales Echo*. Muller went to the scales first. He was fully clothed, and his weight was called as being fourteen stones two pounds. 'That's my boy's weight,' shouted Pa Petersen as Muller stepped down. 'If there's any question about it, then he will strip.'

Jack stepped on to the scales but Pa refused to allow his weight to be called. Although this was within the rules with heavyweights, it was extremely annoying to those people anxious to know his true weight. Those close to the British champion estimated that he would be conceding over a stone to the German.

Although he appeared very tense, Jack said he was confident he would beat Muller in double quick time. The betting boys agreed, and in the pre-fight odds, he was installed as 2-1 on favourite.

During the early evening dozens of sailors from a huge German naval vessel anchored in Cardiff Docks, went ashore to see the fight. They joined the crowds at Ninian Park, estimated to be about 53,000, said at the time to be the largest ever to attend a boxing match in Europe. '*Muller, Muller, Muller,*' they chanted as the boxers were called to the centre of the ring.

Everyone in the crowd had waited in eager anticipation for the fight, but were stunned when Petersen crushed the German in just two minutes, ten seconds of the opening round. Although disappointed that the fight did not last longer, many fans left Ninian Park convinced that Jack carried a punch in his right hand which would floor the best heavyweights in the world.

Petersen started quickly, slamming solid blows into the German's face. Although Muller countered with a right to the body, he walked onto a hard left hook to the chin. Again he countered, this time with two rights to the British champions face. Jack moved sideways and feinted to throw a left. The German covered up but was open to a right to the stomach.

Without a seconds hesitation, Petersen drove it in, hard and true. It was a terrific punch, and Muller sank to the floor clutching his stomach, his face wreathed in pain. Many people sitting at a distance from the ringside thought he had been fouled but this was not so. The punch was perfectly delivered to the solar plexus and gave the German no chance of beating the count.

It was a sensational victory for Petersen, and dispelled the concerns of a number of critics following his fight with Ernst Guehring. Promoter Jimmy Jones was so excited that he immediately cabled American promoter, Jimmy Johnstone, with a view to bringing world heavyweight champion, Jack Sharkey, to Britain.

'It is my ambition to stage a world heavyweight title fight in Cardiff,' Jones told the *South Wales Echo*. 'I have told Johnstone that in Jack Petersen, we have a boxer better than Carpentier.'

Jones was also full of praise for the *South Wales Echo* and *Western Mail* newspapers. He said that without their support in advertising the fight, there would not have been anything like the numbers who packed into Ninian Park.

Immediately after the fight, Jack returned to the Lynn Institute for a massage. He and his father then went to Barry for a supper party. Jack was the most relaxed of the group, darting in and out of the dining room munching apples, apparently oblivious to the fact that he had just destroyed a former European heavyweight champion.

* * *

Jeff Dickson had been at ringside to see the British champion's performance, and he was very impressed. The manner of the Welshman's victory over Muller made a contest with Doyle even more attractive. If Dickson were to stage it, he knew exactly what he had to do.

In previous weeks, the promoter had heaped criticism upon the

Petersens, describing their demands for £5,000 as 'monstrous' and 'ridiculous'. He assured Pa that the fight would never take place unless they became more reasonable. Dickson, however, was one of the shrewdest promotors around. He knew the value of the fight and was determined to stage it at all costs. He therefore swallowed his pride and quickly renewed contact with the Welsh camp.

'Jack is the champion,' Pa reiterated firmly as soon as Dickson contacted him. 'You know our price – take it or leave it.'

Pa knew what he was doing and had no intention of taking a backward step. Well aware that he had to move quickly, Dickson agreed in principle to stage the fight at London's White City on 2 June, on the British champion's terms.

Articles were signed at a meeting at Dickson's office in London on 19 May, and a statement issued to the press to end weeks of controversy and speculation. The previous evening Doyle knocked out Jack Humbeeck in two rounds. Jack and Pa were at Olympia but were not perturbed by what they saw. 'We shall definitely not lose on the second of June,' declared Pa as the meeting commenced.

Within hours of the fight being announced, Doyle amazingly pulled out. He had travelled to Paris to commence preparations but on arrival complained of pains in his back. It was stated that he would be unable to do any serious training for at least three weeks. What was not disclosed was the fact that Doyle required urgent treatment for an infection.

Jeff Dickson intended to re-schedule the fight for the first two weeks in July, but this looked extremely unlikely. Talks had continued between Jimmy Jones, and Madison Square Garden matchmaker, Jimmy Johnstone, and plans were being made for Petersen to box at Cardiff on 26 June. Johnstone suggested American, Hans Birkie as an opponent, and this was agreed by Jack's advisors at a meeting on 20 May.

Promoter Jones was having a difficult time finding an opponent for Jack because everyone he put forward was turned down. Birkie became another casualty when Pa discovered he had a poor record. After some tense negotiations, it was agreed that Jack would face George Cook, the veteran Australian, over 15 rounds at Cardiff on 26 June, even though he had originally been rejected.

Cook was a good test for the young champion. He was one of the toughest heavyweights around and had boxed all over the world. He had only been knocked out once in the preceding five years, that being by the massive Primo Carnera. In his last contest, George lost a highly disputed decision to Walter Neusel at the Royal

Albert Hall. Amongst his victims, was the current European champion, Paulino Uzcuden.

The Petersen-Doyle fight was eventually re-scheduled for 15 July, but because of the postponement, Jeff Dickson called upon both men to deposit £2,500 as appearance money. In reporting the story one London newspaper claimed that Dickson had added a further condition, that if Petersen was beaten by Cook, he would forfeit his deposit. The paper claimed Jack had agreed to do so.

It was in fact an absurd story because in effect it would have meant that Jack would wager £4,500 to nothing that he beat Cook. He was guaranteed £2,000 for each of three fights by Jimmy Jones on condition he remained undefeated.

As he got down to serious training, Jack was again joined by Gypsy Daniels as his chief sparring partner. Former Cardiff rugby forward, Goff Retter, a close friend of Pa's was also hired. He was also a well known wrestler and weight lifter who had such immense strength, it was claimed he could pull a car along with his teeth, and hammer six inch nails through a block of wood with his bare hands.

Pa Petersen insisted that having Retter at the camp was not a gimmick, but designed to test Jack's strength at inside work. 'We know Cook's style of boxing,' he declared, 'and are looking for ways and means to counter him.' Apart from being a top class wrestler, Retter was also a useful boxer. In the week he worked with Jack, they had some brisk exchanges as the British champion concentrated on fighting at close quarters.

With less than two weeks to go, Petersen's training schedule was seriously disrupted when Gypsy Daniels had to withdraw from the camp with a carbuncle on his back. Despite great efforts by William E. Allen, who toured the Rhondda on Jack's behalf, it seemed impossible to find a replacement.

Allen had greatly admired Jack ever since his amateur days and had a genuine desire to help him get proper training. He approached a number of men, including Welsh light-heavyweight champion, Randy Jones, and Clydach Vale prospect, Tommy 'Kid' Farr, who was training to meet Gunner Bennett on the Cardiff bill. Neither was interested in sparring with Petersen.

For a week Jack was forced to do the bulk of his work on the heavy bag. Only during the last two days of training did he get help from former Welsh middleweight champion, Jerry Daley (Penygraig) and Albert Donovan (Cardiff), one of the few men to have beaten him as an amateur.

During the week prior to the fight, William E. Allen persuaded

George Cook to write some articles for the *South Wales Echo*. He described how he seconded Leo Bandias in his fight against Petersen in December 1931. George disclosed that after the fight, Pa Petersen told him; 'You are the last fighter I would think of letting my Jack meet. Not only are you so damn tough, you have had more experience than any other fighter this side of the Atlantic.'

Pa admitted to Allen that he made the remark, but now considered Jack sufficiently experienced to face the Australian.

* * *

Despite his busy schedule, Jack remained in constant demand for personal appearances and charity work. He received a tremendous ovation when he presented the prizes at an amateur show at St. Peters Boy Scouts Boxing Club in Cardiff. He applauded generously throughout the contests, and genuinely appreciated the efforts of all the young boxers.

He attended an event at Mountain Ash for the crowning of the May Queen, and two days before the Cook fight, was present at Abergavenny Hospital boxing promotion. The event at Market Hall was the main attraction during hospital week, and Jack received warm applaus when introduced into the ring by William E. Allen.

He then took part in a three rounds exhibition with his father during which they delighted the audience with a touch of comedy. The gloves they used were later auctioned and raised thirteen guineas. An autographed photo of Jack brought a further five pounds.

Many people naively believed Jack always gave his services free, and were surprised when it was revealed that he charged £25 for attending the Mountain Ash and Abergavenny events. 'We are not in the boxing business for nothing,' explained Pa when the subject was raised. He disclosed that they asked for £25 appearance money which did not include sparring. For a three rounds exhibition, their fee was £100.

'If it is an exceptionally deserving charity, we do not hesitate to give the money back,' explained Pa, 'but in cases where we are told that Jack's attendance means an addition to the funds of immensely more than twenty-five pounds, and they persist in asking for his services, then we expect them to meet our terms.'

* * *

On 12 June, Len Harvey beat Eddie Phillips for the British light-heavyweight title vacated by Petersen. He immediately issued a fresh challenge to Jack, offering to increase the side-stakes to £1,500. Len said he would also agree to the Petersen's earlier demands of the fight being on a winner-take-all basis.

As Jack was already contracted to meet Cook and Doyle, the challenge was rejected. This prompted Charlie Rose to write to Jimmy Jones stating that Harvey was prepared to meet Petersen for side-stakes of £500 irrespective of the outcome against Cook. The promoter ignored the proposal.

Meanwhile, the Board of Control received a letter from the National Boxing Association in America stating that they were withholding recognition of Maxie Rosenbloom as world light-heavyweight champion pending a decision by the Board in London that he first meets Jack Petersen. Some months earlier, the Board had submitted Petersen's name to the N.B.A. as a logical challenger for the title. It had since become clear that Rosenbloom was reluctant to defend against him.

At a meeting on 22 June, the Stewards decided to notify the N.B.A. that since submitting Petersen's name, Len Harvey had won the British light-heavyweight title. He should therefore be nominated as a logical contender in place of Petersen.

* * *

George Cook arrived at Cardiff the Sunday before the fight accompanied by his wife, manager Charlie Rose, and trainer Wally May. At a gathering at his headquarters, the Claude Hotel at Roath, Mrs. Cook was overheard speaking about Jack Petersen in extremely complimentary terms.

'I think his personality is greater than that of Carpentier, but in a somewhat different way,' she remarked with great sincerity. 'Petersen is gifted with glamour, and must have considerable character to have done what he has for a young man. We shall fight to the bitter end to beat him, but whoever wins it will not mean another enemy.'

Cook scaled 14 stones 5 at the weigh-in at the offices of the *South Wales Echo* in Cardiff. Petersen's weight was called at 'over thirteen stones' but the actual weight never revealed.

A crowd of over 50,000 flocked to Ninian Park where conditions were even finer than when Jack met Heine Muller. Yet there was great disappointment at the British champion's performance. Although he got the decision after fifteen rounds, he was well below form, and never really looked like beating the tough

Australian inside the distance. Cook was never on top at any stage of the fight, but there were times Jack had considerable difficulty with him.

It was a close affair throughout, and at the end Petersen was only just good enough to be declared the winner. He started well enough with his customary speed, scoring with a series of solid lefts to the face. A big right just missed the target, but after more lefts to the head, Cook hung on grimly and was cautioned by the referee.

'Tell him to keep his guard up,' screamed Cook's wife to the cornermen from her ringside seat.

Whilst the opening round was a good one for Jack, the next three were hard, mauling affairs. Very few solid punches were landed by either man. As expected, Cook, who was short and stocky, worked mainly at close-quarters, whilst Petersen tried to dictate matters at long range. It was not pretty to watch because the contrast in styles made it difficult for either man to gain superiority.

In round five, both men were cut, Cook above the left eye, and Petersen below the right. The crowd roared when the Australian suddenly went to the floor, but it was only a slip and he was up immediately.

The British champion hardly landed a punch in the sixth, but rallied well in round seven. Cook's spoiling tactics, however, ensured that neither man gained any advantage.

In round eight, Jack showed some of his old fire, but the tough Australian matched him by anticipating most of his moves and punches.

Petersen again showed plenty of aggression in the ninth but when he caught Cook with a tremendous right to the head, the Aussie hit back viciously. Jack retreated and hung on grimly. Cook was giving an amazing display of strength and stamina for a man fourteen years older than his opponent.

The Welshman began round ten with several heavy rights, and for a while Cook was unable to hold him off. Then, yet again, he displayed another of his characteristic rallies, and was punching Petersen around the ring at the bell.

During the interval there was a protest from the Australian's cornermen when they saw champagne being poured over Jack's head. They feared it would get into their man's eyes, so the referee went to the British champion's corner and wiped a towel over his head.

Although Jack had the edge in round eleven, Cook was far from beaten, and landed some solid right digs to the ribs. The pace dropped in the twelfth as both were intent on cancelling out each others close work.

Cook scored freely at the start of the thirteenth during which Petersen missed badly whenever he threw his right. It was the same at the start of the next, as the British champion became frustrated at his lack of success. Midway through the round, however, he staggered Cook with a powerful left and right combination. The crowd roared because at last the Australian looked to be in serious trouble. Petersen's punches, however, were wild and well wide of the target, and Cook again dodged and ducked out of trouble and weathered the storm.

Before the start of the final round, Mrs. Cook left her ringside seat and climbed to the ring apron. 'Keep your guard up,' she yelled pointing an admonishing finger in her husband's face. 'And fight like hell.'

As though obeying his wife's demands, George shot from his corner and waded into Petersen with wild abandon. This was his undoing, and after scoring with a volley of solid lefts, Petersen let go a hard right to the chin. Cook slumped to his knees for a count of 'three', and was very shaky when he rose. Again, Jack was wild in his attempt to end the fight, and Cook mauled and spoiled to keep out of danger until the final bell.

George Cook had played his part in a tense, absorbing fight, and received a big hand as he left the ring. Although Petersen got the decision, everyone knew it had been close. What was not revealed was the fact that Jack was again having trouble with his right hand.

In training he knew something was wrong, but it was not serious enough to call off the fight. Against Cook, however, he lacked the confidence to use both hands as he would have liked which effected his performance. The fact was only revealed in later years as a guide to the fact that when a boxer does not put up a performance equal to his best, there may be a perfectly valid reason.

Although they said nothing in public, Jack and Pa were extremely concerned about the injury. In the days following the fight Jack had further treatment on the hand, and also for bruising to his jaw. He knew that a dramatic improvement would be needed if he was to overcome the threat posed by Jack Doyle in just three weeks time.

7

AN IRISHMAN NAMED DOYLE

Negotiations for the fight between Petersen and Jack Doyle had been long and tense. Although Jeff Dickson believed he had an agreement for the contest to go ahead on 12 June, things were far from settled.

Doyle was no fool, and realised he was the man to draw the crowds. He knew that White City Stadium, who by this time were his managers, would profit handsomely from gate receipts. He therefore demanded an identical purse to that of the champion.

In February 1932, with the help of Dan Sullivan, Doyle had bought himself out of the Army to concentrate on a career as a professional fighter. Sullivan first spotted him boxing for the Irish Guards and immediately believed he was a heavyweight champion of the future. Jack left the Army with an unbeaten amateur record of 28 victories, 27 coming by knockout. When he turned professional, Sullivan became his manager.

They started off successfully enough, but the relationship soured somewhat in October 1932. A few days after he had beaten Jack Pettifer, Doyle discovered that Sullivan had sold his managerial contract to White City Stadium for the pricely sum of 5,000 guineas. Without any discussion with his fighter, Sullivan had struck up a deal with White City Stadium chairman, Brigadier General A. C. Critchley.

As the fight with Petersen approached, things were made more difficult for Doyle because Sullivan still thought he should collect his 25 per cent manager's fee. As far as Doyle was concerned, that ended when Sullivan sold the contract.

The Irishman became increasingly angry with Sullivan and Critchley, and therefore went it alone in conducting negotiations regarding his purse. By-passing them, and promoter Jeff Dickson, he spoke with Francis Gentle, a Director of White City. Agreement was eventually reached that the Irishman would receive a purse of £3,000 net, excluding training expenses.

Still not prepared to trust anyone, Doyle insisted that the agreement be confirmed in writing. Gentle confirmed the deal in a letter of 29 June 1933, after which Doyle finally agreed to the fight.

The Irishman was clearly envious of the success Petersen had achieved. From his training camp at Taplow, he made no secret of the fact that he intended to knock him out as quickly as possible. The majority of the critics, however, fancied the more skilful Petersen to retain his title. By the day of the fight he was a 6-4 on betting favourite.

On paper, it appeared an absurd fight to be staged for the British heavyweight title. As a professional, Doyle had just 15 rounds experience in ten fights. Yet, in other ways, it was the most attractive heavyweight contest for a very long time.

The style of the flamboyant Irishman, and the manner of his victories, had captured public imagination. Five victories in the first round, five in the second, eight coming by clean knockout, convinced the fans he was a world beater. Doyle was an extremely confident individual with tremendous physical attributes. He received massive publicity, his photo appearing in every possible publication. The only concern amongst his fans was that he was wayward and headstrong and therefore difficult to handle.

Writer and historian, Gilbert Odd, was convinced that Doyle enabled Petersen to command the massive purse he negotiated. In his view, Doyle was in fact entitled to the larger share:

'The size of the purse is determined by the drawing power of the boxers ... There is no question that Doyle is the man who attracts the spectators.'

The comments were unfair to the Welshman, as the writer seemed to forget Jack's own tremendous drawing power. It was the fight itself which warranted the massive purse because it was the greatest attraction in heavyweight boxing for years. Petersen, as champion, was therefore entitled to the lions share.

Jack had an incredible following and had achieved everything asked of him. He already had two notches on the championship belt, and badly wanted to make it his own property within the space of just twelve months. The demand for tickets was therefore enormous, and no indoor arena in the country could have housed the numbers expected to attend.

The two boxers had three opponents in common, but Doyle had beaten them all in much quicker time; Bill Partridge (rsf.1), George

Slack (ko2) and Jack Pettifer (ko2). The Petersen camp were well aware of the Irishman's pulling power when they conducted their negotiations. That was why they held out for the massive purse which they were eventually paid.

Unbeknown to outsiders, Doyle's medical problem was causing him considerable discomfort. It also seriously affected his training. Nevertheless, he was convinced that the sheer power of his punches was sufficient to beat Petersen. A good luck telegram from former world heavyweight champion, Jack Dempsey, gave him further encouragement.

* * *

Petersen travelled to London during the afternoon before the fight. He was accompanied by Pa, John Woods, and Danny Davies, and when they arrived at Paddington Station, a huge crowd were there to greet them. They took their usual precautions of staying overnight in a quiet hotel away from well-wishers. They even took their own food which had been specially prepared. Pa never took chances before a fight and would not risk Jack being upset by strange food. He also believed that it was possible efforts could be made on behalf of an opponent to 'get at it.'

The following morning, hundreds of excited fans gathered in the street outside Jeff Dickson's office in the west end of London to see the principals arrive for the weigh-in. Both were jostled and cheered loudly, and there was such a crush that police struggled to clear the way to enable them to get through.

Never before in the history of British boxing had two men so young fought for the heavyweight championship. Petersen was 21 and Doyle just 19. When they came face to face inside Dickson's office, both were very calm and polite. They bowed, shook hands and smiled.

'I hope you are well,' said Petersen.

'I am very well thanks,' replied Doyle, 'How are you?'

'I am exceptionally well thank you very much,' was the British champions reply.

With another slight bow they went to the scales. Petersen's weight was called at 13 stone 6. Doyle, who scaled 15 stone 3, also had a three inch advantage in height.

By early evening the area around White City was at a standstill. All roads leading to the stadium were jammed by long lines of cars and taxis. People spilled from the pavements, and there was chaos as police attempted to control the heavy masses.

WHITE CITY STADIUM

JEFF DICKSON PROMOTION

WEDNESDAY, JULY 12th, 1933, at 8 p.m.

THE GREATEST HEAVY-WEIGHT NATURAL EVER STAGED IN GREAT BRITAIN
FIFTEEN (3 min.) ROUNDS CONTEST
For the Heavy-weight Championship of Great Britain

JACK   JACK

PETERSEN v. DOYLE

WALES (Holder)   IRELAND

Grand Special Fifteen (3 min.) Rounds Return Contest

JACK (KID) BERG v. CLETO LOCATELLI

These men recently met in a Ten rounds Contest at the Royal Albert Hall, Locatelli getting a very close decision.

Inter-British Heavy-weight Ten Rounds Contest
CHARLIE SMITH (DEPTFORD) v. BEN FOORD (SOUTH AFRICA)

POPULAR PUBLIC PRICES (including Tax)
Covered Stands: 5/-, 8/6, 12/6, 15/-. Ringside: £1-4s., £1-16s., £2-8s.

Seats can be booked at the White City Stadium ; Harringay G.R.A. ; and at Messrs. Keith Prowse, Alfred Hays, District Messengers, Webster and Waddington, Webster and Girling, all Agencies ; Jeff Dickson's Offices, 8 and 10, Cecil Court, Charing Cross Road, W.C.2 (Temple Bar 5523 and 8922). Birmingham ; Jim Murphy, Farcroft Hotel, Rookery Road, Handsworth (Northern 0967)

Poster advertising British heavyweight championship between Jack Petersen and Jack Doyle.

Although the crowd was later described as being the largest ever to attend a fight in Britain, Jeff Dickson was disappointed. He had expected a gate of at least 80,000 but in the end it was estimated as being between 60,000 and 70,000. Whatever the true number, thousands were unable to get in. Welsh and Irish fans were there in their thousands, and everything seemed set for a memorable contest.

The fight attracted a tremendous amount of betting. Huge amounts, including two of £6,000 and £3,000 were placed on Petersen to retain his title. Most newspapers also fancied the Welshman to win.

There was an almighty roar from the wildly cheering crowd as Doyle emerged from his dressing room. Clad in an emerald green dressing gown, he waved his arms and punched the air as he strode jauntily towards the ring. The roar became deafening as he climbed through the ropes and stripped off his gown.

Born at Cobh in County Cork, Jack was the first man from Eire to challenge for the British heavyweight title. He qualified because at the time of his birth, the country came under British rule.

Although only 19, Doyle was a showman. Wearing immaculate

green satin trunks with a white waistband, his initials embroidered in gold on each leg alongside a shamrock, he bowed to the audience and blew kisses to ladies sitting at ringside. He didn't appear to have a care in the world and chatted cheerfully to everyone around him, including the Master of Ceremonies.

The Irishman's mood, however, soon changed because as the seconds ticked by there was no sign of Petersen. It was a deliberate ploy and one of the oldest in the game. All of five minutes elapsed before the British champion appeared, but instead of unnerving Doyle as was intended, it made him extremely angry.

Many prominent dignitaries were seated at ringside, including ex-king Alfonso. Every leading boxer of note was there including heavyweights, George Cook, Walter Neusel, Larry Gains and Don McCorkindale. When introduced from the ring, Neusel and McCorkindale both issued a challenge to the winner.

Throughout the introductions, Doyle was noticeably on edge, and barely took his eyes off Petersen on the other side of the ring. The mood in which he entered the ring, had gone.

After the introductions, referee, Mr. C. H. Douglas, called them to the centre of the ring and gave a very pronounced lecture. Jogging up and down, Doyle paid no attention to what was being said. He was extremely fired-up and itching for the opening bell to send them into action.

The fight started at a tremendous pace as they exchanged a barrage of punches in the centre of the ring. Petersen banged away at the Irishman's stomach and at the same time managed to avoid several wild punches which were thrown back at him. Knowing the Irishman would start quickly, Jack continued to punch away in an attempt to gain the early ascendancy. As Doyle lunged forward, he was caught by a solid left jab to the face. He then swung a right which missed the target, but another vicious right aimed at the jaw caught Petersen on the side of the neck.

As he continued to attack, Doyle left himself wide open, and Petersen scored with several solid blows to the ribs. Doyle held on and they wrestled, punched, pulled and tugged, both ignoring the referee's orders to break. Twice Mr. Douglas pulled them apart and cautioned them, but each time Doyle completely ignored him. He was fighting mad and couldn't hear a word. All he wanted to do was get back into the fight.

On the second occasion, Mr. Douglas had barely finished speaking when the Irishman lunged at Petersen who quickly grabbed and held on. Once again they were scrambling all over the ring, hitting and holding, until the referee managed to pull them apart. Doyle was the culprit, and this time he was severely lectured by Mr. Douglas.

Again the Irishman was not listening. His fiery eyes were fixed firmly on Petersen, and when they were ordered to 'box on', he rushed forward lashing out in all directions.

The champion scored with a beautiful left to the chin followed by a straight right. Doyle immediately responded with a swinging right to the body which went low, prompting Mr. Douglas to warn him to keep his punches up. There was no complaint from Petersen who crashed another right to the chin.

Head down, Doyle responded with another wild heavy punch which landed well below the belt. Referee Douglas dived in to caution him but took a punch on the shoulder in the melee. The Irishman was by now so out of control that he ignored the official and attacked Petersen viciously with both hands.

His back to the ropes, the British champion hit back with a left and right combination, but more swinging punches from the Irishman had him reeling and in serious trouble. Doyle, however, was so erratic and out of control that he failed to hit the target when the champion looked about to be taken.

Another wild right crashed into the Welshman's right thigh, and as Mr. Douglas stepped in to admonish him, Doyle drove a powerful left into the champion's groin. Pushing him firmly aside, the referee gave him a final warning.

'Have you gone crazy Doyle?' he yelled. 'Do as I tell you and keep your punches up or out you go!'

Despite vigorous protests from Petersen's corner, the champion himself never once complained. He was a true sportsman in every sense and was genuinely trying his hardest to make a clean fight of it. Instead of going to the floor and taking advantage of the blatant low blows, he continued to try and outbox his wild opponent.

As the bell sounded for the end of an incredible first round, the referee was forced to grab hold of Doyle as he was about to throw another wild punch at his stricken opponent. Relieved to get some respite, Jack pulled himself upright and limped to his corner, clearly in pain from the effects of the powerful shots which had strayed well below the target.

The crowd booed loudly as the Irishman returned to his corner with Mr. Douglas hot on his heels. He talked long and hard to the boxer and his chief second, and before walking away, made his intentions abundantly clear. 'You understand now,' he said firmly. 'If he hits low again, no matter where, I shall disqualify him.'

The referee had already given Doyle a great deal of latitude because any one of five blows were bad enough for him to have been thrown out. The fouls had been so blatant that at the bell many people in the areas nearest the ring were screaming for the Irishman to be disqualified.

Had it been a non-title affair, the referee's task would have been easy. Yet in a contest of such public interest, he was in a difficult position, and therefore reluctant to rule Doyle out so early.

It is debatable whether Doyle heard a word Mr. Douglas said during the interval because at the bell for round two he tore into Petersen with wild abandon. Although he was met with crisp punches to the chin, the Irishman's response was to throw two more wild punches which landed low.

'Stop', shouted referee Douglas as he attempted to pull them apart. Doyle, however, was completely out of control, and head down, he bundled Douglas aside. Lashing out wildly, he tore into Petersen and wrestled him across the ring into a neutral corner where they indulged in a wild hitting free-for-all.

The referee chased after them still trying to call a halt, but could do nothing. Using the ropes well, Petersen hit back viciously, driving Doyle to the centre of the ring. There, they stood toe-to-toe in a vicious two-fisted rally, each taking heavy punches to the head.

Eventually, Mr. Douglas got between them and pushed Doyle backwards. He ordered both men to their corners and indicated that he had disqualified the Irishman for low blows. There was a storm of booing when the official announcement was made because many people sitting at a distance from the ring had not seen what prompted the referee's decision.

Immediately after the announcement, Doyle went to the British champion's corner and apologised for his behaviour. 'I'm sorry,' he said smiling ruefully as he shook hands with Jack. 'It's alright,' said Pa. 'We shall see one another again soon I hope.'

Pandemonium broke out and the protests continued long after the boxers were back in their dressing rooms. Years later, Gilbert Odd described it as the worst uproar he had ever witnessed at a boxing arena.

Petersen came out of the fight with tremendous credit. He landed the only clean blows, but Doyle's tactics prevented him from showing his true ability. His face was wreathed in pain as every low blow hit home, but the fact that he did not collapse said a great deal for the magnificent condition he was in. Yet despite everything, he battled away with the courage which was so characteristic of him.

Back in his dressing room Doyle was beseiged by reporters

desperate for his comments. Choked with emotion, the Irishman made no excuses for his defeat.

'Knowing so many of the folks from Ireland were watching, I just sailed right in,' he remarked. 'I told myself I would finish it quick. I suppose I did hit low because everyone says I did, but it will not happen again.'

He claimed that youth and inexperience contributed to his downfall, but remained convinced he could still beat anyone in the world.

The following morning several reporters visited Petersen at his hotel. He was pleased to see them, despite having spent a sleepless night due to excruciating pain in his groin and lower abdomen. Although he expressed great disappointment that the fight ended as it did, he was nevertheless delighted to have won. It meant that in exactly one year, he had made the championship belt his own property.

Jack showed the reporters the protective cup he wore during the fight. Although it was made from heavy aluminium strengthened with wire and covered with thick leather, it bore a dent thought impossible to make unless hit with tremendous force by a hammer.

Pa Petersen said that fouls were always an unfortunate feature of a fight. 'We don't like to win like that,' he said, 'but it's all in the game.'

Jack agreed, but was in no doubt that he would have eventually emerged the winner. 'I am certain that had the fight gone another round, I would have knocked him out,' he added politely.

As the years passed by, Jack was constantly asked about his fight with Doyle, and invariably gave the same reply:

'It was a travesty and tragedy of a boxing match from every point of view. I would like to forget all about it.'

Always the diplomat, he did try to understand matters from Doyle's side. 'There can be no doubt that he was anxious to win, and win quickly,' said Petersen quietly, 'but poor Doyle lost his head completely. Let us put it down that the occasion was altogether too big for him.'

On returning to Cardiff later that day, Jack was greeted at the Central Stadium by a large enthusiastic crowd. Still in tremendous pain, his first appointment was with his doctor near to his home at Barry. Examination revealed severe bruising from the lower part of his stomach almost to his knees. The doctor was amazed that he was able to stand after sustaining such damage.

Jack was advised to take a complete month's rest and told that he would be in no condition to fight again for several months. It was a severe set-back because he was due to meet Walter Neusel at Cardiff on 31 July. Negotiations were also at an advanced stage for him to fight Maxie Rosenbloom for the world light-heavyweight title in America during the autumn.

Immediately after the Doyle fight, there had been an exchange of telegrams between Welsh promoter, Jimmy Jones, and Rosenblooms advisors. The next day it was announced that terms were practically agreed. The Americans had even invited Petersen to have a warm-up contest against Jack Sharkey. Pa, however, rejected the offer because Sharkey had only recently lost his world heavyweight title to Primo Carnera.

After Jack's visit to his doctor, his backers had a meeting with Jones, and it was agreed that the fights with Neusel and Rosenbloom would have to be postponed indefinitely. In justifying the decision, Pa told the *South Wales Echo* they would not consider a world title fight until Jack had returned to peak fitness. 'That will take a long time,' he added.

Meanwhile, a film of the Petersen-Doyle fight was shown at Cardiff a few days later. It revealed that Jack was hit with no less than fourteen low blows, any one of which could been expected to floor him because of their sheer power.

In his column in the *South Wales Echo*, William E. Allen made the point that not enough credit was given to Petersen for the gallant way in which he stood up to the savage attack.

'He stood up unavengingly with not a word of protest from his mouth,' wrote Allen. 'Yet it was not until he reached his home in Barry that he felt it necessary to seek the attention of his doctor.'

* * *

Whenever a boxer is disqualified during a fight, it is customary for his purse, or a significant proportion of it, to be withheld pending an enquiry. Within three minutes of Doyle's disqualification, the British Boxing Board of Control Steward in charge, Lord Tweedmouth, ordered promoter, Jeff Dickson to send the Irishman's full purse to the Board of Control.

An enquiry took place at the Board offices at 68 Dean Street in London the following week. The matter was of such interest, that dozens of reporters waited outside for the outcome.

Among the matters considered was a report from referee, Mr. C. H. Douglas, himself a Steward of the Board. His report concluded with the statement; 'I consider Doyle's offence rather a serious one, and was caused by him completely and totally losing his head.'

Doyle attended the enquiry and expressed his sincere regret for hitting Petersen low. He pleaded with the Stewards not to punish him financially, explaining that such a penalty would place an intolerable burden upon his parents in Cork who depended on him totally for financial support.

The enquiry lasted for more than four hours, after which Doyle was suspended from boxing for six months and ordered to forfeit £2,740 of his purse money. The balance would be divided equally between himself and his mother, and paid at the rate of £5 per week throughout the duration of his suspension.

It was one of the severest punishments ever imposed upon a British boxer by the governing body. Jack Petersen, however, agreed with the decision. In an interview some years later, he said, 'I thought they were quite right. They were good stewards and extremely fair. Doyle deserved what he got. It was a very important fight and drew more people than any other contest I can recall.'

Doyle was devastated but refused to accept the Board's ruling. At a hearing in the King's Bench Division of the High Court on 8 March 1934, he contested the legality of the decision. Mr. Justice McKinnon ruled in the Irishman's favour and ordered the Board of Control to return all his purse money to him.

The judge ruled that as purse money had been agreed by word of mouth, no valid legal contract had ever been in existence. In his judgement, the Board of Control's action was illegal.

The Board immediately served notice of appeal which was heard on 10 July 1934, by the Master of the Rolls and two Appeal Judges. The judgement of Mr. Justice McKinnon was overturned meaning Doyle would never receive the balance of his purse.

Six years later, the Irishman wrote his account of events in the *Sunday Pictorial*:

'I fouled Petersen in the first round. I admit that now, freely. I was warned that I would be disqualified if I persisted. I did persist. I fouled him again in the second round, more than once. I was ordered back to my corner, disqualified and disgraced.'

Although he did not reveal the problem, Doyle claimed he was ill and should never have gone into the ring to face Petersen:

'. . . . so I fought. I knew I had one chance, a knock-out in the first two rounds. My strength would not last beyond that. At all costs I must knock Petersen out in six minutes. A colossal task when you consider the strength and determination of Jack Petersen . . . .'

Doyle never fought for the British heavyweight again. Although he boxed on and off until 1943, he had just twelve further fights over ten years, of which he won seven.

Petersen was frequently asked about the fight with the Irishman, and although never bitter, he clearly never forgave him. In 1990, when aged 79, and President of the British Boxing Board of Control, Jack was quoted as saying: 'Doyle must have hit me low fourteen times in all, and the punches put a huge dent in my protector. Had I not been wearing it, I would never have fought again. He could have crippled me for life. The fight itself was an absolute farce. It was a disaster as far as British boxing was concerned.'

Yet Jack Doyle was never a dirty fighter. He was an excitable, flamboyant showman, but very young and inexperienced. His demise was a loss to British boxing.

8

TASTE OF DEFEAT

During his enforced lay-off following the Doyle fight, Jack again went to sea to aid his recovery. This time it was a family holiday aboard the luxury yacht, '*Stella Polaris*', sailing in and out of the capitals of Northern Europe. Although he loved the new experience, Jack would still have preferred the carefree, simple life on a tramp steamer with the fine manly companionship it always provided.

When they visited Copenhagen, Jack met many old friends from his amateur days, including the hall porter of the hotel where he stayed with the British Amateur team in November 1930. The Danish sporting press turned up for interviews when they knew he was in town, and the British champion was feted and treated as a hero.

On returning home, Jack was refreshed and full of enthusiasm, but got the impression that heavyweight boxing in Britain was dead. Anxious to get back into the ring, he resumed light training in the autumn. He had talks with promoter Jimmy Jones who planned to stage a series of top class shows in South Wales throughout the winter.

Jones intended to ease Jack back with a relatively undemanding contest, but when he announced that the British champion would meet Peter Van Goole of Holland at Greyfriars Hall, Cardiff, on 18 December, there was a storm of criticism. Many fans wrote to the *Western Mail* and *South Wales Echo*, and William E. Allen once again became an influential figure.

In one of his columns Allen said the fight with the Dutchman was absurd. So in an attempt to help Petersen get a testing opponent, he travelled to London and had talks with Charlie Rose. Allen hoped to reach agreement for Jack to face Eddie Steele, the young Norwood heavyweight who had given Walter Neusel a good fight in 1932.

Meanwhile in Paris, the first steps were taken to match Petersen with Len Harvey who had boxed at The Palais des Sports on 16 October on a Jeff Dickson promotion.

Len did not particularly like Dickson, but on the way to Le Bourget Airport, his wife suggested to the promoter that he matched him with Petersen. Florence Harvey, known affectionately as 'Blossom', insisted that Len was so eager for the contest he would fight for nothing. In a subsequent telephone conversation with Dickson, Len agreed to the fight on condition the promoter paid his training expenses.

Before making contact with the Petersen's, Dickson knew from past experience they would demand a substantial purse. Pa's terms were £2,000, and once again Dickson had plenty to say, claiming purses of that level were killing the game all over the world. Pa stuck to his guns because he knew it was a fight many people had looked forward to for a long time, and would draw a capacity crowd.

Negotiations were tough, and one night Pa and Dickson were locked in debate from 8 pm until one in the morning in a room at the Savoy Hotel in London. Voices were raised as the promoter's frustration grew, but Pa refused to relent. He was a hard businessman and not in the game to line the promoters pockets. If Dickson wanted to stage the fight, he would have to meet the champion's terms.

The promoter eventually gave in, and when Pa Petersen caught the early morning train for South Wales, he had a contract on his terms safely in his pocket. The fight was set for the Royal Albert Hall on 30 November 1932, and every ticket was sold days in advance, assuring Dickson of financial success.

* * *

Whenever he could, Jack continued to make personal appearances at functions organised for charity. He attended a dance at Treorchy in aid of the Frank Moody Fund, and was guest of Honour at a St. David's Day dinner at Pentre. Suddenly, however, he became involved in a rare bout of criticism and controversy.

On 23 November, he failed to attend a boxing tournament at Judges Hall, Trealaw, organised in aid of Tonypandy Catholic Church Fund. The organisers were extremely angry because they had fully expected Jack to attend and present the prizes.

It was claimed that shortly before the show commenced, a telegram was received in which it was stated that training for his forthcoming fight with Len Harvey had prevented the British champion from attending. In announcing Petersen's absence to a disappointed audience, Reverend Father Crowley said, 'I have here a telegram received just before the show which I will not bother to read to you, but it contains some such rot as "strenuous training".'

Father Crowley was very bitter as he addressed the audience;

'I feel absolutely confident that you will not blame me, or the Welsh Amateur Boxing Association, that Jack Petersen is not here to present the prizes. I had a definite promise a few months ago that he would carry out this duty. Because I feared the match with Len Harvey might bring about a last minute change of plan, I held up advertising the matter for some weeks. We would not dream of stating on posters that Jack Petersen would be here if we did not have a definite undertaking to this effect. The day before yesterday, and again as late as this morning, I received assurances that he would fulfil his promise.'

The situation caused a great deal of bitterness, and Father Crowley even commented that had Len Harvey made such a promise, he would have attended. At that point the audience broke into prolonged applause.

The following day, Father Crowley's remarks were printed in the *South Wales Echo* and prompted an immediate response from Pa Petersen. In a letter to William E. Allen he said:

The reply to the detrimental remarks made in today's *South Wales Evening Mail* and *South Wales Echo* by the priest at Trealaw last night is; that no arrangements were ever made direct with Jack Petersen or his father.

A gentleman well known in sporting circles, some time ago asked if Jack would appear, and was told that if there was nothing to prevent him, he would be pleased to do so. He has made a large number of these appearances and is only too ready to help those who are endeavouring to raise money for good purposes.

This gentleman was told that on account of the Harvey fight, Jack would not be able to appear at Trealaw. No communication has been received by Jack regarding his appearance, and if the promoters had done the right thing, they would have gone to the right source and approached Jack direct in a proper business-like manner.

It is very painful for the lad, whom you know has gone all over the district giving his assistance, and it is very questionable as to whether any similar appeals in the future will be considered by Jack or his advisers.

The scornful remarks are unmerited, and evidently the speaker knows little of training, or the importance that is attached by the serious professional boxer to such a fight as Jack is entertaining in only a week hence.

* * *

Although Jack had been in light training, the lack of sparring partners again became a problem. At first he worked with Charlie Bundy (Treherbert), but in a fight against Eddie Manning at Bargoed, Charlie sustained a badly cut eye which prevented him from sparring for several days. As Jack had nobody, Manning was offered the job, as were Randy Jones and Tommy Farr, but all refused. Eventually, Eddie Phillips agreed to join the Welsh camp. It was a good appointment because Eddie had given Harvey a good fight in June when they met for the British light-heavyweight title.

Harvey was by far the most experienced man Jack had been asked to face. He began fighting for pay in 1920 when he was just 12 years old, and in 13 years had taken part in 118 fights, losing just eight. He was an experienced ringman with a cool calculating brain.

In 1926, he challenged Harry Mason for the British welterweight title, but was held to a draw. He became middleweight champion in 1929, beating Alex Ireland in seven rounds, and defended the title eight times, losing it to Jock McAvoy in April 1933. The

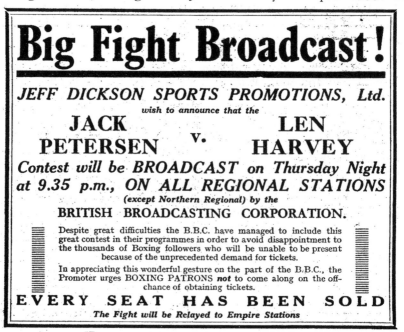

The BBC advertised that the fight would be broadcast on all regional stations.

previous year he put up a great display against Marcel Thil of France for the world middleweight title, losing on points.

Len became British light-heavyweight champion in June 1933, outpointing Eddie Phillips at Olympia.

He had been accepted by the British Boxing Board of Control as the leading contender for the heavyweight title as soon as the fight was announced. He trained at The Black Bull at Whetstone, convinced he had the beating of Petersen whom he had been chasing for months. The bookies didn't share his confidence making Jack 2-1 on favourite to retain his titles.

The Royal Albert Hall could only accommodate 10,000 fans, so on the morning of the fight newspapers advised those without tickets not to travel to Kensington. The fight was sold out ten days earlier, but despite the warnings, hundreds wandered around the entrances in the hope of getting in. Touts did a roaring trade with tickets changing hands at three times their face value.

Many fans remained in the streets outside merely to hear the result of the fight. Those who had stayed at home had the benefit of a radio commentary by Lionel Seccombe on the London, Scottish, western and midland regions of the BBC.

Both men received splendid receptions as they entered the ring, and support was evenly divided. The fight was one for the connoisseur, a battle between brains and brawn which kept the full house absorbed from start to finish.

For the first five rounds, Petersen wasted a lot of energy trying to land his big punches. He was looking to take Harvey out with one shot, but his judgement of distance was poor. Len was too skilful, and either rode the shots or avoided them by clever movements of the head and good footwork.

Petersen started with his customary fire, and after only a minute of the opening round clipped Harvey on the chin while he was off balance. Len took a count of 'three', and hung on tightly for the remainder of the round.

There was little in it during round two, but in the third, Harvey opened up and caught Jack with a solid left hook to the chin. Petersen immediately hit back with something like his usual fire, and by the bell, was fighting strongly.

For the next few rounds, Harvey concentrated on defensive boxing, but at the same time was scoring points. His tactics, however, annoyed the referee, Mr. C. H. 'Pickles' Douglas, who warned him on a number of occasions for leaning on, and holding and hitting. In the sixth round, Mr. Douglas issued a final warning. 'For the last time Harvey,' he shouted, 'don't hold.'

From that point in the fight, Len stepped up the pace and boxed in the style he was known for. He beat Petersen to the punch, and drew blood from his nose and mouth. The Welshman's attacks fizzled out and his fan's became silent as he appeared to have no answer to the skilful challenger. Harvey jabbed, hooked and uppercut almost at will, and was much too clever at close quarters, a fact Jack would always concede in years to come.

Midway through round eight, Jack was caught by a hard right to the head. As he reeled backwards, blood streamed from an ugly gash above his left eye. The Welsh supporters groaned in dismay when they realised how bad the cut was. From that point, Petersen was fighting a losing battle. His timing was severely handicapped by a continuous flow of blood into his eyes. Unlike his previous fights when he was in trouble, he did not fight back with the same guts and determination.

In the tenth, the champion became extremely frustrated, and after forcing Harvey to the ropes, blatantly butted him under the chin. It was so uncharacteristic of Jack, and his action brought a storm of booing which continued to the end of the round, throughout the interval and into the start of round eleven.

The hostile demonstration clearly affected Petersen who showed little of the fighting spirit the fans had come to expect. Pa knew the title was slipping away, and screamed advice from the corner, only to be admonished by the referee.

Although Jack did make desperate attempts to land his big punches during the last two rounds, he was either too wild, or found the challenger too elusive.

Len continued to box beautifully until the final bell, and there was tremendous cheering when Mr. Douglas raised his arm as the winner. Jack had no argument with the decision, and being the sportsman he was, immediately went to Harvey's corner and congratulated him.

It was Petersen's first taste of defeat as a professional, and it hurt. As he sat in his dressing room after the fight, he was very dejected, but retained his dignity. 'I have no complaints at all,' he said. 'Harvey boxed masterly, although I am sure that but for the mishap to my eye, I would have won.'

Jack was particularly moved when Len walked into the dressing room and spoke to him in the most sporting and gentlemanly terms. Whilst they already had great respect for each other, it was the beginning of a friendship that would last for the rest of their lives.

From that moment, Jack had one ambition – a return with the

new champion. Yet in his heart, he knew he had to climb the ladder all over again.

Jeff Dickson recognised the potential rewards from a return contest. Immediately after the fight he offered Harvey the chance to defend his newly won title. 'The fans will be clamouring to see you and Petersen in action again,' said the promoter. 'And I will pay you as much as I had to pay him tonight.'

Len refused the offer saying that he wanted to meet Larry Gains for the British Empire title. He argued that if he beat Gains, there would be no hall in London big enough to house the crowd who would pay to see Petersen try and win back his title. Dickson knew it was sound business sense, so his immediate plan was to contact Gains.

Before the Petersens left the Royal Albert Hall, Pa confronted Dickson and demanded a return. The promoter told him that Harvey had other plans, so they would have to wait.

Two weeks later, Harvey gave a champagne party at the Stadium Club in Holborn. The press and many leading personalities in boxing were invited. Jack Petersen was also a guest, and he and Len met for the first time since their fight. They shook hands warmly and openly complimented each other.

'A great boxer and a gentlemen,' was how Jack referred to his conqueror.

'A good sportsman,' replied Len, 'and as soon as I have fought Gains, he can have a try to regain the championship. We might be fighting for two of them by then.'

In typical warm, gentlemanly fashion, Jack stooped to kiss Mrs. Harvey on the cheek, and asked her to ensure that Len kept his promise. 'You don't have to worry about that,' she replied. 'When my husband says a thing, he means it.'

In mid-December, Jack attended a big boxing show at Merthyr Labour Club Stadium, staged in aid of the Frank Moody Testimonial Fund. It had been organised by the Welsh National Sporting Association in conjunction with the *Western Mail* and *South Wales Echo*.

Despite his defeat by Harvey, large crowds turned out to give Jack their support on what was his first public appearance since losing the British title. He climbed into the ring with Moody, and both received thunderous cheers from a crowd of over 2,000.

In acknowledgement, Jack made what was a long speech for him. 'I am very glad to be here to support such a good cause,' he said. 'I thank you for your wonderful reception. I am particularly pleased to see my old friend Frank Moody looking so well again.'

The two first became friends when Jack was still an amateur, and Frank gave him some valuable advice and guidance. He said that his attendance was his way of expressing his gratitude, and spent the remainder of the evening at ringside watching the boxing.

* * *

Early in 1934, Jerry Walsh acting on behalf of Jimmy Jones, announced that the first fight of Petersen's comeback campaign would be against Dutchman, Peter Van Goole, at Greyfriars Hall on 29 January. Only two months earlier, the Dutchman was considered an unsuitable opponent for Petersen, but opinion had now apparently changed.

The promoter based Van Goole's suitability on the fact that he had recently gone the distance with Jack Pettifer, previously lasted the course against Charlie Smith, and on the continent had drawn with Hans Schonrath.

At a meeting at the Board of Control office in London on 10 January 1934, concern was expressed about making application to the Ministry of Labour for a work permit for Van Goole. The Stewards felt there were boxers in Britain more suitable as opponents for Petersen.

Charles Donmall, General Secretary of the Board, wrote to members of the Welsh Area Council asking for their comments regarding the suitability of Van Goole. Most considered him unsuitable, and as a result the Board notified the promoter that application would not be made for a work permit.

The controversy regarding Van Goole originated from a Belfast promoter following his knock-out in four rounds by Larry Gains in July 1933. It was claimed his performance was so bad that he should never be permitted to box in Britain again.

Concerned about his reputation as a promoter, Jones eventually decided against Van Goole. Instead he attempted to match Petersen with Seaman Rowles of Chatham, who was serving in the Royal Navy. Rowles quickly agreed terms but his application for special leave was refused, adding to the growing frustration of the Welsh promoter.

Meanwhile, several men Jack had beaten on his way to the top were only too willing to face him again. Reggie Meen was anxious to prove that his form at Wimbledon was all wrong, while Charlie Smith and Harry Crossley expressed their willingness to face the Welshman anywhere to try and prove themselves worthy title contenders.

Petersen (right) has Larry Gains on the defensive during their fight at White City on 10 September 1934. Referee is Mr A. S. Myers.

Larry Gains (right) cleverly avoids Petersen's left jab during their fight at White City on 10 September 1934.

Jack Petersen with Harry "Kid" Furness, a veteran of over 200 fights and a pupil of Jem Mace.

Jack Petersen and his fianceé, Betty Williams shortly after announcing their engagement in January 1935.

Jack with his pet Bull Mastiff dogs.

George Cook is floored by Petersen in the first round of their fight at the Royal Albert Hall on 17 December 1934.

Petersen (right) and George Cook embrace at the end of their fight on 17 December 1934. Referee Percy Moss is about to raise Jack's hand as the winner.

George Cook (left) leans back to avoid Petersen's left lead during their fight at the Royal Albert Hall on 17 December 1934.

Petersen (left) ducks under a left hook from Walter Neusel at Wembley on 4 February 1935.

Petersen is floored by Walter Neusel at Wembley on 4 February 1935.

Referee Mr C. B. Thomas pushes Walter Neusel away after the towel had been thrown in from Petersen's corner during the eleventh round of their fight at Wembley on 4 February 1935.

Walter Neusel (left) and Jack Petersen shake hands after signing contracts for their fight on 25 June 1935. Seated are Paul Damski (left), Wembley promoter Arthur Elvin, and Pa Petersen.

Jack Petersen (left) and Walter Neusel pose on Wembley football pitch after signing contracts for their fight on 25 June 1935.

Jack Petersen (left) and Neusel shape up to each other during their fight at Wembley on 25 June 1935.

Len Harvey (left) signs the contract for his fight with Petersen (far right) on 29 January 1936. Sydney Hulls (standing) and Arthur Elvin look on.

Jack Petersen (left) spars with Johnny Summers at the Lynn Institute for his fight with Jock McAvoy on 23 April 1936. Billy Diamond (left) watches.

Referee Arthur Myers counts over Jock McAvoy during the final round of his fight with Jack Petersen at Earls Court on 23 April 1936.

The challenges suited the Welsh camp fine, and they wasted no time in drawing up an ambitious comeback campaign of three fights in a month. As there were prospects of huge gates at Cardiff, Greyfriars Hall was selected as the venue for contests with Smith and Crossley under Jones' promotion on 29 January and 26 February 1934 respectively. A return with Meen would take place at Leicester on 12 February.

* * *

Determined to put the Harvey defeat behind him, Jack was back in light training within two weeks. As soon as the contest with Smith was agreed he got down to the heavy stuff. For a change he had no problems getting sparring partners and was joined at the Lynn Institute by Alf Luxton, a young heavyweight from Birmingham, Phil Barnes and Alf Powell, a Lieutenant in the Royal Welsh Fuseliers stationed at Tidworth.

Powell, who came from a Monmouthshire family, was Army heavyweight champion. By assisting Petersen, he was also getting himself fit for a regimental competition. He was a terrific puncher, and in a secret try-out at the Lynn Institute on 24 January, really put the former champion through his paces. One punch to the chin had Jack reeling into the ropes, but as he let his punches go, Petersen badly cut the soldiers face.

In another brisk session, Phil Barnes also sustained a nasty injury when a thumb caught him in the eye. Within seconds it swelled to the size of an egg and he had to withdraw from the camp.

Despite his heavy training schedule, Jack still found time to travel to London on 15 January and box an exhibition at the Stadium Club with Charlie Bundy in an event in aid of the Middlesex Hospital. He was still a tremendous favourite at the Club, and before the exhibition, was introduced in the ring to Prince Arthur of Connaught.

* * *

The fight with Charlie Smith generated tremendous interest, the lowest priced seats at two shillings and sixpence being sold out within a few days of going on sale. On the day of the fight, hundreds of fans descended on the Barry Hotel in Cardiff where the weigh-in was held at 2 pm. Many were disappointed because the weights of the boxers were not announced.

Before the fight, fans arriving at Greyfriars Hall were confronted by huge barricades, erected to prevent scenes of disorder encountered the previous year. Groups of police were on duty at every entrance to ensure that only ticket holders gained admittance.

Inside the hall, amid a smoke thickened atmosphere, there was great excitement and heated conjecture about who would win. Preceding the main event was a dull affair between Panther Purchase and Leo Phillips. The crowd became very restless, although there was one lovely moment of comedy as the two boxers were locked in a wrestling hold. It was reminiscent of a rugby scrum, and as referee, Mr. F. R. Hill, danced around the boxers, a wag in the crowd shouted, 'Throw the ball in Bob.'

Jack gave a brief wave to the crowd as he climbed into the ring, and both men looked very tense as they posed for photographs. Pa Petersen then added to the tension by going to Smith's corner and lodging a complaint about his right glove. This was upheld by referee, Mr. C. B. Thomas, and a new one was sent for.

Most of the leading boxing critics in the country were at Greyfriars Hall, and witnessed one of the greatest sensations in the history of British boxing. Petersen threw just two punches to record the quickest ending to a heavyweight contest in Britain. It was over in 16 seconds, including the count.

Jack shot from his corner and attacked Smith before he was barely off his stool. He threw a left to the face, feinted to throw another, but instead crashed a tremendous right to the point of the chin. The speed of the punches was incredible.

Eyes glazed, Smith fell forward on to his face, his limp outstretched arms slipping down his young opponent as he fell. The count was a formality.

Petersen was back with a vengeance, and Pa danced excitedly in the ring as he adjusted his son's dressing gown. It was a devasting victory, and Charlie did not regain consciousness until after Jack had left the ring. His first words to his cornermen as they treated him were, 'When do we start?'

'Petersen is the greatest fighting machine since Dempsey,' remarked Dan Sullivan, manager of Smith immediately after the fight. 'He was giving away two stones, fighting a man who has travelled the world and reputed to be the craftiest man fighting.'

In his dressing room some while later, Smith was dumb-founded and in tears. 'The left of Petersen was nothing,' he sobbed, 'but after that I remember nothing.'

Although he was bitterly disappointed, Charlie did not hesitate to praise Petersen. 'I wish him all the luck in the world,' he said. 'That he will one day win a world title is my sincere hope. He is a wonderful boy, and no boxer breathing could have stood up to the crashing right he unleashed on me.'

It was the perfect return for Jack, and his handlers were convinced the Harvey defeat was no more than a temporary setback. It was therefore back to the gym to prepare for Reggie Meen in two weeks time.

* * *

On 3 February 1934, disturbing rumours circulated in South Wales that Jack had been either seriously injured, or in fact killed, in a car crash at Newport the previous evening. Offices of the *South Wales Echo* and other local newspapers throughout the region were inundated with calls from anxious fans.

As soon as he heard the rumour, William E. Allen went straight to the Lynn Institute. As he arrived he could hear Pa Petersen shouting instructions to somebody who was pounding the punchbag. Allen went inside, and to his relief found Jack alive and well, engaged in a training session. He related the story about how Jack was supposed to have come to grief the previous evening.

'Not me,' said Jack with a smile. 'I'm alright,' and he explained how he had been at home at Barry all evening playing cards.

Meanwhile, the schedule of fights for Petersen continued to grow. Jeff Dickson announced that just ten days after facing Harry Crossley at Cardiff, Jack would fight Ben Foord, a young South African heavyweight, at the Royal Albert Hall.

* * *

On 8 February, Len Harvey won the British Empire heavyweight title by beating Larry Gains on points. The public were already clamouring for a return between Harvey and Petersen, and Dickson knew he now had a ready made money-spinning double championship fight if he could arrange it.

The promoter contacted the Petersen camp, who agreed in principle for the fight to be staged at the White City on 4 June, which was the Monday of Derby week. Agreement still had to be reached with Harvey, however, and there was also a potential problem with the British Boxing Board of Control.

A couple of days later, Board general secretary, Charles Donmall, wrote to all parties involved in the forthcoming Petersen-Harry Crossley fight stating that the contest would be recognised as an eliminator for the British heavyweight title provided it was

113

conducted strictly in accordance with championship conditions. Donmall, however, went on to say, 'The winner of the contest will not be recognised as the leading contender for the championship until the Board has given further consideration to other challengers.'

Pa Petersen was furious, and in a conversation with William E. Allen, angrily remarked, 'Who but Jack could logically be considered as an opponent for Harvey?'

* * *

Against Reggie Meen, Jack was again in devastating form, scoring his second quick win in the space of two weeks. He had rarely fought with such determination and venom, and his tearaway style thrilled the crowd of 10,000. He was so fast and strong that Meen had no answer to the furious onslaught. Punch after punch found their target, and as the courageous man from Desborough tried to cover up, his gloves and arms were remorselessly battered down.

Somehow Reggie did find the strength to catch Jack with a crashing right to the chin midway through the round. The crowd roared with excitement as Petersen reeled against the ropes, and momentarily looked in serious trouble. Typically though, he hit back with a tremendous right to the jaw which sent Meen crashing to the floor. Although he was up without a count, he looked finished. Scarcely able to raise his arms, he bravely tried to fight on but was a sitting target.

Petersen waded in and unleashed another volley of punches from both hands, forcing Meen to the floor on two occasions. Only the bell to end the opening round saved him from a certain knockout.

It was only a matter of time before Petersen finished it, but as they came out for round two the scenes were amazing. Both sets of cornermen stood on the ring apron shouting and gesticulating as their fighters smashed away at each other.

Suddenly, Jack threw a hard left hook to the solar plexus and Meen went to the floor. Some people thought he had been hit low because he was clutching his stomach as he sank. Referee, Jack Smith, was perfectly positoned, and proceeded to count Meen out.

As the Desborough man was struggling to get to his feet, a fight broke out near his corner. It started when one of his supporters rushed to the ringside screaming that he had been fouled. A number of Welshmen promptly set about him and a fierce fight raged until it was broken up by security men.

114

Back in his dressing room, Jack faced a crowd of reporters. 'This is the way I must finish my fights,' he told them. 'I must show the public I am a fighter, and I shall win back my championship by the fighting road. Only by quick finishes can I get through my programme, but I shall do it.'

* * *

A few days later, it was revealed that the partnership between Jack and Danny Davies had come to an end. Davies was not in the corner during the recent fight with Meen. It was reported that Jack had decided to ignore advice from the corner and fight his own type of battle. 'I can see how a fight is shaping as I go along,' he told inquisitive journalists.

* * *

Within a couple of days of beating Meen, Jack was back in full training. With two important fights lined up within the space of ten days, he was more determined than ever. By increasing his work rate on the bag and in sparring, he became stronger and reached an extremely high level of fitness.

In a public try-out five days before meeting Crossley, he really set about Phil Barnes and Eddie Steele, the young protege of former heavyweight champion, Phil Scott. Both were competent boxers, but Barnes in particular, was given a real going over. Wearing 20 ounce gloves, Jack flattened him with a single punch, knocking one of his teeth clean through his lower lip. The way he performed made onlookers wonder how he came to lose against Harvey.

With just three days to go, the Board of Control caused further annoyance by issuing a statement saying the fight between Petersen and Crossley would not now be recognised as a title eliminator. They contended it was not being staged under championship conditions.

Jimmy Jones was furious, and argued that the Board had imposed what he considered improper conditions. He objected strongly and added, 'We will carry on with the contest and let events look after themselves.'

Jerry Walsh was also very critical of the governing body. He pointed out that the majority of the British public recognised Petersen as the logical challenger to Len Harvey, especially as he was back to top form. Referring to the Crossley fight, Walsh said,

115

'They meet over fifteen three minute rounds under championship conditions. The referee will be properly qualified and licensed. If Crossley beats Jack, could the Board say he was not entitled to a shot at Harvey?'

The attitude of the Board was viewed with contempt by many followers of boxing, and had angered both camps. In an attempt to defend the decision, Charles Donmall told a press gathering in London that the Board had not appointed the referee or any other officials. They were not supplying the gloves or tapes, so the fight was therefore not under championship conditions.

It was a weak argument because the Board had known about the fight for some weeks. Furthermore, every newspaper in Britain carried stories regarding public interest in a return between Petersen and Harvey. Should Crossley subsequently beat Jack, it was claimed that he would automatically become the logical contender.

* * *

Crossley caused a bit of a scare in Cardiff the day before the fight when rumours spread that he had not arrived as expected. The promoter was so concerned that he began to look for a late substitute. It transpired that Crossley was staying at a Penarth hotel where he had gone to avoid pressmen and well-wishers.

'I am fit and well,' he told reporters when he was eventually located, 'and you can assure Welsh boxing enthusiasts that Petersen will not find me as easy to dispose of as Smith and Meen.'

* * *

Petersen and Crossley weighed-in at the Barry Hotel, headquarters of the Welsh Area of the Board of Control, at 2 pm on the day of the fight. As was a regular feature of fights involving Jack, no weights were announced.

Another full house saw the Welshman box along entirely different lines to his usual style. He knew how tough Crossley was, so there was none of the blistering opening attack everyone had come to expect. Instead, he was cautious, controlled, and boxed to a carefully contrived plan of upright boxing and straight short arm punching.

Although there were times when he was out of range with his left leads, Jack's sustained attacks gradually wore down the tough Yorkshireman. Apart from courage, Crossley had little to offer other than spoiling tactics which only delayed his inevitable defeat.

For a while in the sixth, Petersen showed boxing ability of the highest order, overcoming the cleverness of Crossley who kept turning sideways to present a difficult target. As the fight wore on, the Yorkshireman took a terrible hiding as Petersen's accurate short arm punching continuously jolted back his head.

The seventh was a thrilling round and remembered long after the fight was over. His left eye bleeding badly, Crossley was cautioned for holding as he attempted to smother Petersen's relentless attack. He was groggy on the ropes, nothing more than a chopping block, as Jack slammed home swings, hooks, crosses and jabs. Yet the game Yorkshireman was determined not to become another of his horizontal victims.

Eventually, like a giant tree surrendering to a woodman's axe, he toppled over. He rose at 'nine' only to be clubbed to the floor by another whirlwind attack. With the count at 'eight', he climbed wearily to his feet and kept the Welshman at bay until the bell.

Bets were taken during the interval that the next round would be the last, but a lot of money was lost. Jack was too wild and missed with his best punches as the skilful Yorkshireman weaved and ducked.

Crossley's pluck earned him loud cheers in the ninth as Jack slogged into him. Eventually he went down again for a count of 'eight' but gallantly refused to give in. When the bell ended the round he was still on his feet.

The inevitable ending came in round ten when Harry was nothing more than a punch bag. As he reeled from rope to rope, sheer fighting instinct kept him more or less upright. Eventually a vicious left flush on the mouth sent him to his knees for 'nine'. To everyone's amazement, the grand old fighter climbed to his feet again. Battered and bleeding, he stood unsteadily in front of Petersen who rushed at him like an enraged tiger. Crossley went down for a count of 'four', and when another jolting punch forced him to his knees in sheer exhaustion, referee Jack Smith stepped in.

'That will do,' he said as he put his arms around the courageous Yorkshireman and led him to his corner. His face cut and badly bruised, Crossley was scarcely able to twist his features into a smile. He had been hammered unmercifully into a state of complete helplessness.

Harry was surely one of the gamest losers ever seen in the ring. As he returned to his dressing room, the Cardiff crowd gave him one of the finest ovations he received in his long and honourable career. The applause for Petersen was mild in comparison.

'What a fine fellow,' said Jack respectfully after the fight . 'How in the world he stood up to my punching, I cannot understand. Game? I've never seen anything like it.'

Crossley was equally complimentary about his conqueror. 'What a fighter,' said the badly bruised Yorkshireman in his dressing room. 'I've never come across a man with such a terrific right hand punch; and what speed!'

* * *

Against Ben Foord at the Royal Albert Hall ten days later, Jack reverted to his familiar cyclonic start to a fight. Although looking almost frail in comparison to the big South African, he had only one idea in his head – win as soon as possible. Like a human tornado, he threw punches from all angles, smashing through Foord's defence. Had he picked his punches and not let his impetuosity upset his timing, he would have destroyed the South African early in the fight. Instead, Ben remained calm and weathered the opening attacks.

In round two, Jack was forced to take some heavy shots as they traded punches in the centre of the ring. Then, as they broke from a clinch, Foord landed a hard swinging right which re-opened an old wound over Jack's left eye. It was a nasty injury, and the South African made it a target for his heavy right swings. A number found their mark, and as the fight progressed, the eye swelled badly and continued to bleed.

During the fourth, Petersen became angry and frustrated by the rough-house tactics used by the South African. Stepping up the pace, he lashed out viciously and floored Foord for a count of 'seven' with a right to the jaw. On rising, Ben was hit with punches from all angles, and his nose bled badly as he reeled under extreme pressure.

As Foord sagged to his knees from another battery of punches, he wrapped his arms tightly around the Welshman's waist. In frustration, Jack chopped him heavily on the back of the neck with a rabbit punch. It was an act completely alien to his character, and the crowd booed their disapproval.

Two rounds later, Petersen offended again in even more blatant fashion. This time, he had Foord's head locked tightly under his left arm, and using his right, punched him heavily on the back of the neck. Again, the crowd booed loudly, but incredibly, like the first offence, it drew no caution from the referee.

Petersen was being tested to the limit in a rough, hard fight, but his fitness was incredible. Foord was again in serious trouble in the seventh when he was rocked by heavy right hands. Incredibly, he recovered quickly and drove a crashing right under the heart which shook Petersen to his toes.

From this point of the fight, Jack used his left jab more. It appeared that he had damaged his right because he rarely used it. In the ninth, he bled profusely from his cut eye, and came off second best in a vicious exchange as Foord somehow mustered the strength to trade punches.

From the tenth, however, the South African became an open target and absorbed a terrible amount of punishment. Rounds eleven and twelve were very one-sided as Petersen pounded him at will.

In the thirteenth, Foord was knocked through the ropes on to the apron of the ring, but gallantly climbed to his feet at 'eight'. He was defenceless as Petersen moved in again, and at last the referee mercifully called a halt. Many fans thought it should have been stopped earlier, and Jack later remarked that it gave him no pleasure to continue hitting an opponent who was hopelessly beaten, yet too brave to quit.

Always a true sportsman, Jack assisted Foord to his corner after the fight had been stopped. Later, he was full of praise for the bravery of the South African.

'No words of mine can tell of his enormous courage,' he told reporters. 'No man can ever put up a gamer fight. I felt sorry for Foord, and could scarcely force down the lump in my throat as I helped him back to his corner. If the day comes that I must take a beating so terrible, may I take it like he did.'

Although he eventually got the job done, Jack had lacked his usual sharpness. There were times when he had the South African at his mercy only to let him survive. A number of critics believed his strenuous programme of fights was taking its toll. Foord, however, like Harry Crossley before him, displayed incredible courage, and the capacity crowd gave him a tremendous hand as he left the ring.

A fight a fortnight had been Pa Petersen's plan for the comeback, and Jack was scheduled to meet Vincent Hower of Germany at Greyfriars Hall on 26 March. Examination of his injured left eye, however, revealed that the damage was more serious than at first thought.

'My eye is in such a condition that it will not be able to heal within a fortnight,' Jack told a *Sporting Chronicle* reporter when he arrived back at Cardiff the following day.

The eye which had been damaged against Len Harvey, and aggravated in subsequent fights with Crossley and Foord, was a worry. Further specialist examination revealed that it would be some weeks before Jack would be fit to box again. The fight with Hower was therefore cancelled.

Despite the set-back, Jack remained very sought after. Harry Levene had watched his fight with Foord and promptly issued a further challenge on behalf of Larry Gains. In a letter to William E. Allen, he said he was even more convinced that Gains would emerge the winner, and offered to put up a substantial side-stake. Larry had outclassed Ernst Guehring before knocking him out in seven rounds on 5 March, and Levene pointed out that a year earlier Petersen only beat the German on points.

Jeff Dickson, meanwhile, announced that he was bringing former world light-heavyweight champion, Tommy Loughran, to Britain. He intended matching him with men of the calibre of Petersen and Len Harvey. The Welsh camp, however, showed no interest in such a fight. Jack had scored four successive inside the distance victories, and the only contest he was interested in was a return with Harvey.

9

CHAMPION AGAIN

Shortly after Jack's victory over Ben Foord, Welsh light-heavyweight champion, Tommy Farr, contacted the *South Wales Echo* stating he fancied his chances against his fellow Welshman. Farr was training to fight Jim Winters at Greyfriars Hall on 26 March 1934 in an eliminator for the British light-heavyweight title. He said that if successful he was prepared to deposit a substantial side-stake for a fight with Petersen.

This was just the beginning of what would become a personal crusade by Farr of constantly issuing challenges to Jack. Tommy was regarded as a promising young fighter, having lost only two of his last 18 contests. Many of his fans were convinced that if he had the financial backing of Petersen he would be even better.

Although Jack had no interest in meeting Farr, he and Pa were present at Greyfriars Hall for the Winters fight. Tommy won by a close decision but was clearly not in the class of the former heavyweight champion.

Immediately before the fight, Jack was introduced from the ring. His left eye heavily plastered, he waved and smiled broadly to the cheering crowd of 4,000. He drew roars of laughter when he bent down and squared up to a youngster in Winter's corner. Yet when the M.C. called upon him to make a speech, Jack became very embarrassed and withdrew to a neutral corner. Despite his efforts to avoid the issue, the M.C. was insistent, much to the amusement of the crowd.

'Thank you very much for your support,' said Jack shyly. He would rather have had a dozen hard fights than go through that ordeal again.

Jack's eye injury responded well to specialist treatment, and on 9 May he and Len Harvey signed contracts for a return contest at the White City on 4 June during Derby week. He was extremely happy because they had planned for it, schemed for it, and fought four times to get it.

Pa had sat at ringside with Charlie Rose the night Harvey took the Empire title from Larry Gains, and suggested it was time Len and Jack had a return. Rose agreed, but matters were delayed when representation was made to the Board of Control on behalf of George Cook and Don McCorkindale.

After a lengthy meeting, the stewards ruled that Harvey must defend both the British and Empire titles against Petersen. Both men were, however, required to sign a declaration agreeing that the winner, before entering into any further agreement to defend the British title, would meet the winner of a fight between Cook and McCorkindale.

Although Jack never claimed he was 'robbed', he always privately considered himself unfortunate not to have got the decision over Len when they met six months earlier. He was therefore determined to do everything within his power to win the return, or quit boxing altogether.

Otto Von Porat, a magnificently toned and proportioned Norweigian heavyweight, was engaged to assist Petersen in his preparations. Standing six feet three and weighing over 14 stones, he had won an Olympic gold medal in Paris in 1924. He was very quick and powerful and really put Jack through his paces, landing as many solid punches as he took.

With only two weeks to go before the fight, Von Porat caused a minor sensation when he re-opened the cut above Jack's left eye. Although it was not serious, it remained a closely guarded secret, and was treated with a specially prepared substance.

Although he had lost his British title to Len Harvey Jack was still the most sought after heavyweight in Britain. Just a week before he faced Len again, he was offered £5,000 to meet Walter Neusel in Germany. He was also offered an attractive amount to agree to a contest in South Africa, possibly against Ben Foord. Attractive though the offers were, they were completely ignored because the young Welshman and his handlers were committed to preparations to meet Harvey.

The contest between Jack and Len had been the talk of the country ever since it was announced. Daily features from both camps appeared in most national newspapers, as did interviews with both boxers. Jeff Dickson considered it to be the most attractive fight he had made in six years of promoting.

'Judging by present bookings, nothing I have ever staged, either in Britain or on the Continent, approaches this fight as an attraction,' he said excitedly. 'I really believe it will draw the biggest crowd in the history of boxing in Europe.'

Bookings far exceeded anything he had anticipated even in his most optimistic moments. His office was inundated with calls for tickets, and his decision to stage the fight at the White City was more than justified. Capable of holding crowds of up to 100,000, it was already established as a successful boxing venue.

Petersen and Harvey agreed to be put on a percentage of the gate. When ticket sales went so well, it was rumoured that Dickson bought their agreed percentages outright, costing him a great deal of money. This was, however, discounted by Norman Hurst writing in the *Sporting Chronicle*. 'That story can be taken with a grain of salt,' he wrote.

When Harvey failed to agree to a £500 side-stake, Pa Petersen was extremely angry. 'This is the last time we will take notice of Harvey's talk about backing himself. I never heard of a champion wanting odds of 7-4.'

The British Boxing Board of Control appointed Mr. C. H. 'Pickles' Douglas to referee the contest. According to a number of newspaper reports, this did not meet with the approval of Pa Petersen. In *Sporting Life* on 2 June 1934, under the headline 'ANYONE WHO CAN COUNT TO TEN WILL DO,' it was claimed that Pa had sent a written protest to the Board of Control, and also notified the promoter.

He was alleged to have told reporter Stanley Longstaff; 'I have had no reply, and it was not my intention to say anything in public, but that the Board choose to ignore my protest, I am glad of the chance to say what I think about the whole situation. I did not ask for Douglas – he was the man wanted by Harvey.'

Pa was further quoted as saying that the decision given to Harvey by referee Douglas in November 1933, was contrary to the views of many ringsiders. 'I have been given to understand that the appointment will stand. I have objected on principle. Anyone who can count up to ten should be able to handle this fight without any trouble. If Harvey's father can roll off ten words, he will do,' the report concluded.

Similarly worded articles also appeared in the *South Wales Echo* and *London Star*. In the *Sporting Chronicle*, however, Norman Hurst was convinced that Pa Petersen made no objection to the appointment of Mr. Douglas. Having been curious about the affair, he was the only journalist who took the trouble to check with the Board of Control. When he telephoned, he was assured by a Board spokesman that no letter of protest had been received from Mr.

Petersen. Hurst went on to establish that Jeff Dickson's publicity department had in fact released the story about Pa having sent a letter to the Board.

* * *

The weather on the day of the fight was ideal for an open air contest. Although there had been some dark clouds and a few spots of rain earlier in the day, by evening it was fine and warm.

Although the crowd did not quite reach Jeff Dickson's estimate of 100,000, it was not far short. The organisation was first class and stewarding was undertaking by 200 cowboys and cowgirls who were taking part at the White City Rodeo Show.

Petersen was first into the ring, but it was more than five minutes before Harvey arrived tightly clad in flannel trousers and a dressing gown. By this time, Jack was showing signs of impatience, and feeling the effects of a cutting wind which blew across the open stadium.

Harvey was soon under pressure as Petersen went on the attack looking to take command early. Len was forced to use all his defensive skills to avoid being swept away. He hung on desperately, and within the first minute received a warning from Mr. Douglas. He weathered the storm by clever boxing, and late in the round hurt Jack with a good left hook. Another landed flush on the chin as the bell ended an interesting opening session.

The contrast in styles made it difficult for both men. Harvey tried to work inside away from Jack's heavier punches, whilst the Welshman wanted to dictate matters from long range. Petersen was warned for holding in the second round, whilst Harvey was spoken to on three occasions for low blows.

Harvey's spoiling tactics frustrated Petersen in the third when he was loudly booed after he chopped three solid punches on the back of Len's neck, drawing him another stern warning. Although there was little sparkle, it was becoming a rugged but intriguing duel as Len smothered most of the heavy punches Jack threw at him.

The fifth was the first round in which there was any real fighting. Petersen was already getting fed up with the course of the fight, and shot aggressively from his corner at the bell. He threw a vicious right to the body followed by a right to the jaw.

Harvey was badly shaken and before he could move out of range Jack drove another hard right to the stomach. Len was going through a difficult period, and as he tried to hold on, the Welshman threw a short-arm right to the head with tremendous force. It caught Len full in the face causing him to cling on desperately. When the referee Douglas pulled them apart it was seen that the champions left eye was almost closed.

Petersen piled on the pressure trying to force a finish but even with only one good eye, Harvey was too clever to be caught again. The bell didn't sound a moment too early for the champion and as he returned to his corner, his eye was a mere slit. His cornmen worked feverishly but could do nothing to bring down the swelling. Although few people expected him to continue for long, Len looked surprisingly fresh as he came out for round six.

Sensing his chances to become champion again, Petersen was quickly on the attack although to his credit he made no attempt to take advantage of Len's handicap. All Harvey could do was hold on to avoid the big punches being thrown at him.

It became a mauling affair with plenty of rough work from both men, and eventually Mr. Douglas called a halt and issued a stern warning. 'Let us have a boxing match not a brawl,' he snapped loudly. 'If you don't stop holding when I tell you, I will be forced to send you both from the ring.'

When the action resumed, a right hook from Harvey reopened the injury on Petersen's left eye. It bled profusely and suddenly he was having to defend. Harvey boxed brilliantly for the remainder of the round despite being able to see out of only one eye.

His injury patched up, Petersen attacked viciously at the start of round seven. He threw himself at Harvey and a left hook landed flush on Len's closed eye. The effect was instant, and the flesh beneath the eye swelled rapidly into an ugly lump. Harvey, however, had no intention of giving up his titles without a fight, and the courage he displayed to survive the round was amazing.

Although Petersen attacked strongly in round eight, he was caught with several solid punches to the head which slowed him. At close quarters though, Harvey's head was continuously rubbing dangerously into Jack's face prompting angry protests from the Welsh corner.

In the ninth, Harvey appeared to blatantly butt the Welshman, again bringing blood streaming from his damaged left eye. Referee Douglas swiftly stopped the action and severely warned the champion. 'This is the last time I will warn you Harvey,' he snapped. 'Next time, out you go.'

By round ten, Harvey's eye was swollen to the size of an egg. It was a grotesque sight, and there were calls from ringsiders for him to quit, or the referee to intervene.

Another heavy attack from Petersen in the eleventh sent Len to his knees and he took a count of 'five' clinging to the Welshman's legs. His eye was getting worse all the time and he was in an extremely bad way. Still he would not quit, and throughout the twelfth he took a terrible hiding. Despite taking heavy punches from all angles, he courageously stayed on his feet.

Finally Mr. Douglas had seen enough, and when the bell ended the round, he followed Harvey to his corner. 'I strongly advise you to give in otherwise I shall stop you coming out for the next round,' said the referee.

There was no protest from Len. He merely nodded his head in agreement and instructed his cornerman to throw in the towel.

When Mr. Douglas raised Jack's right arm, he took two delighted leaps into the air, then ran back to his corner. He was overjoyed as he hugged Pa tightly before going to Harvey and shaking hands.

Both men left the ring to tremendous applause. It was the first time in 122 contests that Harvey had lost inside the distance, and the crowd recognised the courage he had shown.

This was a particularly important victory for Petersen because not only had he regained the British title, but he showed considerable restraint throughout the fight. He proved he had learned the art of defence, yet when the openings came still showed all of his natural aggression.

In his hotel room after the fight, Jack paid warm tribute to Harvey. 'He is one of the gamest men ever seen in the ring,' he remarked. 'How he kept up such a magnificent fight for seven rounds with one eye out of action, beats me. He is a grand fellow.'

Pa Petersen paid tribute to both men when he said, 'Tonight you saw two of the best heavyweights in this country for the past twenty-five years.'

Harvey's eye injury was so bad that he spent the following day in a dark room with compresses being applied at regular intervals. A specialist subsequently confirmed that no permanent damage had been caused, but advised extreme care for some while.

The injuries they sustained prevented both Jack and Len attending Sir Harry Preston's charity boxing tournament at Brighton the following weekend. Both had been invited as guests of honour.

* * *

Never before in Wales had there been so much interest in a fight. The result was so eagerly awaited that every local office of the *South Wales Echo*, throughout South Wales and neighbouring

Monmouthshire, was beseiged by hundreds of Petersen admirers anxious to know the result. Scenes at offices at Cardiff, Barry, Newport, Pontypool, and elsewhere were remarkable. Traffic was completely held up by dense crowds of people awaiting special late editions of the paper carrying the result.

There was tremendous cheering at each office when newsboys eventually emerged carrying bundles of papers. As they were distributed, wild excitement spread amongst the crowds when they realised Petersen was champion again.

Some years later, Jack would admit that this was the only occasion when he went into the ring 'seeing red'. There was so much to wipe out, and he was determined Harvey would pay. He had learned a lot from their first fight, and this time he was able to dictate the terms. He resolutely refused to become embroiled in close quarter work and this had a noticeable effect on Len.

* * *

When Jack arrived at Cardiff Great Western railway station shortly after 3 pm the following day, a huge crowd was there to greet him. Nearly 100 policemen had been specially deployed to control them, and they had great difficulty in containing a stampede through the booking hall as Jack's train pulled in. There was tremendous cheering and clapping when the new champion appeared, and shouts of 'Good old Jack.'

Smiling broadly, Jack showed few signs of battle other than the damage to his left eye. As he walked from the station he was surrounded by a posse of policemen. When told of the condition of Len Harvey's eye, he was very concerned. 'That's not too good,' he said sympathetically. 'His eye must be pretty bad.'

A Police Superintendent had arranged for a friend of Jack's to drive him to his home at Barry. Accompanied by a *South Wales Echo* reporter, they drove from the station to resounding cheers and waving.

As they arrived at his house, Jack said, 'Good old Barry. Thank goodness to be back. When you leave Barry for London, and then return you wonder why you ever went to London.'

Once again, the damage to his eye upset Jack's immediate plans. An examination the following day revealed that the injury was more serious than at first thought. The wound, about one and a half inches long, was deep and very close to the eye. Jack was told he would not be able to do any serious training for several weeks. Four important contests, all with lucrative purses, therefore had to be postponed.

127

On the advice of his Cardiff doctor, Jack also consulted Sir Harry Gillies, a Harley Street specialist. He established there was no permanent damage to the eye, and vision was perfection every respect. Jack was advised to rest until the injury was completely healed, after which he could train and fight again when he felt fit.

Meanwhile, there had been suggestions that Harvey's eye had been damaged by a lace from Petersen's glove. 'Ridiculous,' snapped Pa angrily when the suggestion was put to him by a *South Wales Echo* reporter. 'To begin with, laces are not used in boxing gloves. They are tied with tape, a material that is not likely to scrape an eye. I want you to emphasise this in your paper because such a statement can only have been uttered in order to detract from the merit of Jack's victory.'

Two days after the fight, it was Derby Day at Epsom racecourse in Surrey. Both Petersen and Harvey attended the event, and quite by chance, bumped into each other. They chatted happily, not only about their fight, but also about trying to select the winner of the big race. In his typically sporting fashion, Jack expressed concern about Len's eye, and wished him a speedy recovery.

Following Jack's victory over Harvey, hundreds of letters poured into the Lynn Institute every day. Many came from fans, whilst others contained offers of fights in all parts of the world. One came from a well known London sportsman who claimed he had won £1,500 on a double bet. He backed Windsor Lad to win the Derby, and the Cardiff lad to win the fight!

* * *

The British Boxing Board of Control meanwhile, had become concerned about articles in particular publications containing the remarks allegedly made by Pa Petersen over the appointment of 'Pickles' Douglas to referee the fight with Harvey. Pa and promoter, Jeff Dickson, were called before the Stewards to explain the situation.

During the hearing reference was made to the articles which appeared in the *Star*, *Sporting Life* and *Sporting Chronicle* on days leading up to the fight. Pa reminded the Stewards that they knew neither he nor Jack had sent any letter of protest to the Board concerning the appointment of Mr. Douglas. Reports in the press were therefore entirely erroneous. Furthermore, he had not given any interviews, or informed any member of the press that he had lodged a protest against the appointment of the referee.

Dickson told the stewards that publication of the articles had followed communication from his press bureau. He produced a telegram from Pa Petersen dated 31 May 1934 which read; *'Do you agree with Douglas refereeing or shall I put in a protest?'*

The promoter said he telephoned Pa and advised him not to lodge any protest. He understood Pa to reply, 'I have already sent it out.'

Seeing the situation as a possible way to boost interest in the fight, Dickson informed his press agents who made up a story from it. Explaining to the Stewards what he considered necessary bally-ho to promote a big fight, he insisted that the press greatly enlarged the story sent to them.

Pa Petersen then called Harry Jones to testify on his behalf. He told the Stewards that on the morning of the fight, he telephoned the Board of Control office and asked if a denial could be sent in respect of the false publication saying Mr. Petersen had objected to the referee. He was told it was too late for the Board to issue a statement, but the matter would be noted and reported to the Stewards.

A copy of the notice sent out by the promoters press bureau was produced and found to be almost identical to the eventual articles. The Chairman told the Stewards that the *Sporting Chronicle* was the only paper to have enquired of the Board to establish if the statement received was accurate.

Norman Hurst, who wrote the *Sporting Chronicle* article on 4 June, was then called and asked to explain his reason for writing it. The journalist said that when his paper received details of the alleged protest by Mr. Petersen, he was asked to look into it. Wishing to ascertain if the statement was accurate, he telephoned the Board of Control and was told that no such protest had been received from Mr. Petersen.

The Chairman then asked Mr. Hurst if he was surprised to know that he was the only journalist to have taken the trouble to enquire whether the statement attributed to Mr. Petersen was correct. Hurst said that although papers took every possible precaution against publishing false information, they would, on receiving a story from a source such as the promoter of a contest, take the same as being authentic.

After a lengthy deliberation, the Stewards unanimously agreed that Pa Petersen be absolved from blame. They concluded that Jeff Dickson Promotions were entirely responsible for the inaccuracy of the reports, and were fined £10. Dickson accepted the Board's decision, and at his request the Stewards agreed not to issue a statement to the press.

* * *

Early in July 1934, it was agreed that Jack's future ring interests would be looked after solely by his father. The syndicate which had backed him since he turned professional, was to break up. It had always been known that neither sponsor had the slightest desire to make money from the enterprise, but as time passed, a number of differences arose which were not in keeping with the original ideas.

At an early stage, members of the syndicate realised Jack had a problem with his nose which caused him difficulty in breathing. He was sent to a prominent specialist in London who strongly advised an operation and a long rest. It was claimed that Pa refused to agree to the operation.

There was further concern to the syndicate when Jack's left eye, damaged in the fight with Len Harvey in November 1933, kept re-opening in later fights. They insisted that he saw Sir Harold Gillies with a view to being given the best possible advice about treatment. Again, it was claimed that an operation was refused.

Members of the syndicate were also said to have been irritated by a number of statements made by Pa. There was press speculation that his exuberant enthusiasm had become exceedingly difficult to handle, thus contributing to the eventual break-up of the syndicate.

Whatever the differences were, matters remained private and were dealt with in gentlemanly fashion. Speaking at a specially arranged luncheon in London, Willie Blackwood said, 'It is impossible to say anything very definite about Jack Petersen's future plans. The syndicate which has been looking after him for the past two and a half years, will go out of existence, and his future will be settled by himself and his father. We feel that now Jack is of age, he is able to look after his own affairs.

Jack was presented with a beautiful gold cup estimated to be worth at least £300. It was a striking piece of workmanship, the base bearing gold plaques to commemorate each of his professional championship victories.

Making the presentation, Mr. Malcolm McDonald, Parliamentary Secretary to the Dominions, and son of the Prime Minister, said that Jack was the admiration of all British sportsmen. A gold cigarette case was presented to his father.

In response, Pa said, 'It's easy to spend millions in money and forget it, but this gift will forever be a reminder of an association marked with happiness throughout.'

The break up of the syndicate was purely for personal reasons, and not because of any major dispute between the parties. 'They remain my very good friends,' emphasised Pa in paying special tribute to Willie Blackwood and Harry Jones. 'When guidance is wanted, we shall not hesitate to refer to them again, and we know it will be forthcoming gladly.'

Thanking the syndicate who had been his advisers since he was 19, Jack said, 'I'm happy indeed that their faith in me has been justified.'

Jack knew it would be a while before he fought again, so he decided to go on another cruise. He joined the Canadian Pacific steamer '*Montrose*' and spent an enjoyable and refreshing three weeks. When he returned home in early August, he was fit and ready to defend his British Empire title against Larry Gains.

The first moves to stage the fight had occurred within a week of Jack beating Len Harvey. Harry Levene, who managed both Gains and George Cook, travelled to Cardiff and had talks with William E. Allen with a view to persuading Petersen to defend the title against Cook. Although Cook was recognised by the British Boxing Board of Control as the official challenger, Allen knew Gains was a much bigger attraction. He was anxious to regain the title, and he and his backers were convinced Petersen would be easy prey. Larry had been at ringside when Jack beat Harvey, and issued a challenge before the Welshman left the ring.

Allen suggested matching Petersen with Gains, and if he retained his title, he should then face Cook. Levene could not lose, so it was agreed that Allen should put the proposals to Pa Petersen.

Jeff Dickson was anxious to stage the fight at the White City on 10 September, so with Allen acting as go-between, negotiations with Pa began. As an added incentive, Dickson said he wanted to match the winner with former world heavyweight champion, Primo Carnera.

In June, Carnera lost the title to Max Baer, but was looking to re-establish himself and gain a return. The promoter insisted that if the fight went ahead, it would be staged in Paris because there was no arena in Britain large enough to take it.

Dickson travelled to America and guaranteed Carnera a purse of £6,000, or 32$^{1}/_{2}$ per cent of the gate, to meet the winner of Petersen and Gains. His manager, Luigi Soresi, agreed subject to receiving a better offer to box in America. Provisional arrangements were made for Carnera to sail to England on 4 August, but everything fell through when he was offered a fight with Vittorio Campolo in Buenos Aries on 30 November.

Whilst in America, Dickson became acquainted with Doc

Morris, Sports Editor of the *New York Daily Mirror*. Acting on behalf of a syndicate of wealthy sportsmen in Bermuda, Morris had secured Max Baer's signature to fight any heavyweight in the world. He saw Petersen as a colourful fighter who would help draw a crowd large enough to make a promotion a financial success.

Morris handed Dickson contracts asking that he put them to Pa Petersen. Although Jack was being offered $25,000 plus expenses for two people, Pa rejected it when he met the promoter in Cardiff the following week. 'Wait until the Gains fight is over and done with,' he remarked, 'then we'll see.'

The main obstacle was a condition in the contract that in the event of the contest going the full distance, the decision would be awarded by a majority of newspaper writers present at ringside. This was stipulated because Baer was already under contract to the Madison Square Garden Corporation to defend his title under their direction.

A few days later, Pa met William E. Allen at the Lynn Institute, and both were amused at the offer of $25,000. 'I think Dickson must have got a bit mixed up in the coinage values between American and English,' said Pa. 'What we had in mind was £25,000 (pounds), and for that sum we will fight any man in the world.'

He was quick to point out that $25,000 (dollars) was equivalent to about £5,000, and they could earn that amount for any fight in London or Cardiff.

Anxious to push Jack into world championship reckoning, Dickson then proposed to match him with American Steve Hamas in London. He said the winner would challenge Max Baer for the title the following year.

There was also newspaper speculation that the Welshman would meet British middleweight champion, Jock McAvoy. Such reports were angrily denied by Pa Petersen. 'It's all moonshine,' he snapped. 'Such a match is absolutely stupid.'

Meanwhile, Jack's potential at world level attracted the attention of former world heavyweight champion Jack Dempsey. In a cablegram to well known British sportsman, Sir Harry Preston, he said; *'Would like to get Jack Petersen under my management. Think I can guarantee him championship within two years. Would appreciate seeing his father. Find out what can be done about this.'*

Preston promptly contacted William E. Allen who immediately went along to the Lynn Institute. 'Over there, they know there is only one challenger from Europe for Max Baer's championship, and that is Jack,' said Pa Petersen when Allen told him of Dempsey's interest.

132

Pa said they would go to the United States if terms were acceptable, whether it be under Dempsey's management or anyone else's. 'We are prepared to fight Baer or any other fighter who cares to come along,' he added.

* * *

Despite all the speculation about future contests, Jack concentrated on training for the fight with Gains. Yet again, there was a shortage of genuine heavyweights for him to spar with, and the only man to accept the generous wages offered was Reggie Meen, and that was only during the last few days.

Despite the difficulty, Jack did not remain idle, and received great support from Charlie Bundy and South African Eddie Pierce, although both were much smaller than Gains. During mid-August he and Bundy boxed a fiery exhibition at the annual tournament at Cardiff staged in aid of Nazareth House.

Bundy was a capable and experienced fighter and he performed so well in work-outs with Jack that Pa Petersen told the *South Wales Echo* he believed he was good enough to fight for the British light-heavyweight title. The remark immediately brought an angry response from Tommy Farr, who was due to defend his Welsh light-heavyweight title against Bundy at Judges Hall, Trealaw on 14 September.

'As long as Mr. Petersen is so full of confidence as to the ability of Bundy,' said Farr, 'a more practical way of dealing with the position would be for him to back Bundy for £50 to £100 a side. As a businessman, Mr. Petersen will appreciate the increased value of the match to the public if genuine side-stake money is put down.'

'Now,' continued Farr, 'there is no moonshine about this challenge. If Mr. Petersen would lodge his money with Mr. W. J. Phillips, Secretary of the Welsh Branch of the British Boxing Board of Control, it will be covered immediately.'

Tommy then raised another controversial issue by asking when the Welsh Area Council were going to call upon Jack to defend his Welsh heavyweight title.

'Every other champion has to defend his title every three months according to the regulations,' said Farr. 'Petersen has been Welsh champion for two years, yet no action has been taken in this direction by the Welsh Area Council. It may have been that no boxer with sufficient ability was available,' he continued, 'but there is one who is not afraid to tackle Petersen for the title, and he is myself.'

Farr, from a deprived background in the mining community of the Rhondda, was becoming critical of the Petersens' at every opportunity. He was known to have a chip on his shoulder, and there was a hint of jealousy over his fellow Welshman's achievements.

'I think it is only fair that this point should be expressed,' continued Farr, 'because it must be remembered that during the period when Petersen was without his heavyweight crown, no attempt was made to get him to defend the Welsh title.'

* * *

In early September, Jeff Dickson took legal action against the BBC over what he described as an illegal broadcast of Petersen's fight with Len Harvey at the White City. Concerned that the same situation could occur with the Gains fight, he applied for an injunction restraining the BBC from broadcasting any report or comment of the fight.

His application was heard by Sir Boyd Merryman sitting as an occasional Judge at his house, the living room being used as a temporary court.

After reading papers before him, the Judge said he understood that on one previous occasion, the BBC had paid to broadcast a fight, but on another they were not prepared to pay anything. Instead, they had people in the arena, who at intervals, went outside to a telephone over which was re-constructed a broadcast of the fight for which they had refused to pay a fee for the privilege.

Although the Judge made no order, the BBC gave an undertaking; 'not to induce, or endeavour to induce, any person to breach any contract between Mr. Jeff Dickson and themselves, and not directly, indirectly or by their offices, servants or agents, to commit any tresspass.'

No order was made as to costs.

* * *

Interest in the fight was enormous, and the crowd was expected to be the largest ever to attend a boxing contest in Europe. The Petersen's therefore ensured they were paid accordingly, although the financial agreement they struck with Jeff Dickson remained a closely guarded secret.

Jack knew he had to beat Gains convincingly to guarantee moving towards a world title shot. Failure would not only ruin those plans, but financial offers amounting to many thousands of pounds would be withdrawn.

There was, however, still great concern about the recurring injury above Jack's left eye. So, in the weeks leading up to the fight, a number of experiments were conducted. In particular, a special preparation of tough transparent, flexible super-imposed skin was applied to the area of the injury. The substance, which continued to harden whilst applied, was only visible from a distance of about three feet.

* * *

Jack was a great dog lover and often when out running he was accompanied by his pet Bull Mastiff. He spent a great deal of his relaxation time grooming the animal for the open competition at the Bedwellty Show at Bassalleg on 3 September. It was his first such venture but he was rewarded with two first prizes.

* * *

Larry Gains was a veteran of 102 fights of which he had won 85 and drawn three, 48 victories coming inside the distance. Born in Toronto, Canada, in December 1900, he had boxed all over the world since becoming professional in 1923. He had the distinction of knocking out Max Schmeling in two rounds in 1925, and in 1932 took a ten rounds decision from Primo Carnera.

Gains won the British Empire title in 1931 with a second round knockout of Phil Scott, successfully defended it against Don McCorkindale and George Cook before losing it to Len Harvey. Although well into his thirties he was still regarded as one of the cleverest heavyweights in Europe.

In an interview with William E. Allen, Petersen admitted being fully aware of the task he faced. 'Gains is the biggest proposition I have ever faced,' he said. 'Nevertheless, I am confident in myself for I am boxing faster than ever, and I am stronger and harder.'

Gains was desperate to regain the title, and stayed at a cottage in a little village five miles from Market Bosworth with his sister and mother who did all his cooking. He engaged some of the best sparring partners around, including George Cook, Scottish champion, Alex Bell, Charlie Belanger of Canada, and Ernie Simmonds from Birmingham. In a series of articles in the *Empire News*, Larry claimed he trained like never before.

During sparring, Gains never wore a headguard, and in his final session three days before the fight, he sustained a cut above his

135

Poster advertising Petersen–Gains fight for the British Empire heavyweight championship.

right eye from a clash of heads with Belanger. The injury required two stitches, but he could not afford to pull out of the fight. Every effort was therefore made to disguise the wound, including painting over the eyebrow. Such a good job was done that Larry passed the pre-fight medical examination by a Board of Control appointed doctor.

* * *

On the day of the fight, there were huge early morning crowds at Cardiff and Newport stations. Boxing fans from the Rhondda and Monmouthshire valleys queued to board conjested trains headed for London. They were the crowds who travelled everywhere to see Jack Petersen fight.

His meeting with Gains had really captured public imagination in both Wales and England. It was an intriguing contest between an experienced technician and an exciting young champion with a tremendous punch. The build-up was like an international football match as thousands wearing Petersen caps and rosettes descended on White City bringing traffic almost to a standstill throughout most of the day.

The principals met at Jeff Dickson's office at noon for the weigh-in. Accompanied by the promoter, they walked to the scales, shook hands and posed for photographs, but neither weighed.

That evening about 70,000 inside the stadium cheered wildly as searchlights picked out the boxers as they made their way to the ring. Gains was first through the ropes wrapped tightly in a white dressing gown trimmed with gold, a huge green maple leaf emblazoned on the back. It was all of five minutes before Petersen appeared clad in a gold robe with three leeks woven in silk across the back.

Len Harvey was among celebrities introduced from the ring, and challenged the winner with a side-stake of £500.

Pa Petersen, meanwhile, crossed the ring to Gains corner. 'That's a lot of vaseline you've got on that eyebrow,' he snapped, reaching up to thumb it away.

'Don't you open it up,' replied Gains pushing Pa away. 'Let your boy do it.'

Word had reached Pa about the injury Gains had sustained in training, and on returning to the corner told his son to make the eye his target.

There was a scrappy start to the fight, and referee, Mr. A. S. Myers, warned Petersen several times in the opening round for hitting with the back of the glove. Gains was then severely warned for swinging Jack to the floor in retaliation. Larry was a crafty exponent of the noble art and knew every trick in the book. He was clearly intent in keeping out of trouble, which had the effect of making Petersen look poor.

The champion landed few solid shots in the opening two rounds, but made Gains right eye his main target. Left jabs reopened the cut in the second round, and it became steadily worse as the fight developed.

In the third, Jack became frustrated at the Canadian's spoiling and elusive style. Desperate to land a solid punch, he became wild and erratic, and at times Gains' skill made him look very raw.

As they came out for round four, the referee suddenly stepped between them. 'What's this?' he enquired pointing to black smudges on Gains' cheek and shoulders. The Canadian was taken back to his corner where his seconds were ordered to wipe the substance off. It was later revealed that during the interval between rounds three and four, a preparation of chloride of iron had been used to seal up an old wound which had reopened on Larry's cheek.

When the action resumed, Gains scored with stiff short arm punches. The fight, however, was not living up to expectations. By this stage, thrills were few and far between, partly because Petersen knew he could not take chances against a man of Gains' experience. He was therefore unusually restrained and biding his time whilst boxing well within himself.

The challenger stepped up the pace in the sixth, opening up with heavy punches from both hands. A vicious right to the chin had Jack unsteady for a few seconds, and he was kept on the defensive for most of the round.

Larry continued to attack in round seven and crashed home several good punches to the head. At this point thousands of Welshmen suddenly feared for Petersen who was groggy and twice sent reeling across the ring from powerful left hooks.

The bout was being fought mainly at long range, and there was remarkably little clinching. Gains was clearly ahead at this stage, but towards the end of the round, the champion hit back. Arms working like pistons, he scored heavily and had the Canadian defending for all he was worth.

Jack continued to attack in the eighth, driving home a series of solid lefts which brought blood streaming from Gains nose. Petersen was in wonderful condition, a tribute to his father's patient care. He was boxing a controlled, intelligent fight, and by gradually applying the pressure, he slowed Larry considerably.

The course of the fight changed dramatically in round nine when the champion was at his very best. Punching with great power, he caught Gains with shots from all angles. Only great defensive skills enabled the challenger to stay clear of serious trouble.

It was, however, the beginning of the end for Gains. Although he hit back strongly at one stage during the tenth, he was badly hurt by some heavy body shots. At the bell he looked resigned to defeat as he walked unsteadily to his corner.

A perfectly timed left to the face at the start of the eleventh shook Gains badly. A continuous stream of solid left jabs kept him on the defensive, and by this stage he was being completely outboxed. He took terrible punishment in round twelve, and few men would have stood up to such a battering. Yet Larry hung on desperately, and despite his power and superiority, Petersen could not find the punch to finish it.

As the bell ended a very one-sided round, Gains legs almost gave way as he staggered to his corner. His lips were cut and badly swollen, blood trickled from his nose, and the cut above his right eye was an ugly sight.

The fight should have been stopped at this point, but incredibly Gains came out for the thirteenth. He immediately set about the champion in a do-or-die effort, but faded badly as Petersen hit back. Larry was punched all over the ring but gallantly refused to go down. Big punches sent him tottering into his own corner as the bell sounded, not a second too soon.

Blood streaming down his face, Gains was defenceless and out on his feet. He didn't know where his corner was, and had to be assisted to his stool by his seconds. Glassy-eyed and unable to utter a word, he looked appealingly into the eyes of his manager, Harry Levene. His right glove clung to the top rope whilst his left arm hung loosely at his side.

Larry's wife, sitting at ringside, could stand it no longer, and dashed up the ring steps. 'Why don't you stop the fight?' she screamed anxiously at Levene as he threw water into Larry's face trying frantically to bring him to his senses.

'Stop the fight, stop it,' yelled Lisa when it was obvious nothing could be done to revive her man for another round. Her frantic appeals succeeded, and before the bell sounded for round fourteen, the towel was thrown in as a token of surrender.

Larry was totally dejected and so weak that his seconds had to support him all the way back to the dressing room. Yet it was no disgrace to lose in the way he did. Few men could have withstood the battering he did during the last four rounds. He was a courageous, lion-hearted fighter who gave everything against a very fit, powerful and brilliant young champion.

As Petersen raised his arms in triumph, thousands of Welshmen broke into singing the Welsh National Anthem. There was tremendous excitement, and he was mobbed all the way to his dressing room.

Once again, Jack was quick to heap praise on an opponent. 'I would like to take this opportunity of saying how fairly Larry fights,' he told newsmen. 'There is nothing about Larry Gains in the roped square which does not conform to the best traditions of British boxing.'

It was a new Jack Petersen on display against Gains. More restrained than in many of his previous fights, he was content to just keep his left hand pushing into the Canadian's face. In the early rounds, he threw so few rights that many of his fans feared a re-occurrence of the injury suffered in the past. It was a mature, controlled performance against a man he knew would not go over easily.

Later that night, Gains and Levene went to the Trocadera in London's west end with friends. They were having a meal when Pa Petersen approached their table. After exchanging pleasantries, Pa bought drinks for everyone.

'Larry, I think you're a wonderful man,' said Pa sincerely. 'I would pay you £100 a week to teach Jack some of the tricks you pulled on him tonight. So how about it, will you come down to Cardiff with us?'

'Pa, it's no good,' said Gains politely. 'You see, I still think I can beat your boy. I'm just praying for the chance to fight him again. That's why I can't teach him.'

Accepting Larry's rejection with a smile, Pa raised his glass of champagne and said, 'In that case Larry, here's to the next time.'

In a further article in the *Empire News* the following Sunday, Gains said his injuries contributed to his downfall. He claimed that after his eye was cut, a solution used to stem the bleeding got into the eye causing intense pain. There were two occasions when a thumb accidentally caught him in the other eye rendering him defenceless to Petersen's punches. Despite everything, he accepted defeat gracefully.

'I would be a poor sort of sportsman if I started to offer a bundle of excuses for my defeat,' he wrote.

Although Gains had a further 30 fights before retiring in 1939, he and Jack never fought again. They did remain firm friends, and frequently met at dinners and ex-boxers association functions.

* * *

In an article in the *News Chronicle*, Jack said he had never been so keyed up before a fight, or more encouraged by the roar his fellow Welshmen gave him as he went to the ring. 'I am well satisfied,' he remarked on reviewing the fight. 'I consider it the greatest of my triumphs.'

In the *South Wales Echo*, William E. Allen was generous in his praise of Petersen; 'I've never seen him give a more perfect exhibition of boxing. Gains was outwitted and outfought in ten of the thirteen rounds.'

When Jack returned to Cardiff, more than 1,000 excited fans were at the station to greet him. He was loudly cheered, but when asked about the fight, would only say, 'I feel fine.'

The interest in Petersen was phenomenal, and throughout the week a film of the fight was shown to packed houses at most cinemas and suburban halls in Cardiff.

The British champion was swamped with invitations to fight in all parts of the world. America was clamouring to see him, and amongst those anxious to secure his services was Jimmy Johnstone, matchmaker for Madison Square Garden. In a cablegram to Pa, he said; 'Would like to use Jack at the Garden sometime this season. Cable. Alright?'

Another cable was received from Jack Dempsey with his proposals for a business arrangement. He said that if he could manage Jack, he would take him to the United States and allow him to acclimatise for a couple of months. The plan would then be to give him an easy fight, followed by one against a world rated fighter. Provided Jack kept winning, he would get a world title fight within two years.

Dempsey said he would want a five year contract with the privilege of a further five years if the Welshman became champion. 'If I did not think he had the possibility of becoming champion, I would not be willing to waste my time,' said Dempsey.

Pa insisted he would not be baffled by loud noises from America, and the only way they would go there would be for a world title fight. 'Jack has one or two other jobs over here first,' he told William E. Allen.

* * *

The day after he beat Gains the British Boxing Board of Control ordered Jack to defend his titles against George Cook. Managers were given until 25 September to arrange the contest otherwise it would go out to purse offers. Pa Petersen and Harry Levene, however, quickly reached agreement with Jeff Dickson for the fight to be staged at the Royal Albert Hall on 17 December.

Born in New South Wales in 1898, Cook had already challenged, unsuccessfully, for the Empire title against Joe Beckett in 1922, Phil Scott (1926) and Larry Gains (1933). This time, he had a new incentive because the British Boxing Board of Control ruled that he would become the first man from an overseas dominion permitted to fight for the British heavyweight title under a new residential qualification rule.

In the meantime, Petersen continued to receive offers to fight in America. In late October Pa received another cablegram from Jimmy Johnstone offering Jack a fight with Maxie Rosenbloom for the world light-heavyweight title. It was well known that the Welshman could easily make the limit of 12 stones 7, and many critics in the States believed that if the fight went ahead, he would be favourite to win.

Johnstone, who had long sought to get Jack across the Atlantic, promised that if he beat Rosenbloom, he would be matched with Max Baer for the world heavyweight title without having to meet any of the leading contenders. Although it sounded an exciting prospect, Pa remained sceptical. He was not convinced that the terms offered would make the trip worthwhile.

Rosenbloom, meanwhile, was matched with Bob Olin in New York on 15 November in what would be the ninth defence of the title he won back in June 1930. Within a few days of the fight being made, Pa received a further cable from Johnstone; *'Cable terms to fight winner of Rosenbloom-Olin light-heavyweight championship contest. Match to come off sometime December or January – 15 rounds for title.'*

Again, Pa showed little interest in the latest offer.

News of a possible world title fight, however, dramatically increased the demand for Jack to make public appearances. As it was not possible to accept every invitation, priority was given to the most deserving causes.

On 7 November, he attended a matinee performance in aid of the *Western Mail* and *South Wales Echo* Gresford Relief Fund at Cardiff Empire where he boxed a three rounds exhibition with Charlie Bundy. The following day, he travelled to Swansea, having agreed to box exhibitions at the Hospital Sportsmans Bed Fund Boxing Tournament.

It was Jack's first visit to the town since becoming heavyweight champion, and a lengthy programme of events was organised for him. The people of Swansea loved him, and he was cheered wherever he went. Within an hour he had signed hundreds of autographs and shaken countless numbers of hands.

Jack arrived at the new Guildhall shortly after noon and was greeted by the Mayor, Alderman Edward Harris, and the Deputy Mayor. During a tour of the building he and Pa showed great interest in some Viking designs.

After signing the visitors book, they were taken to Messrs William Edwards store in Oxford Street, one of Swansea's most modern buildings. Jack was delighted when shown a window display of his numerous boxing trophies.

Hundreds of people had gathered in the street, and the champion was mobbed as he left his car. Once inside the store he was surrounded by excited employees seeking his autograph. On reaching the boardroom, Jack turned to a local newspaper reporter and smilingly offered him the post of bodyguard against autograph hunters.

'It's the same everywhere we go,' explained Pa.

On leaving the store, Jack had to fight his way through cheering crowds as he made his way to the Hotel Metropole where he was the guest of a group of 60 prominent Swansea sportsmen. During lunch, he was presented with two photographs taken during his tour of the Guildhall by a local photographer.

'My word, that's quick service,' he remarked. 'You certainly do things well here in Swansea.'

Alderman W. D. Rees, Deputy Mayor of Swansea, said they were delighted to meet Jack who was an example to all young men by his clean way of living. He had put Wales on the map, and the people of Swansea were thrilled that he had agreed to visit them and help the hospital.

After lunch Jack and Pa visited the local headquarters of the British Legion after which they went to the hospital. Jack toured the wards, and at his request, visited the children's ward. He loved children, and the youngsters had looked forward to the hour long visit he had promised. There was a huge demand for his autograph, and for several of the older children, he drew caricatures of himself.

After leaving the hospital he visited the Castle Hotel at Neath in the company of the owner, Owen L. Harries. His visit was a surprise to the principal and guests at a wedding reception. The champion autographed two photographs of himself and presented them to the bride and groom, and wished them long life and happiness.

The final engagement of the long day, was at the Mannesmann

Hall, where Jack boxed exhibition bouts with Swansea heavy-weight, Jim Wilde, and Charlie Bundy. Using 20 ounce gloves, the champion gave the large audience a wonderful demonstration of his class and ability. Neither of his opponents could do anything against his fast left jab, and he also opened up with the occasional big punch.

Petersen thoroughly enjoyed himself and was in good spirits. The next bout was a four rounds exhibition between Young 'Kid' Jones (Pontardawe) and Young Driscoll (Abercrave). Jack acted as second to Jones, whilst Pa agreed to look after Driscoll.

Everything was conducted in a good spirit, and, during one of the intervals, Pa called across the ring to Jack, 'Tell your man to stop using his right.' Jack smiled and half pulled off his jacket as if to challenge his father to a fight. At the end of the contest each raised their boy's hand as the winner, but after light-hearted consultation, agreed that the verdict was a draw.

At the end of what had been a full and demanding day, Jack expressed his gratitude for the receptions they had received from the people of Swansea. 'I have been warmed by their hospitality,' he said before leaving. 'I am told it is characteristic of west Wales sportsmen, but frankly, they swept me off my feet.'

10

THE TEUTON TERROR

During late November 1934, London promoter Arthur Elvin announced that Petersen would top his bill at Wembley Sports Arena in the New Year against one of the world's top four heavyweights.

Meanwhile, in the United States, Maxie Rosenbloom lost the world light-heavyweight title to Bob Olin on points. A few days later, Pa Petersen received a letter from Jimmy Johnstone offering Jack $12,500 to meet Olin for the title. As it amounted to just under £3,000, the offer was promptly rejected.

Pa told Harry Lascelles-Carr of the *Western Mail* he believed American heavyweights, Steve Hamas and Art Lasky, could be persuaded to meet Jack in London or Cardiff. They were the top two contenders for the world title in '*Ring*' magazine's November rankings, with Petersen rated at number six.

'*Ring*' editor, Nat Fleischer, had some respect for Jack, and in his yearly summary the following month, wrote:

> Petersen, the British menace, must be given serious consideration by the other heavyweight contenders. He has a good record, as far as foreign competition goes, even though his list of victims includes several who couldn't stand up in this country. The fact remains that he has clashed with the best of competition abroad and has come through triumphantly, and that makes him an outstanding fighter. His most notable victories were k.o.'s over Reggie Meen, Larry Gains, Len Harvey, Ben Foord, Charlie Smith and Harry Crossley.
>
> Petersen may not be a world beater, but he has displayed a brand of fighting that, for the first time since Phil Scott was at the helm, has enabled England to have one of its heavyweights so far up in the ranking.

Boxing in America, at a time of depression, was not, however,

RATINGS FOR THE MONTH OF NOVEMBER

These are my ratings for the month ending November 17:

Heavyweights	Light-Heavy-weights	Middleweights	Welterweights
World's Champion	World's Champion	World's Champion	World's Champion
Max Baer	Bob Olin	Marcel Thil	Jimmy McLarnin
1—Steve Hamas	Maxey Rosenbloom	Teddy Yarosz	Kid Azteca
2—Art Lasky	Tony Shucco	Young Corbett	Cerefino Garcia
3—Primo Carnera	Joe Knight	Paul Pirrone	Bobby Pacho
4—Max Schmeling	Al Gainer	Oscar Rankins	Harry Dublinsky
5—Patsy Perroni	Ambrose Palmer	Carmelo Candel	Tony Falco
6—Jack Peterson	John Henry Lewis	Vince Dundee	Bep Van Klaveren
7—Natie Brown	Johnny Miler	Jock McAvoy	Eddie Kid Wolfe
8—Johnny Risko	Tait Littman	Fred Henneberry	Willard Brown
9—King Levinsky	Fred Lenhart	Freddy Steele	Tiger Burns
10—Lee Ramage	Al McCoy	Lew Halper	Jack Carroll

Lightweights	Featherweights	Flyweights	Bantamweights
World's Champion	World's Champion	World's Champion	World's Champion
Barney Ross	Freddy Miller	Al Brown	Title Vacant
1—Tony Canzoneri	Baby Arizmendi	Sixto Escobar	Midget Wolgast
2—Frankie Klick	Mike Belloise	Speedy Dado	Jackie Brown
3—Young Peter Jackson	Nel Tarleton	Pablo Dano	Benny Lynch
4—Tiger Humery	Petey Hayes	Young Tommy	Valentin Anglemann
5—Cleto Locatelli	Petey Sarron	Louis Salica	Maurice Huguenin
6—Lew Ambers	Joe Conde	Star Frisco	Young Siki
7—Eddie Cool	Johnny Pena	Baby Quintana	Tommy Pardoe
8—Lew Massey	Henry Armstrong	Little Pancho	Joe Mendiola
9—Tracey Cox	Merv Blandon	Joe Tei Ken	Bobby McGhee
10—Benny Bass	Jackie Wilson	Henry Moreno	Phil Milligan

Ring magazine monthly ratings for November 1934.

sufficiently attractive to Jack to be guaranteed as much as he could demand in Britain. If a fight with either Hamas or Lasky came off, he would earn substantially more than offered by Jimmy Johnstone.

* * *

In preparation for the fight with George Cook, the British champion was assisted by Eddie Steele (Norwood) and Bert Ikin (Stoke), who had recently beaten Reggie Meen. He was also joined by Mickey Callaghan who gave up the chance of winning a novices competition for the experience of sparring with Jack.

In his final try-out, the Welshman looked exceptional. Wearing 20 ounce gloves, he gave both Steele and Ikin a terrible hiding. Knowing Cook would be no push-over, he really let his punches go, and used his left jab with great accuracy.

Petersen and Cook met at Jeff Dickson's office at 2 pm on the day of the fight but did not weigh. This was becoming a regular feature for fights involving Petersen, although there was never any dispute. 'What does it matter about the weights,' said Jack when the subject was raised by a pressman.

Jack was a picture of coolness as he climbed into the ring, and even waved to friends sitting at ringside. Yet for most of the fight there was a listlessness about him. He started well enough, and after only a minute crashed a beautiful right hook to the chin sending Cook to the floor. The tough 'Aussie', however, was up at 'two' and fiddled his way through to the end of the round.

Although Cook had a sound defence, Petersen was unusually restrained, and it became a dull fight by his standards. There was very little real action during the opening rounds, and in the fourth there was a shout from ringside, 'He's not trying.'

In the fifth, Jack was sprung into action when Cook hurt him with a solid right into the pit of his stomach. He hit back immediately with a two-fisted attack, but it was only brief.

'Come on Jack,' shouted frustrated fans during round six. He did shake Cook with a crashing right to the chin in this round, but it was one of the few occasions he threw the punch, peferring instead to use a prodding left jab.

A left hook from Cook opened a gash on Jack's top lip in the seventh. The injury appeared to inject some urgency into the champion's performance, and from this point he gave a clever display of boxing. Left after left pumped into Cook's face in rapid succession, although there was rarely an opening to land the right.

There was both excitement and tension in round eight when Petersen went to the floor following a brisk exchange of punches. As referee, Percy Moss, waved the Australian away to take up the count, Jack was on his feet claiming it was a slip.

When ordered to box on, Cook rushed straight at the Welshman and caught him with a solid right to the chin which had him reeling. The excitement was intense, but the bell sounded before Cook could do any further damage.

During the interval, former world welterweight champion, Ted 'Kid' Lewis' rushed to Cook's corner screaming at him to go straight out and finish the job. Lewis obviously knew nothing about Jack's ability to absorb punishment and hit back when the going got tough.

Throughout the next three rounds, Jack jabbed Cook silly, and in the eleventh opened a cut under his left eye.

Petersen was hurt in round twelve by a heavy right to the body, and throughout the thirteenth Cook attacked strongly to the body with both hands.

The crowd saw something of the real Petersen in round fourteen which was by far the most exciting of the fight. He crashed a right to the temple which had the challenger reeling into the ropes. Another big right caught him flush on the chin sending him heavily to the floor. Cook was in serious trouble, but his tremendous strength prevailed, and he was amazingly on his feet at the count of 'six'.

Although he was decidedly groggy, George was tough and knew how to survive. He weaved and ducked away from the onslaught, and Petersen was unable to land the one punch needed to finish it.

Cook did little more than defend throughout the final round, but did so skilfully. At the final bell, he was still on his feet. Although he lost the decision, the veteran Aussie got a wonderful ovation which continued as he made his way back to the dressing room.

Despite the fans disappointment, Pa Petersen was perfectly satisfied with the outcome. 'We want boxing experience,' he said. 'We cannot get it in the gymnasium, so we have to get it in the real ring. We had it tonight.'

'The old man is a great fellow,' continued Pa referring to Cook. 'He can teach us something.'

William E. Allen was so concerned about Jack's performance that he went to the dressing room straight after the fight. 'Is something wrong with Jack?' he enquired.

'Definitely not,' replied Pa. 'Jack went in to box and I did not tell him to open up until the twelfth round.'

Although Jack lacked the fire his fans had come to expect from him, he showed he was a greatly improved boxer and not just a fighter with a big punch.

The British champion returned to Cardiff early the next day, but Pa stayed in London. He went to collect their purse of £2,000 from Jeff Dickson, and then had a meeting with Sydney Hulls who was matchmaker for Wembley promoter, Arthur Elvin.

Talking to reporters, Pa was still full of praise for Cook. 'George gave us a great fight,' he said. 'He is a clean and honest fighter.' He confirmed that Jack was not going to America, but likely to fight Walter Neusel at Wembley in the New Year. The German had offered to deposit a side-stake of £500 with the Board of Control for a fight with Petersen.

* * *

Once again the British Boxing Board of Control Stewards became concerned about remarks attributed to Pa Petersen in a newspaper article. A reporter from the *London Star* claimed to have met Pa at his hotel the morning after the fight with George Cook. Pa was quoted as saying:

> Jack would have knocked Cook out any time he liked but I told him there was to be no knockout unless Cook got too cheeky.
>
> Jack is only a baby in the game but he does what I tell him. As I have been in the game for over 45 years, I am not talking through my hat. I was confident of success long before the fight began, but I told Jack he could learn a lot from Cook who knows all the tricks, and Jack did as I told him. It was a grand experience for him but he was never in any danger. It was like a cat playing with a mouse.
>
> We would pay Cook almost any sum he asked to come and box with Jack. But why should we make this offer again while people are willing to pay Jack £2,000 for a fifteen rounds lesson as they did last night.

The alleged remarks infuriated Cook's wife who told the *Star* reporter: 'His remarks are an insult. The truth is, Jack Petersen never looked like a champion. George showed up all his limitations. It's absurd to say Petersen deliberately withheld a knockout blow, because last night George represented £20,000 to Petersen. He ran away from George.'

George Cook was amused by Pa's comments rather than angry. 'Pa Petersen is just one big bluff,' he remarked. 'I am willing to fight Jack any time, any place. He can't knock me out.'

His claim was backed by manager, Harry Levene, who immediately challenged Jack to a re-match over any distance. He also offered a side-stake of £200 that Cook would not be knocked out.

The Stewards of the Board of Control wrote to Pa asking if his comments in the newspaper were correct. A response was received from a firm of solicitors acting for Pa. The explanation given was accepted by the Stewards, but they refused to release the details.

* * *

On New Year's day 1935, it was officially announced that during the Christmas holiday Jack had become engaged. His fiancee was Miss Betty Williams, an attractive 18 years old young lady who lived with her parents at 18 Ninian Road, Cardiff. She was keen on sport and had represented her schools at hockey and La Crosse.

In his young days, Jack had a good friend, Nibbs Williams, who was a cousin of Betty. Two years earlier she joined him and Jack for an evening out. Jack and Betty became close friends, and their engagement was of great happiness to both families.

Betty was the elder of two sisters and knew a bit about boxing. Her father, a retired Cardiff auctioneer, had once been a backer of Freddie Welsh.

* * *

In early January 1935, Pa Petersen wrote to Nat Fleischer, editor of *Ring* magazine, taking him to task over comments he made about Jack not being ready for a shot at Max Baer's world title. Pa was also critical of the fact that the British champion was not rated as the number one contender in *Ring* magazine's list of rankings.

'If you want to put boxing back on the map, a Baer-Petersen fight is the one you should go after to bring back the million dollar gate,' declared Pa. 'We want to fight Baer and put boxing on top of the world again.'

'As I told Jimmy Johnstone, the only thing that will bring us to America is a world championship fight with Baer,' continued Pa. 'If you read through his record, you will see that my boy has beaten more champions than you have ever seen in America.'

Fleischer replied saying it was of great amusement in America to think of Petersen increasing world interest in boxing should he win the world heavyweight title. Commenting on Pa's statement that Jack had a better record than Georges Carpentier when he fought Jack Dempsey for the title, Fleischer insisted there were at least five American heavyweights who he considered capable of beating the British champion. He based his opinion on information gleaned from respected British writers and sportsmen.

In one of his columns, Fleischer wrote:

'When Pa Petersen names the champions beaten by Jack, and places his faith in his boy's fighting ability as a world beater on victories or knockouts over such champions as Harvey, Crossley, Muller, Schonrath, Gains, Pettifer, Power, Bandias and Doyle, he fails to take into consideration that from the entire list only Harvey and Gains are worthy of recognition among the top flight.'

Fleischer pointed out that Harvey was only an overgrown middleweight who failed to make any impression when he boxed in the United States in 1931, and both Schonrath and Pettifer had been beaten in the States.

A number of other American journalists also made uncomplimentary remarks about Jack's ability at world level, but by doing so, Pa reckoned his boy had been given the best advertisement possible.

Fleischer, however, remained critical of Jack. In another article, he wrote;

> 'It would be suicide to put Jack in against Baer. He has only beaten a series of bums dug up from the graveyard. Despite this, however, I have heard favourable comments about Jack who is liable, in time, to put Britain on the boxing map. But until he has beaten some first and second rate American heavyweights, he will be given no consideration for a tilt at Baer's title.'

Fleischer said many of the names on Jack's record meant nothing in the States. 'Pettifer could not even get a six round preliminary contest in New York,' he remarked.

In a conversation with Harry Lascelles-Carr of the *Western Mail*, Pa Petersen made it clear that he would not allow Jack to go to America like Carnera, to be exploited by American boxing magnates. 'He is ready to fight every one of America's first and second rate heavyweights in England.' insisted Pa. 'But why should we go to America when he can get bigger purses over here?'

Pa pointed out that Baer had not defended the title since winning it from Carnera the previous June. Instead he was boxing four round exhibition contests to pay off his debts. 'There's no need for Baer to fight in such farces when he can come to England and fight Jack with a guarantee of £15,000 or 40 per cent of the Wembley gate which will amount to approximately £40,000,' said Pa.

'It will be a nice holiday for him, and as he will be only meeting a little schoolboy of 23 years old, a veritable novice, not considered good enough to meet America's leading heavyweights, the champion would earn £40,000 for nothing.' Pa said that after Jack had fought Walter Neusel, it was hoped he would face world number one contender, Steve Hamas.

* * *

Jack commenced training for the Neusel fight during the first week in January, but again experienced difficulty getting sparring partners. Anxious to get the best available men, Pa again attempted to recruit Tommy Farr who was due to meet Eddie Phillips for the British light-heavyweight title the night Jack faced Neusel.

Farr again rejected Pa's offer, and at a meeting at the Lynn Institute, Harry Lascelles-Carr said there appeared to be considerable animosity between Farr and the Petersens. Pa firmly denied this saying they would be only too pleased to give Tommy

151

EMPIRE POOL
AND SPORTS ARENA
WEMBLEY
MONDAY, FEB. 4th, at 8 p.m.

WEMBLEY STADIUM LTD.
PRESENT
ANOTHER ALL-STAR PROGRAMME

INTERNATIONAL HEAVY-WEIGHT CONTEST
15 (3-Min.) ROUNDS

WALTER NEUSEL
(THE GERMAN BLONDE TIGER)
v.
JACK PETERSEN
(HEAVY-WEIGHT CHAMPION OF GT. BRITAIN)

HEAVY-WEIGHT CONTEST—8 (3-Min.) ROUNDS

BEN FOORD v. ED WENSTOB
(The South African Sensation)   (The Fighting Canadian Cowboy)

MIDDLE-WEIGHT CONTEST—8 (3-Min.) ROUNDS

ERIC SEELIG v. AL BURKE
(The Jewish Refugee Boxer)   (Southern Area Champion)

6 (3-Min.) ROUNDS CONTEST

HERBIE HILL v. REGGIE HALL
(Wembley)   (Bristol)

AND FURTHER NOVICE HEAVY-WEIGHT CONTESTS

SEATS (NUMBERED & RESERVED) 12/-, 24/-, 36/- & 63/-

BOOK NOW

WEMBLEY STADIUM BOX OFFICE (Wembley 1550), PRINCES RESTAURANT, PICCADILLY (Regent 8141)
and the usual Ticket Agencies and Libraries
ALL 3/6 and 6/- SEATS HAVE BEEN SOLD

Poster advertising the contest between Jack Petersen and Walter Neusel on 4 February 1935.

the opportunity to spar with Jack as part of his preparation to meet Phillips.

'We all know Eddie's tricks,' said Pa, 'and are only too willing to give Farr the advantage of our knowledge which we had to pay for.'

Although only 22, Tommy was a determined and strong-headed young man with the experience of more than 130 fights. When Lascelles-Carr told him of Pa's comments, he said, 'I have had many offers from Gains, Cook, Harvey and Neusel to help them in their fights with Petersen. I have always refused because I do not want to assist a foreigner to beat a Welshman. For the time being I must refuse Mr. Petersen's kind offer because if I beat Eddie Phillips I hope to secure a fight with Jack. At such a time I feel I must look after my own interests. As my ambition is to win the British and Empire heavyweight titles, I will not spar with Petersen.'

Following Farr's refusal, Eddie Phillips was recruited to spar with Jack, angering many Welsh boxing enthusiasts. As Phillips was a Londoner, it was considered an act of treachery, and he should not have been allowed such quality preparation before meeting another Welshman for a British title.

* * *

Walter Neusel was two years older than Petersen and had been a professional since 1930. He was no stranger to British rings, and held victories over George Cook, Harry Crossley, Reggie Meen, Jack Pettifer, Gypsy Daniels (twice), Bobby Shields, Gunner Bennett, Eddie Steele and Guardsman Gater. He also beat Larry Gains in Paris in 1932. He boxed in America during 1934, creating a good impression with points victories over King Levinsky and Tommy Loughran, and a draw against Natie Brown. At one stage, he was expected to face Primo Carnera for the world title, but his hopes were shattered when he was beaten in nine rounds by Max Schmeling in Hamburg in August 1934.

When Neusel arrived in London to face Petersen, he had a credible record of 40 victories from 45 contests, 23 coming inside the distance. He had drawn two and lost three. He set up camp at the Star & Garter, Windsor, but his weight of 15½ stones was of concern to promoter, Arthur Elvin.

Anxious that the German was fully fit when he faced the British champion, Elvin bound him with an agreement that he would weigh-in at no more than 14 stones 2. Failure to meet that weight would result in a forfeit of £250. This was the first and only time in the history of British boxing that such a stipulation was made for heavyweights.

A number of critics thought Neusel could be weakened by having to lose so much weight, which would aid Petersen. The Welsh press certainly fancied Jack to win in quick time.

Interest in Jack was again incredible, and crowds flocked to the Lynn Institute daily in the hope of seeing him train. When he wound up his preparations on 30 January, scores of London and provincial pressmen were present. Jack didn't disappoint them, and did four rounds with George Brennan, Bert Ikin and Norman Baines. He then spent an hour doing strenuous ground exercises, skipping, muscle stretching using developers, and shadow boxing. When he finished he was almost as fresh as when he began.

Jack travelled to London the day before the fight and stayed at what he described as his lucky hotel at Harrow. In a telephone call to William E. Allen on the morning of the fight, Pa Petersen said, 'Jack is very fit. He has had his usual walk, usual breakfast, and expects to gain his usual victory.'

Petersen and Neusel met in London at 12 noon for the weigh-in, and there was a tense period because of the clause in Neusel's contract regarding his weight. Wearing only thin carpet slippers, he stood on the scales, carefully supervised by Sydney Hulls. Ten seconds elapsed before Hulls announced, 'Neusel is exactly fourteen stones, two pounds.'

Pa Petersen had been watching closely, and nodded in agreement. Jack did not weigh, but it was announced that he scaled a little under thirteen stones.

Looking in magnificent condition, Neusel said he was fit and confident of victory. He insisted that the weight reducing had not weakened him.

The fight was a tremendous attraction and every seat was sold more than a week beforehand. Amongst the crowd of 11,600, a record for an indoor promotion in Britain, was a wonderful gathering of notable sportsmen and boxing enthusiasts. Wembley had gone a long way to become the largest sports centre in the country, and this fight proved to be its biggest success to date. Gate receipts totalled nearly £10,000, and hundreds of fans who arrived without tickets, were turned away.

The atmosphere inside the Empire Pool was electric, and Petersen received the most wonderful reception as he climbed into the ring. It was a crucial fight for him, and victory was essential if he was to progress in the world rankings. Sydney Hulls and Arthur Elvin were convinced that if he beat Neusel, they could persuade Max Baer to defend his world title against Jack in London during the summer.

As they were called to the centre of the ring by referee Mr. C. B. Thomas, Neusel objected to the amount of vaseline smeared across Petersen's eyebrows and forehead. It was promptly reduced by Pa at the referee's request.

The fight opened at a terrific pace as Petersen shot from his corner and landed a series of punches before the German got started. Two good lefts also found Neusel's face, but he replied with a heavy, swinging right which hurt Jack. Looking very strong, Walter made the body his main target, and the weight of his punches frequently had the Welshman backing away.

The British champion started round two quickly, scoring with three sharp lefts to the face but the German was unperturbed. His face utterly expressionless, he strode forward purposefully, still concentrating his attack on the body.

Midway through the round, Jack shook Neusel with a solid right to the jaw. As he followed up with a barrage of punches, the excitement was intense. The crowd were on their feet frantically yelling the Welshman on. Although groggy, Neusel smothered and held on effectively, and by the end of the round was fighting back strongly.

Predictably, Jack shot from his stool at the bell for the third. He caught the German with a vicious combination to the head but missed widly as he followed up. The force of his desperate swings threw him off balance and Neusel seized the advantage. A heavy right sent Petersen to his knees, but he was up without a count.

The crowd roared as the Welshman fought back. 'Hit him, hit him,' yelled Pa from the corner steps, but Jack was too wild and erractic to be effective. He was fighting as though it was do or die. Neusel was unperturbed, and continued thumping away to the body. One heavy right made Jack gasp, and two more solid punches landed as the bell ended the round.

The pace slackened in the fourth as the British champion became more cautious. He looked better when he concentrated on his left jab rather than seeking to have a war with his heavier opponent.

Suddenly, Neusel waded in with heavy shots to the body, but Petersen countered brilliantly. Two vicious rights to the German's left ear hurt him, and the ear quickly became red and swollen. By the end of the round, however, Jack looked tired, and his left eye was showing signs of damage.

By comparison with what had occurred before, the next three rounds were quieter, although both men were still battling hard. Jack was very tired in the sixth but still used his left jab to good effect.

As he came out for round eight, Petersen must have known that he faced a hopeless task. Yet he never gave up trying. His courage kept him going, and he stood up magnificently to the terrible body punishment dished out by the powerful German. By the end of the round, however, Jack was falling apart. He was extremely tired, and his nose was bleeding heavily.

Displaying incredible courage, Petersen started the ninth by scoring with five left jabs without reply. Neusel rocked back on his heels and hung on grimly as Jack attempted to follow up his advantage. Both men were extremely tired, and a lot of heavy clinching and mauling developed. As the crowd began to heckle, referee Thomas pulled them apart and told both men to clean it up.

The warning was effective and brought about instant action. Neusel resumed his attack to the body, and twice before the end of the round caught Petersen with vicious punches. By the bell he looked in serious trouble, and literally fell to his stool.

The British champion refused to give up, and at the start of round ten, forced Neusel to the ropes. As he followed up, swinging wildly, he was caught by a savage, chopping right which opened a terrible gash above his left eye. As Jack reeled across the ring with blood streaming down his face, the grimly determined German strode forward lashing out with both hands. Petersen was almost doubled up by a right to the pit of the stomach, and was driven around the ring as punches rained on him from all angles.

Still Jack refused to quit or go to the floor. In a frantic effort to get back into the fight, he swung a wild right which missed badly. The force of the blow threw him to the floor, and when he rose, Neusel closed in and piled on the pressure. Again Jack hit back, and the crowd were on their feet as he staged a desperate rally towards the end of the round.

Almost blinded by his own blood, Jack staggered the German with a barrage of tremendous punches, but in his excitement and desperation, became too wild. Many punches missed their target, and Neusel remained calm under pressure, and by the bell was punching back.

Pa worked frantically on Jack's damaged eye during the interval, and by the bell for round eleven, had stemmed the flow of blood. Neusel, though, was not to be denied, and was out of his corner like an angry tiger. Gamely, the British champion tried to keep going by using his left jab, but the German was too strong. Two telling blows were pumped into his face, and the gash above Jack's left eye reopened bringing blood spurting down his face.

Sensing his opportunity, Neusel smashed a vicious right to the jaw which shook Jack badly. As he reeled across the ring, the German followed him unleashing heavy punches from both hands. Petersen was in a bad way. His knees sagged, his arms were limp, and his gashed eye was a ghastly sight. His courage was incredible as he was pursued by a man almost as tired as himself, yet inspired by the sense of imminent victory.

Right after right crashed into Jack's face, and a short, yet powerful punch, sent him briefly to the floor. Even then he was up without a count, only to endure another vicious battering. Backed into his own corner, the Welshman took punch after punch full on the chin.

The entire fight had been waged amid an ever increasing volume of cheering and shouting, but culminated in wild excitement. As Jack was smashed helplessly on the ropes, he desperately tried to stop the might of Neusel with one wild right but missed and stumbled to the floor. Grasping the middle rope, he gamely pulled himself upright and swung a left. It missed badly and the impetus swung him completely round to be at the German's mercy.

There was no way Jack could recover. He staggered about the ring, his face covered in blood. Only his tremendous courage and pride kept him on his feet. From ringside seats, hysterical women screamed for the fight to be stopped, but amazingly referee Thomas showed no sign of stepping in.

Realising Jack's strength had left him, Neusel lashed away with both hands. All found the target and the Welshman tottered on the ropes like a drunken man. Finally, the battering became too much for Pa. He had suffered agonies watching the son he idolised taking such terrible punishment, so wisely, albeit belatedly, he threw in the towel.

Although beaten, Jack came out of the fight with his reputation higher than ever. He fought furiously and courageously, and until his left eye was cut in round ten, he was in with a chance. At the end the referee had him two rounds ahead, his scorecard reading $47^1/_2$ - $46^1/_2$.

Throughout the final round, and for at least ten minutes after the fight was over, the huge arena echoed with the cheers of thousands who knew they had seen one of the greatest heavyweight fights for years. Although the middle rounds had appeared dull, it was only because they were overshadowed by the sheer brilliance of the first three and last two when the ferocity of the two men continually brought the crowd to their feet.

The cheers for the two men were deafening, but there was no denying that Jack had been beaten by a heavier and much stronger man. Although he boxed cleverly and often landed powerful punches, the fight exposed his limitations as a heavyweight at world level. Not for the first time he displayed incredible courage, but the fact remained, he was just not big enough.

Jack's defeat surely ended his dream of challenging for the world heavyweight title. It proved to be a disastrous night for Welsh boxing because at Mountain Ash, Tommy Farr failed in his bid to become British light-heavyweight champion, going down on points to Eddie Phillips.

Jack's 18 year old fiancee listened to a broadcast of the fight at her Cardiff home. It was his first fight since their engagement and she could not bear seeing him being hit, so she stayed at home. The following day, she told a reporter she was not 'the most disappointed girl in the world' because she had every confidence in Jack. 'He knows how to lose, and that makes me all the more proud of him,' she added.

Although Jack was disappointed at losing to Neusel, he was by no means dismayed. At noon the following day he went to a tailors shop in London to be measured for new suits prior to returning to Cardiff. To a *South Wales Argus* reporter who met him he said; 'Neusel is certainly a tough customer. It was a slice of bad luck when my old wound re-opened. But for that I might have brought about a different result – who knows?'

Pa Petersen was angry at reports in a number of morning papers that the defeat meant the end of Jack's career. In an interview with a *Western Mail* reporter he said;

'It is utter rubbish. The boy is only 23, and last night was a wonderful experience for him. Neusel is a grand fighter, and it is men like him Jack must meet.'

'He will be quite fit to fight again in a short time, but we are in no hurry. We are still seeking the world title. After Jack has had a holiday, we shall challenge Max Baer again.'

As was customary following his fights in London, a large crowd gathered at Cardiff railway station to see Jack return. Extra staff and police were on duty, but it was all to no avail because the beaten champion did not arrive. Instead he left the train at Newport and was taken by car to his home at Barry.

There was some concern in South Wales because nobody knew where Jack was. Several reporters called at his house, but their knocks were ignored. The fact was, Jack was resting and nothing was going to persuade him to give interviews. Eventually he conveyed a message to the group outside his house through a friend. 'My father, who is still away from home, will conduct that side of the business.' With that, he asked to be left in peace.

In the press, there was considerable concern regarding the severity of Jack's injured eye. One London newspaper believed it could be the end of his career. That story was quickly dispelled when a prominent South Wales doctor conducted an examination. Although the injury had bled profusely, it was expected to respond to careful treatment and heal without difficulty.

Jack also required treatment for damage to his right hand. Within a few days, he flew to Jersey where he saw Sir Herbert Barker, described as the world's most eminent specialist in manipulative surgery. He was familar with Jack's problem, having seen him the previous year. After a minor operation, the injury which had troubled him for some while, healed well.

* * *

The fight between Petersen and Neusel created so much interest that a film of it was shown for an entire week at the Gaumont Movietone News Theatre at Shaftesbury Avenue in the heart of London's west end.

DON'T MISS LONDON'S
ONLY LONG-LENGTH FILM

OF

PETERSEN

v.

NEUSEL

SHOWING ALL THIS WEEK

AT THE GAUMONT-BRITISH

MOVIETONE
NEWS THEATRE

Shaftesbury Avenue, W.I

RINGSIDE SEATS 7d. and 1/-

A film of the fight was advertised in London newspapers.

Within a couple of weeks Jeff Dickson announced that he planned to stage a big open-air show at the White City in early June during Derby week. High on his list of preferred top-liners was a return between Petersen and Neusel.

Len Harvey, meanwhile, continued to press for a rubber match with Jack. 'I don't know what the public think when they read about Jack Petersen and Walter Neusel being described as the best two heavyweights in the country,' he remarked. 'I thought I came in somewhere. I've beaten Jack and he has beaten me. So, what about a third meeting that everyone talks about?'

Harvey suggested a contest for £500 a side, or whatever stakes Jack would agree to. 'If he comes in at light-heavyweight, I'll lay odds of 6-4 on the result,' said Len.

Pa Petersen laughed when told of the offer, and made it clear they wanted £5,000 to meet Len again. 'I am not at all interested,' he snapped. 'Harvey can try all he likes to get publicity for himself, but frankly I wish he would leave us alone.'

When William E. Allen conveyed Pa's message to him, Harvey asked if the demands would be reduced if he agreed to make 12 stones 7. 'I am prepared to make a match, put up £500 forfeit, and lay odds of 6-4 on myself,' said Len. 'Failing that, I am willing to meet Petersen for £500 a side, and that offer also goes to Walter Neusel or any other heavyweight in Europe.'

Pa was still not interested, and said that despite the Neusel defeat, they were still in a position to negotiate. 'If Harvey wants to fight at light-heavyweight, then he can meet Eddie Phillips or Tommy Farr. Why doesn't he get Bob Olin over here for the world title?'

'If Jack ever fights at 12 stones, 7, it will only be for the world title,' continued Pa. 'We are not concerned with small fry, we have no time to spare.'

London newspapers continued to publish elaborate stories about Jack, including the fact that he was definitely fixed up to go to America. This was angrily denied by Pa who told the *South Wales Echo*, 'We have no such plans. We will have our next fight here in June, not in America.'

There was so much speculation by the newspapers that in later years Jack often remarked that much of what was written about him was pure fabrication.

A few days after Len Harvey's latest challenge, the Petersens received a cable from the United States offering Jack a fight with Bob Olin for the world light-heavyweight title. Pa immediately rejected it because the terms were again unacceptable. He told the

South Wales Echo that he did not rule out the possibility of Jack meeting Olin, but only in England.

Refusing to be denied, Len Harvey issued a further challenge, and offered to lay £700 to £400 on the result. A few days later, he increased his offer to £1,400 to £800 on discovering that the Petersens had received the offer to meet Olin.

'It has been suggested that Petersen will meet Olin for the world title in the summer,' Len told the *South Wales Echo*. 'It is also suggested the American would need a couple of fights before he meets Jack. Well, I'm prepared to meet Olin with a side-stake of £500.'

Eddie Phillips and his manager Sam Russell were also unhappy at the prospect of Jack meeting Olin. 'We object to Petersen having first claim on the world light-heavyweight title,' Russell told the *Western Mail*. 'Surely he must beat Phillips before meeting Olin.' They issued a challenge to Jack for £500 a side at 12 stones 7.

* * *

By the middle of March 1935, Pa was in negotiations with three promoters for Jack to have a return fight with Walter Neusel. Although Jeff Dickson was desperate to stage the contest, Pa eventually reached agreement with Arthur Elvin for it to go ahead in the open air at Wembley Stadium on 25 June.

Although the injuries to Jack's left eye and right hand necessitated a lengthy break from sparring, he worked daily to maintain his strength and fitness. Once given the all-clear, he sparred with Bert Ikin and Norman Baines, nicknamed 'King Kong' because of his massive build and tremendous strength. Eddie Steele was also recruited to help increase the British champion's speed.

The return fight with Neusel was such a tremendous attraction that special trains were organised from all parts of the country, in particular South Wales. Working men, including miners, dockyard workers, bus and train drivers, saved up through their clubs for weeks to enable them to travel to London. It was anticipated that more than 10,000 Welshmen would be at the fight. An extra 20,000 seats were erected in the stands and an additional 6,000 on the ground.

The popularity of Jack Petersen was incredible, and thousands of letters poured into newspaper offices in London and South Wales praising his courage. Few of his fans believed the crude but powerful German, was the better man.

That view was shared by Tommy Farr who had been at The Star

WEMBLEY STADIUM
TUESDAY, JUNE 25, at 8 p.m.

BRITAIN'S GREATEST OPEN-AIR PROMOTION

Return Contest—15 (3 Min.) Rounds

WALTER

NEUSEL

(Germany)
versus
JACK

PETERSEN

(British Empire Heavy-weight Champion)

Empire Light Heavy-weight Contest—15 (3 Min.) Rounds

EDDIE PHILLIPS *v.* **ED WENSTOB**

(Light Heavy-weight Champion of Great Britain)   (Canada)

AND STRONG SUPPORTING PROGRAMME

Prices of Admission :—

| Special Ringside Enclosures | £5/5/0 & £3/3/0 | Ringside Seats 36/-, 24/- |
| Stand Seats (Numbered & Reserved) 24/-, 12/- & 6/- | Stand Seats (Reserved but Unnumbered) 3/6 | Room for 50,000 at 2/6 |

BOOK EARLY to Secure the Best Positions

Tickets available from Box Office, Wembley Stadium (Wembley 1550); Princes Restaurant, Piccadilly (Regent 8141), and from the usual Ticket Agencies

Poster advertising the return contest between Petersen and Neusel on 25 June 1935.

162

& Garter at Windsor, watching Neusel train. 'Between you and me, Neusel moves like a carthorse,' Tommy told the *South Wales Echo*. 'And the fact that he has been wearing sponges in his gloves, indicates to me that his hands are not too good.' Tommy said he had backed Jack to stop the German. 'Wish him all the best and luck from me,' he continued. 'I think you will see a Petersen-Farr fight after all.'

With less than two weeks to go, Jack was given an extra incentive to beat Neusel. On 13 June, James J. Braddock caused a major upset in America by taking the world heavyweight title from Max Baer. Arthur Elvin and Sydney Hulls promptly commenced negotiations with Braddock's people for him to defend his title against Petersen at Wembley provided Jack beat Neusel.

Jack and his father arrived 15 minutes late for the weigh-in at Piccadilly in London's west end. Pa promptly said he saw no reason why Jack should go to the scales. 'This is a heavyweight fight,' he snapped, 'and what weight they are makes no difference.' Paul Damski, manager of Neusel was unconcerned. 'I don't mind,' he said. 'I can tell you Walter is fourteen stones one and a quarter pounds.' It was believed that Petersen weighed only 12 stones 9.

Neusel was wearing a bandage around his neck. He had been suffering from a boil which had been lanced at the weekend.

Although the attendance was well over 60,000, it fell way short of the promoters original estimate of 100,000. During the afternoon, a terrible thunderstorm hit London, with fork lightning illuminating the sky. Heavy rumblings of thunder could be heard for miles around, and rain fell in blinding torrents for several hours. Although it cleared up a few hours before the fight was due, ticket sales on the night were seriously affected.

As the programme of events commenced, rows of famous sportsmen in evening dress huddled close to each other in their ringside seats. Those who had taken waterproofs were rewarded because there was another heavy deluge before the big fight started.

* * *

For thrills, the fight will be remembered as one of the greatest heavyweight contests ever seen in a British ring. It was another full bloodied and punishing battle, and the courage shown by both men was incredible. It was a fight which neither deserved to lose.

Mr. C. B. Thomas, who was again the man in charge of hostilities, later described it as the most sensational heavyweight battle in Europe for a quarter of a century.

Neusel started quickly, and taken by surprise, Petersen spent the first half minute defending himself against a savage attack. Once he settled, however, there were some furious exchanges, with the British champion getting the better of it. He shook the German with a terrific right to the jaw just before the bell, but as Neusel hit back the old injury above Jack's left eye re-opened, and blood streamed down his face.

Pa succeeded in stemming the flow of blood, and Jack leapt from his stool at the start of round two. He launched a furious attack, and Neusel was badly shaken by a right to the chin. Urged on by Pa slamming his fists on the boards of the ring, the British champion crashed lefts and rights to the chin sending the German reeling along the ropes.

Desperate to finish it Jack became wild, and allowed Neusel to get to close quarters and slam his own big shots to the body.

Midway through the round, blood again poured from Jack's eye injury, and sensing the danger, he slammed home heavy punches to have the German in trouble again. The crowd were wild with excitement, but the bell sounded before Jack could follow up his advantage.

During the third, Walter again concentrated on the body whilst Petersen attempted to use his greater speed to outbox him. A heavy right to the chin shook Jack, but he hit back immediately. In a hectic toe-to-toe rally leading up to the bell, he gave as good as he got, but at a price. Blood again streamed down his face from the injury which looked extremely nasty.

As Jack dropped on to his stool, Pa was waiting with a wad of cotton wool soaked with collodion. His hand shook as he applied it to the injury, and some of the solution leaked into Jack's eye. As the bell sounded for round four, he could barely see.

They were both quickly off their stools and engaged in a fierce slam in the centre of the ring. Jack was badly hampered by not being able to see from his left eye, but then another cut appeared below the right.

Ignoring the injuries and discomfort, the British champion fought with courage and fury which delighted ringsiders. Both men hit out for all they were worth, and it was reminiscent of a bare knuckle street fight. Although he was very tired, and bleeding badly, Jack held his own in a savage round.

Neusel was made to look slow and ponderous during the fifth as Petersen smashed home punches from both hands. The German, however, was prepared to take them in order to force his way to close quarters and hammer away at the body. The

Welshman gasped as heavy shots found their target just above the belt.

Despite having the skill to outbox the German strongman, Petersen again foolishly resorted to a wild two-fisted attack. Whilst it was exciting for the crowd, these were not good tactics. The German was much heavier and stronger, and despite a bad swelling about his left eye, continued to smash heavy punches to the body.

For the first minute of round six, Petersen again boxed brilliantly. Left after left found Neusel's face and made him look clumsy and amateurish. Then Jack again lost concentration and allowed himself to be drawn into a fight. He was rocked by a vicious right, but hit back strongly with good punches of his own. Only Neusel's toughness saved him from going down, but then he fought back. The crowd were on their feet yelling with excitement as big shots crashed against the Welshman's chin.

Neusel was looking to finish it at the start of round seven. He cornered Jack and lashed out with both hands, but the British champion refused to submit. Although he took a lot of punishment, he had an incredible fighting spirit and hit back. He put everything into his punches, but Neusel was exceptionally strong and could take a punch. The excitement reached fever pitch as they traded tremendous shots in the centre of the ring and just before the bell.

Jack again used his boxing skill at the start of the eighth, but couldn't resist reverting to two-fisted fighting. By doing so, he played into Neusel's hands, and was punished heavily at close quarters. Yet again he fought back strongly, and despite their tiredness, they stood toe-to-toe in another fierce rally. At the bell both men went unsteadily to their corners.

Neusel was particularly tired and becoming dispirited. He had hit Petersen with everything, yet he was still standing. His close friend and manager, Paul Damski needed to use all his powers of motivation during the interval to keep him going.

Damski did his job well and the German came out for round nine with renewed energy. He immediately scored with solid shots to the body but as he chased after Petersen, he slipped to one knee. On rising, Neusel was caught with three sharp, hurtful punches to the face.

Spurred on by his success, the British champion cut loose. One tremendous right to the chin shook Neusel badly. Right after right crashed against his chin, and it was amazing that he stayed upright. His face was cut and his knees sagged, yet almost by instinct he kept his arms pumping forward. Several shots caught Petersen as he desperately tried to finish it.

Covered in blood and yelled on by the frantic crowd, Jack drove Neusel to the ropes and hit him with shots from all angles. He gave him a terrible hiding. The German looked out on his feet, yet he refused to go to the floor. His strength and courage were incredible, but at the bell he staggered to his corner shaking his head.

Although ringsiders were unaware of it, Neusel was suffering badly from the effects of the boil on his neck. Petersen, however, knew all about his opponent's discomfort and threw plenty of punches to the raw, sensitive area, particularly in the previous round. Everytime he was caught, Walter winced with agony, and on returning to his corner, desperately wanted to quit.

'I shall die if he hits me there again,' he groaned to Damski, 'It's no use, I cannot go on.'

Damski was a skilful manipulator, and believed Petersen was a spent force. Knowing his man's strength was superior, he implored him to go on. 'Try just one more round for me Walter,' he pleaded. 'You are winning the fight.'

The despondent Neusel shook his blood spattered head. 'No, I am finished,' he said as the bell sounded for round ten. Ignoring his man's plea, Damski pushed him off his stool without another word.

Although Neusel had complete faith in his manager, it was Petersen who looked the more confident. Knowing the German was in trouble he went straight into the attack and caught him with one of the hardest punches he had ever thrown. Most fighters would have been knocked out by the blow, but Neusel was exceptionally tough and stayed on his feet.

Showing incredible speed at this stage of a gruelling fight, Petersen savagely smashed heavy punches to the head. Although in serious trouble, and swaying badly, Neusel still swung his fists in desperation. Enough punches caught the British champion to again bring blood streaming from the cuts around his eyes.

The excitement was electric, as most people believed Jack was about to reverse the defeat he suffered four months earlier. Just half a minute before the bell, however, everything changed as a swinging left and right caught Jack flush on the chin. He was out on his feet, and the dour German mercilessly unleashed punches from every angle until the bell sounded.

The action had all been in Neusel's corner, leaving Jack to stagger across the ring to his stool. Words passed between father and son, and within seconds Pa threw in the towel. What they didn't know was, that across the ring, Neusel was in no condition to continue either. As he slumped onto his stool, he again pleaded with Paul Damski to let him quit. This time the cornerman was about to throw in the towel, but Pa beat him to it.

It was some minutes before Jack recovered, but once on his feet, he walked around the ring acknowledging his army of fans. As he made his way back to the dressing room, he smiled broadly and thanked people for their wonderful support. It was a brave face he put on because he knew that gone were any hopes of meeting James J. Braddock for the world heavyweight title.

The size and strength of Neusel again proved too great. Jack had fought almost the entire contest covered in blood which seeped from the deep gashes around his left eye. Yet he never gave up trying, and in the final round fought himself to a standstill as he strove for victory. The only consolation he gained from the battles with the German, was financial. His purse of £4,000 for the second fight was £500 more than for the first encounter.

11

MARRIAGE AND MORE DEFENCES

The newspapers were full of praise for the courage Jack displayed against Neusel. In '*Boxing*', Ted Scales wrote:

> I don't think I have ever seen any boxer give a gamer display than Jack Petersen. He pulled the fight out of the fire time and again. If points were given for sheer guts, Petersen would never lose.

Despite the beating he took from Neusel, Jack made a remarkable recovery. The following morning Pa told reporters the defeat made no difference to their plans. 'The plain fact of the matter is,' he remarked, 'that on account of circumstances which cannot be controlled, Jack has for the past three years been fighting men much heavier than himself in an effort to uphold the prestige of British heavyweight boxing.'

Jack and Pa, meanwhile, had some lengthy private discussions and agreed that every effort should be made to secure a fight with Bob Olin for the world light-heavyweight title. When they released the news to the press, Pa said they would agree side-stakes of any amount from £1,000 to £2,000.

'If he meets the American as I hope he will,' said Pa, 'he will be fighting a man of his own weight.'

Years later, Jimmy Walsh, one of Jack's trainers, confirmed what many people had long believed. In an interview with a national newspaper he insisted that the heaviest Jack ever went into the ring was 12 stones 12½. Even than, he went to the scales fully clothed, and there were occasions when he had weights in his pockets.

The Petersen's had talks with Arthur Elvin and Sydney Hulls at Wembley Stadium after which a number of cablegrams passed between London and America. Pa and Hulls then went to the States and reached agreement with Olin's manager, Harry Scadra, for the champion to defend the title against Jack in London.

Although Olin was prepared to travel in early July, his European manager, Harry Levene insisted; 'We will be only too pleased to meet Petersen provided Olin's demands are met. He is the champion and entitled to the larger end of the purse.'

Suddenly, however, the New York State Athletic Commission issued a statement refusing to sanction the fight until Olin had defended against either John Henry Lewis or Maxie Rosenbloom. They did agree to review the situation when Rosenbloom was beaten by Hank Hankinson at Hollywood a few days later.

Realising the Petersen-Olin fight was in jeopardy, Harry Levene contacted the British Boxing Board of Control asking that Jack be ordered to defend his titles against either Larry Gains or George Cook. 'His time has expired,' insisted Levene.

There were also challenges from other quarters. Ted Broadribb, the new manager of Tommy Farr, said they were willing to deposit a side-stake of £500 with the *South Wales Echo* if Petersen would agree to a fight. William E. Allen was asked by a sporting syndicate to offer Jack £1,750 to meet Ben Foord in a return contest over twelve rounds.

Len Harvey wrote to the Board of Control and issued yet another challenge to Petersen. At a meeting on 25 June 1935 the day after Jack fought Neusel, the Stewards decided that as he had held the title for more than six months, Len Harvey should meet Eddie Phillips in a final eliminator, and Jack must face the winner.

In the meantime, Petersen had far more important matters to attend to. After his two demanding fights with Neusel, he was in no hurry to get back into the ring. He had originally vowed not to get married until he retired from boxing, but had now changed his mind.

* * *

The wedding of Jack and Betty took place on 9 October 1935, (a Wednesday), at Marshfield Parish Church. From 7.30 am onwards, the lane leading to the little grey church became packed with cars, charabancs and people on foot anxious to catch a glimpse of the champion and his bride. Touts with confetti did a roaring trade.

By 11 am, when the first guests arrived, the crowd had grown to about 3,000. The general public were banned from the church and grounds, and nobody was allowed past the gate without an invitation card.

Burly policemen had a difficult task holding back the rapidly increasing crowds of excited onlookers who lined the road. When

Jack and his best man, Billy Diamond, arrived at about 11.30 am, dozens of women shouting, 'Good old Jack,' struggled furiously to get to him. They had waited hours in the pouring rain and gale force winds, and many broke through the police cordon to grab his hand or slap him on the back.

Handsome and smart in a top hat and tails, the young champion took it all in good spirits. His face wreathed in smiles, he turned and waved before entering the church. Inside, he walked slowly to the flower decked altar in front of which lay a satin cushion bearing his bride's initials embroidered in silk.

Not far behind Jack, came six bridesmaids dressed in blue. They included Barbara Williams, youngest sister of the bride, and Doreen Petersen, Jack's sister. They had an unpleasant time as they awaited the bride. Wind dragged their long dresses through the mud, whilst the pouring rain caused havoc with their hair.

When the bride arrived 15 minutes later, a crowd of excited women, many of whom were crying, surged around her car. Looking pale and nervous, Betty clutched her father's arm tightly as he escorted her to the church entrance. She was closely followed by her bridesmaids, and four ushers who were friends of Jack.

Once they were inside, a group of onlookers made a concerted push, almost sweeping policemen off their feet. Many got into the churchyard and refused to leave.

The packed church was beautifully decorated with masses of gold and bronze chrysanthemums mixed with fern. The ceremony was conducted by the Rev. A. G. Stanley, vicar of Marshfield, who had christened the bride almost 19 years earlier. His gift to her was an ivory prayer book similar to one he gave her mother when he conducted her wedding ceremony in the same church.

A new form of service was conducted because there had been family difficulties. Jack was a Catholic and Betty attended the Church of Wales. In an attempt to resolve the problems, Jack visited the Archbishop of Cardiff who explained that whilst they could marry, any children from the marriage must be brought up in the Catholic faith. When Betty said she would not be able to do this, Jack gave up his Catholic faith. In their wedding service, the bride did not have to promise to obey her husband, and there was no address. The ceremony included the hymns *The voice that breathed o'er Eden'*, and *'Oh perfect love'*.

As the couple emerged from the church they were greeted by a Guard of Honour formed by members of the 1st Rhiwbina Scout Troup of which Jack was still a Rover leader. Their reappearance also brought an end to the crowd's restraint.

The wedding, which had attracted widespread interest, and was later shown on Pathe News at cinemas throughout Britain, ended amid scenes almost unparalleled in South Wales. The couple were mobbed, and wading through deep mud to reach the safety of their car, Jack had to ward off dozens of over-enthusiastic fans. His buttonhole and Betty's bouquet were snatched, and even when they reached the safety of their car, there was no let-up.

Women scrambled onto the running board and threw bags of confetti into the back. All along the narrow one mile journey from the church, there were similar scenes. Only when they reached a main road was the driver able to gather speed and leave the cheering crowds behind.

Nearly 100 guests joined the couple at their reception at St. Mellons Country Club. They included people well known in every section of life in the City of Cardiff. Gifts included a silver tankard from Viscount Tredegar, and a beaver travelling rug from Captain and Mrs. Fletcher of Magram Castle.

The absence of Pa Petersen at his son's wedding quickly set tongues wagging. There were already rumours of a split between the pair because Pa had gone off on a cruise and only returned as Jack went on honeymoon. As Betty was only 18, Pa had advised Jack about getting married too soon, but whatever their other differences, they were kept strictly within the family.

William E. Allen, writing in the *South Wales Echo*, claimed that Jack had become very disgruntled following his defeats by Neusel, and would, in future, handle his own affairs. Yet only a few weeks earlier when Allen made the offer of £1,750 for Jack to fight Ben Foord, there was no indication of a problem.

'That will be just sufficient to pay our expenses,' Pa had said with a smile. He appeared as enthusiastic as ever to discuss his son's affairs, and said he still hoped the delayed negotiations for a fight with Bob Olin would resume.

Jack himself was no more forthcoming, and whenever approached directly with tempting offers, always said, 'I can't do any business – you must see Pa.'

A variety of stories were written concerning a split, but according to Allen, most could be dismissed as being ridiculous. In particular, it was claimed that Jack had finished with the Lynn Institute. Instead he would be trained by Danny Davies at Frank Moody's gym at Pontypridd.

Davies was annoyed when asked if he was to become Petersen's new manager. 'I've not even spoken to Jack,' he assured Allen. 'I know nothing of his intentions or where these reports have come from.'

* * *

Jack looked a picture of health when he returned home after a wonderful five week honeymoon cruise in the Mediterranean. He was very upset when he heard of the differing stories that had been circulating. Anxious to put matters right, he gave an exclusive interview three days later to Allen and Harry Lascelles-Carr.

'In future, I am my own manager,' said Jack. 'I intend to do all my business without reference to anybody.'

It was the first time he had spoken to a member of the press since his wedding day. Paying tribute to Pa, he said, 'My father has been marvellous. No man in the world could have done better. He's fine, but for very personal reasons we have decided to go our separate ways. We are, however, the best of pals, and shall, I hope, continue to be for the rest of our lives.'

Jack handled the situation maturely and with great dignity. It was to their credit that neither he nor Pa ever went public about any differences between them. Such matters are of no concern to anybody else, yet inevitably bring about gossip and speculation as happened with them. There were also suggestions that Jack's new wife wanted him to quit boxing, but he strongly denied this.

'Utter rot,' he declared. 'My wife has done nothing to dissuade me from carrying on in my own way. It is my profession and she intends to give me nothing but encouragement in continuing with it.'

'What are your immediate plans?' asked Allen, pointing out that the Board of Control could order him to defend his titles within a reasonable time.

'I shall be ready to meet all-comers as soon as I have settled down to the new order of things,' replied Jack. Commenting that he estimated he would reach full fitness in about two months, Jack added, 'Whether it be Tommy Loughran, Ambrose Palmer, Maurice Strickland or Len Harvey, I shall be prepared to take them all on in turn.'

The following weekend, Sydney Hulls travelled to Cardiff and had talks with Jack concerning the possibility of future contests. Len Harvey had emerged as the leading contender for his British and Empire titles having outpointed Eddie Phillips over 15 rounds in Plymouth on 26 October. At a meeting on 15 November, the Stewards of the Board of Control ruled that Jack must meet Harvey, and gave the parties one month to arrange the contest. If no agreement was reached, it would go out to purse offers.

Jeff Dickson immediately offered to put up a purse of £10,000 to stage the fight at the White City on 1 June the following year. He offered Petersen £6,000 with the option of 30 per cent of all monies received directly or indirectly, less tax.

The promoter appreciated that if Jack accepted, he would require a warm-up fight. He therefore offered him an additional £1,500 to meet French champion, Andre Lenglet, over twelve rounds at the Royal Albert Hall on 3 February.

Harvey was offered £4,000 or 25 per cent less tax. He was also offered £1,250 to box either Marcel Thil or Lou Brouillard at the Royal Albert Hall on 13 January 1936. Dickson stipulated that if his terms were accepted, neither man should box during a 60 day period preceding 1 June.

When William E. Allen discussed the offer with Jack, he remarked, 'It's a nice offer, but it happens that I am already in negotiations with other people. They have also put some very tempting bait before me.' He therefore intended considering every option carefully before making a final decision.

Jack and Len both believed the fight was worth more than the £10,000 being offered by Dickson. Harvey said he was not prepared to wait around until June 1936, and was supported by the Board of Control who ordered Petersen to defend his titles much earlier.

Within a few days, both men had talks in London with Arthur Elvin and reached agreement for the fight to be staged at the Empire Pool, Wembley, on 29 January 1936.

It was rumoured that Jack accepted a purse of £4,500, but exact details were never revealed. Whenever he conducted business, he insisted on a high level of confidentiality. Harvey certainly agreed to considerably less than offered by Dickson, purely for the opportunity of an early shot at the titles.

After signing contracts, Jack stayed in London overnight. The following morning, he drove to Orpington to view a gymnasium originally built for Jack Doyle. He was impressed, and although he had never previously trained away from Cardiff, he went ahead and ordered specialist equipment.

The intention was to do light training and roadwork in Cardiff before moving to Orpington for sparring. His new home at Cycoed was ideally situated for country runs. A change of circumstances, however, caused Jack to abandon his plans.

Explaining the situation to William E. Allen, he said, 'I am a Director of the Lynn Institute, and now that my father has had to go away on a prolonged holiday because of ill health, I shall need to be in constant attendance in order to take over his work.

Since getting married, Jack had filled out considerably. He told Allen he intended going into the ring against Harvey at about 13 stones 6. He also revealed that his close friend, Billy Diamond, was to become his manager.

Jack commenced serious training immediately after Christmas, and enlisted the help of Charlie Bundy and Bert Ikin. He also extended another offer to Tommy Farr who was training to meet former world light-heavyweight champion, Tommy Loughran. Farr was growing rapidly, and his fight with Loughran was his first at heavyweight.

At first Tommy indicated he would go along to the Lynn Institute, but then failed to appear. When asked by William E. Allen why he had not taken up Jack's offer, he said, 'I've said this before, the only time I'll meet Petersen in the ring is for his titles.'

Most of Jack's training was done behind closed doors, but when outsiders were able to watch him, they were not impressed. He did not appear as mobile as for previous fights, and although Bundy and Ikin were not in his class, they were able to hit him at will.

In his final try-out, Jack took no chances. Wearing a leather headguard and 16 ounce gloves, he failed to impress the critics. One interested onlooker was Paul Damski who took a different view. 'Jack is so keen,' he said, 'I cannot see Harvey beating him.'

Harvey had set up his training camp at the Barn Club, a roadhouse on the Barnet-by-pass in Hertfordshire. His sparring partners were Eddie Steele, Jack Fox and Les Rowlands. He looked impressive, and boxing writers who watched both men train, believed he would win.

In pre-fight betting, Len was made 2-1 on favourite. This was based on his fine display against Petersen in their first fight, and Jack's subsequent gruelling battles with Neusel. It was also thought that Jack could be at a disadvantage without Pa in his corner.

The demand for tickets was again incredible, and within a few days of the fight being announced, Wembley was sold out. The promoter claimed that the cheaper seats could have been sold twenty times over.

In Wales, there was great excitement, and in the pubs and clubs, folk talked of little other than the fight. The fact was that whether he won or lost, Jack Petersen was the biggest individual sporting attraction in Britain.

Huge crowds were waiting for Jack when he arrived at Paddington station during the afternoon before the fight. Accompanied by Billy

Jock McAvoy (left) congratulates Petersen on his victory at Earls Court on 23 April 1936 watched by Billy Diamond (right). Front right is famous cornerman Dick Gutteridge.

Ben Foord (right) viciously attacks Petersen during the opening round of their fight at Leicester on 17 August 1936.

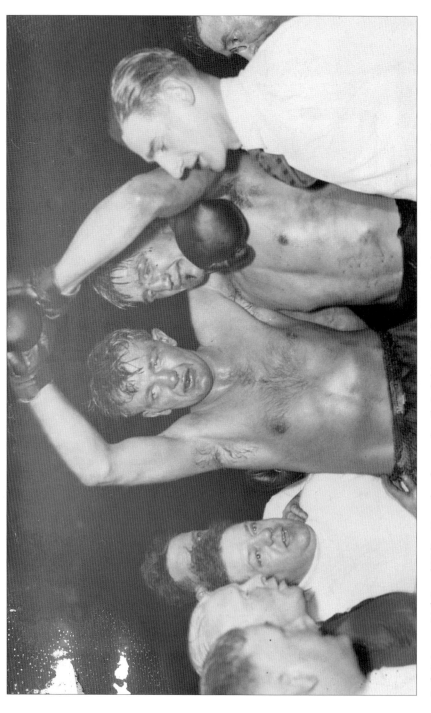

Jack Petersen (right) and Walter Neusel embrace after their fight at Harringay on 1 February 1937 won by the German.

Jack Petersen with two-year-old son John, his wife Betty and baby Michael during
1938.

Walter Neusel (on the scales) shakes hands with Petersen at the weigh-in for their fight at Harringay on 1 February 1937.

Jack Petersen (right) shakes hands with American heavyweight Buddy Baer at the pre-fight dinner for the Tommy Farr – Max Baer contest at Harringay on 15 April 1937.

Captain Jack Petersen with a group of N.C.O.s at one of his physical training courses at Penarth during 1942.

A gathering of great boxers at the Boxing Writers Dinner in London during January 1959. From the left – Joe Beckett, Ted "Kid" Lewis, Ernie Jarvis, Jack Petersen and Dave McCleave.

Former British heavyweight champions honour world champion Rocky Marciano at a gathering in London. From left – Don Cockell, Joe Erskine, Henry Cooper, Len Harvey, Jack Petersen, Johnny Williams and Tommy Farr.

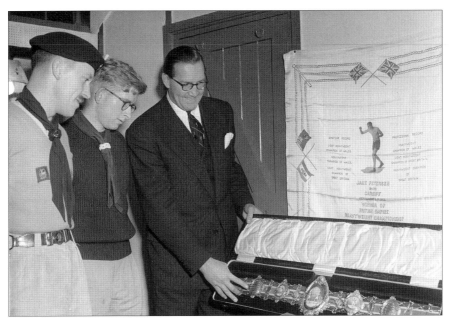

Jack Petersen proudly displays the championship belt he won outright to leaders at a Scout gathering at Well End, Hertfordshire.

Jack Petersen (seated centre) as President of the British Boxing Board of Control. Current Chairman and President, Lord Brooks of Tremorfa and Leonard "Nipper" Read stand fourth and third from the right respectively.

Jack Petersen, President of the British Boxing Board of Control, aged 78 years.

Diamond, he was mobbed and cheered, and had to be escorted through the station by a posse of policemen.

Hundreds more waited in the station yard, and it was several minutes before the British champion reached his car. Once he was inside, a policeman mounted the running board to clear a way through to the street. 'Good luck Jack,' screamed the excited fans as he set off for his regular hotel at Harrow.

* * *

Looking relaxed and happy, Jack climbed into the Wembley ring clad in a green dressing gown with the red dragon of Wales emblazoned across the back. Remembering the courage he showed in his two fights with Neusel, the sell-out crowd gave him a thunderous welcome.

Despite not having his father in his corner for the first time since he turned professional, the Welshman looked extremely confident as the opening bell sounded. Harvey was first to attack, driving Jack to the ropes in his own corner and forcing him to cover up. Then, as so often happened when he was under pressure, Jack hit back viciously.

Three lefts to the face drove the challenger to the ropes, and then a terrific right to the head sent him to the floor. Len took a count of 'five' on one knee, but when he rose he still looked badly shaken. Petersen went all out for the finish, but Harvey's superb boxing skill enabled him to smother the champion's effort.

The knock-down had an important bearing on the course of the fight because Harvey became unusually cautious. He allowed Jack to carry the fight to him during rounds two and three during which he hardly threw anything back.

Jack drew first blood when, breaking from a clinch in round two, he crashed home a solid right which split Harvey's lower lip.

In the third, the crowd got behind the challenger when he suddenly drove Petersen across the ring with a succession of hooks from both hands. Jack hung on tightly, and with his head resting on Harvey's chest, threw several punches to the back of the neck, drawing boos from the crowd.

The fight was by no means a classic, but as it developed, Petersen showed improved skill and defensive tactics. There was none of the recklessness shown in the battles with Neusel. Using his extra height and reach, he was more upright and held his guard high to protect the fragile skin around his eyes. He was unusually restrained, and boxed one of the most disciplined fights of his life.

175

For long periods there was little action, but Harvey did increase the pace in the sixth, and for a while appeared to take control. Skilfully avoiding Jack's left jab, he scored heavily at close quarters. The champion looked distinctly uncomfortable when several solid hooks to the head rocked him.

There were more boos for Petersen in round eight when he again clouted Harvey on the neck and back. Len, however, was doing very little attacking, and Jack scored with several solid punches before the bell.

The challenger was forced to use all his boxing skills to keep out of trouble in the eleventh after he was caught by two vicious rights flush on the mouth. By this stage, the extra weight and strength of the champion were beginning to tell.

Although he was tiring, Len stuck gallantly to his task, and made a brave attempt to turn it around in the twelfth. There were tremendous cheers when he drove Petersen backwards with a heavy right hook to the body.

Petersen was at his very best in round thirteen, and hit Len almost at will. It was a tribute to the challenger's courage that he stayed on his feet in the face of a terrific onslaught. He took a lot of heavy punches, and despite being outfought and outboxed, his spirit remained unbroken.

Gallantly, Harvey tried to match his wits and strength against Petersen in the fourteenth. He attacked desperately with wild swings, but Jack boxed coolly and confidently to avoid whatever was thrown at him.

Harvey staged a grandstand finish in the final round, but again Jack stayed calm. As the challenger launched a frantic last effort to snatch victory, the Welshman was equal to everything he threw. For all of a minute they stood toe-to-toe, but eventually it was Len who had to give ground. In the final half minute, he was defending desperately against a furious bombardment.

At the final bell, Petersen was a comfortable winner, and although he showed good skill and a big heart, Harvey was beaten beyond doubt. Jack was the master throughout, and not once during the fifteen rounds did he cause any real concern to his many Welsh followers. His determination to hang on to his titles, together with new found discipline, won him the day. For a change he came through a fight without any injuries. As he left the ring, Jack was congratulated by Larry Gains, who, putting a hand on his shoulder, said, 'You won all the way Jack.'

Gate receipts were reported to have been £16,000, of which Jack was believed to have received £4,500 plus receipts from film and radio.

* * *

A few days after his victory over Harvey, Jack was again challenged by Tommy Farr, who, two weeks earlier, had gained a dubious points decision over Tommy Loughran at the Royal Albert Hall. In a letter to William E. Allen, at the *South Wales Echo*, Farr said; 'I think I have an excellent chance against Jack. I have had ten fights in ten months, winning nine and drawing one. Petersen has had three in nearly two years and lost two of them.'

Tommy was becoming obsessed about fighting Petersen and was convinced the British champion was ducking him. In an attempt to force Jack's hand, Farr's London connections made moves to try and match Tommy with Walter Neusel.

'To succeed over Neusel,' said Tommy, 'would emphatically put me in line for a fight with Petersen which is the ambition of my life.'

Farr's latest challenge, however, brought about a swift rebuke from Welsh heavyweight champion, Jim Wilde, who accused him of attempting to jump the queue. The Swansea man, who won the title the previous year by outpointing Charlie Bundy, was furious that Farr considered he was entitled to fight Petersen after just one fight as a heavyweight.

'Who the bloody hell does he think he is?' said Wilde angrily. 'Let him fight me first, then we'll know who should fight Jack.'

Away from boxing, Petersen continued to be in demand to attend charity events. At the end of February, he was the major attraction at a special rugby match organised in aid of Pontypridd Police Court Mission and Poor Box Fund. The game was played between a Glamorgan Police fifteen and a team selected by rugby idol, Cliff Jones. Jack kicked off before a crowd of nearly 10,000.

After the match he was guest of honour at a dinner, and made one of his rare speeches. 'I am not any good at rugby,' he declared, 'but I do have an offer to make to Cliff Jones. If he will teach me to play rugby, I will teach him how to box.

* * *

Pa Petersen arrived back in Britain at the end of the month from a trip to Valparaiso. He spent a few days in London during which time he had a meeting with Jack. This prompted speculation that they were about to resume their partnership. Other stories claimed there was a family feud, but if that were the case it was never made public.

William E. Allen was the only journalist to whom Pa spoke, and that was in the capacity of a close family friend. Some days later, Jack told Allen that during the meeting with his father, boxing management was not discussed. Their main topic of conversation had been the business interest Jack had at the Lynn Institute.

Some newspaper reporters believed Jack should concentrate on his boxing to which he responded, 'It is nonsense to say that the business side of things interferes with my boxing. I am quite able to look after my own affairs.'

* * *

In early March, the British Boxing Board of Control announced that Petersen would defend his titles against British middleweight champion, Jock McAvoy, at Earls Court on 23 April.

Stanley Longstaff, a well known sporting journalist, had become matchmaker for Earls Court promotions. Back in January, he had approached William E. Allen seeking help to set up the fight. McAvoy had just beaten Al McCoy in New York, and issued a challenge to Petersen for £500 a side.

Although Jack was training for his fight with Len Harvey, negotiations got underway immediately. He had a series of meetings with Longstaff and agreement was actually reached for him to meet McAvoy before the fight with Harvey took place. The Board of Control gave approval subject to Jack beating Len.

The promoters agreed to put up a purse of £9,000 of which Petersen was guaranteed £4,600. There were, however, contingency clauses in the contracts because at the time McAvoy was in America training to fight John Henry Lewis for the world light-heavyweight title. Although Jock cabled his acceptance to the fight, it was not until 4 March, after a series of cablegrams between Britain and the United States, that he actually signed contracts. He agreed that win, lose or draw against Lewis, he would be on the first available liner back to England after the fight.

It was agreed between the principals that should McAvoy beat Lewis in America, the fight with Petersen would be for the world light-heavyweight title instead of Jack's British and Empire heavyweight titles. Some months earlier Jack had been linked with a possible fight with Lewis who had taken the title from Bob Olin the previous October.

The announcement of the Petersen-McAvoy fight prompted an inevitable comment from Tommy Farr. 'McAvoy is only a middleweight,' he said angrily. 'Not only is Petersen deliberately avoiding me, but the Board of Control are against me as well.'

During the build-up to the fight, Petersen attended a press luncheon at Earls Court. In a short speech he said he was looking forward to meeting McAvoy. Then in typically sporting fashion said, 'I wish him the best of luck in his forthcoming fight with John Henry Lewis.'

McAvoy put up a magnificent display against Lewis at Madison Square Garden on 13 March, but was beaten on points. Had he not injured his right hand in the first round, he may well have won. The injury became a matter of some concern, but on his return to England, an examination revealed it was not serious and would not prevent him training to meet Petersen.

The challenger had the remarkable record of having lost only eight of his 113 professional fights. He had scored 69 inside the distance victories, and been British middleweight champion since April 1933 when he outpointed Len Harvey.

McAvoy had a tremendous following in the north of England, and within a few days of the fight being announced, it was a complete sell-out. The Earls Court management faced the biggest demand for tickets they could remember. Much of the interest came from McAvoy territory, and coach and rail trips were organised in Rochdale, Manchester and surrounding towns.

Boxing promotion was a new venture for ice stadiums, and for the comfort and convenience of fans, a number of major alterations were made inside Earls Court.

The ice surface was removed, and on fight night the arena would be warmed to a comfortable temperature. A massive four-sided clock was installed above the ring to show the three minutes of boxing and one minute intervals; the time keeper would be provided with a microphone so that any count taken up would be heard throughout the arena; amplifiers were installed above and around the ring to convey the sound of blows to every seating area; and every seat would have a parking spot for a hat.

Although Petersen was training to meet McAvoy, Stanley Longstaff suddenly announced that he was planning to bring John Henry Lewis to London to defend his light-heavyweight title against him. Without even considering that Jack might lose to McAvoy, Longstaff said the Earls Court promoters were prepared to offer a purse of £12,000 to secure the fight.

The Wembley promoters, however, had Jack under contract until 15 June. Provided he beat McAvoy they planned to use him to top the bill at an open-air show during the summer. Arthur Elvin (later knighted), revealed that he also wanted to bring John Henry Lewis to London to face Petersen.

179

Activity involving the Welshman was incredible, At the end of March, a London newspaper reported that he had accepted an offer of £6,500 from Jeff Dickson to meet the winner of a fight between Tommy Farr and Bob Olin taking place at the Royal Albert Hall on 2 April. Jack strongly denied the suggestion, and in an exclusive interview with Harry Lascelles-Carr, gave his account of the matter.

'It is quite true. I have had to refuse the largest offer which has come my way for an indoor contest,' he remarked. 'The reason is that Wembley Stadium has an option on my services for my next fight after that with McAvoy. I am bitterly disappointed, especially as I believe I could beat either Olin or Farr,' continued the British champion. 'Still, perhaps I shall meet them in the near future.' Asked by the journalist if he thought he would meet John Henry Lewis, Jack said, 'I will make no plans until after my fight with McAvoy. Then I will have to reach a satisfactory arrangement with Wembley to satisfy my contract.'

Jeff Dickson had been in Paris, and when he returned to London he was extremely disappointed to receive a telephone call from Petersen explaining that he could not accept his offer of £6,500. The promoter had even drawn up a contract which he believed would be accepted. When Jack remarked that he hoped such a contest could be staged in the future, Dickson promised that if Farr beat Olin, he would be willing to pay the £1,000 necessary to get the Welshman released from his contract with Wembley.

Farr outpointed Olin following which he made even stronger claims that he should be matched with Petersen. Dickson immediately made an offer to the Wembley promoters for Jack to be released from his contract. At a press conference he said, 'Petersen against Farr at the White City would be an absolute money spinner, and we intend to stage it in Derby week.'

Everyone knew a fight between the two talented young Welshmen would break all box-office records. A group of wealthy Welsh sportsmen were anxious to match them on an open-air show at Cardiff during the summer. Other promoters in Wales and London were also seeking to sign Petersen. In fact, he received so many genuine offers that had he accepted half of them, he was guaranteed to earn at least £20,000 before the summer was over.

* * *

Despite the pressures of handling his own affairs, Jack trained rigorously at the Lynn Institute. Much of his work was done behind closed doors with only a few close friends in attendance. Amongst his sparring partners was George Cook, recruited because he was the same size and build as McAvoy.

As part of his preparation, Jack watched a film of the McAvoy-Lewis fight on eight occasions. During seven of those he re-ran particular parts in slow motion to carefully study strengths and weaknesses of his opponent.

At the conclusion of his training, Jack broke with tradition by becoming the first British heavyweight champion not to give a public exhibition just before a championship contest. He always disliked being the centre of attention and now he was in charge of his business affairs, he made the decisions.

Instead, he had a secret try-out with Johnny Summers of Leeds. The only people allowed inside the Lynn Institute were William E. Allen, Harry Lascelles-Carr, Billy Diamond, and Mr. F. R. 'Bob' Hill, a leading Welsh referee. After an hour's work, including skipping, floor exercises, ball punching and six vigorous rounds of sparring, Lascelles-Carr described it as the most impressive he had ever seen.

'You will knock McAvoy out in about six rounds,' he told Jack when it was over.

'I would not say that,' replied the champion. 'I've no intention of underestimating McAvoy's prowess. He is a great fighter, and I shall have to be at my best to win.'

A huge crowd was at Earls Court to see the weigh-in which was conducted in the ring where the fight would take place. 'Hello Jock,' said Petersen calmly as his rival went to the scales. 'Well, well, how are you?' responded McAvoy.

Fully clothed, the Welshman's weight was called as thirteen stones, ten pounds, with McAvoy exactly a stone lighter. In the pre-fight betting, the champion was favourite at 3-1 on.

Scores of good luck telegrams, letters and cards arrived at Jack's Kensington hotel. Many came from fans in Wales, but there were plenty from England, Ireland and Scotland, and even some from abroad.

A crowd of about 10,000 witnessed what turned out to be a very tame and disappointing fight. Some critics even described it as the poorest heavyweight title bout of all time. There were no real thrills until the final round, and for much of the time, McAvoy was content to adopt purely defensive tactics.

At 5 foot 9½, and a stone lighter, he proved a small elusive target, as he continually back-pedalled around the ring his face shielded between his gloves.

Although Petersen started well enough, he was cautioned three

181

times during the first three rounds for hitting McAvoy on the back of the head. From the sixth round, there was little real action, and referee Arthur Myers, was kept busy parting them from continuous clinches.

It was not until round eight that the crowd showed any enthusiasm. A solid straight left from the champion rocked McAvoy. Jack followed up with a vicious right upper-cut under the heart, but McAvoy grabbed and held to prevent him from capitalising on his advantage.

In the ninth, after the Rochdale man had slipped to the floor, referee Myers took him aside saying, 'Let's have a little more boxing McAvoy.' His warning had little effect, and in the tenth exchanges were so dull, that the crowd burst into a bout of slow hand-clapping.

'When's the big fight going to start?' shouted one wag from the ringside seats. There was ironic cheering in the eleventh when McAvoy again slipped to his knees, and more slow hand-clapping and booing as the round progressed.

The challenger's best punch of the fight came in round thirteen when a hard left hook to the chin rocked Petersen. Yet there was no sense of urgency about the challenger, and he allowed Jack to recover.

The fight was completely devoid of science or excitement, and in the fourteenth Petersen fell to the floor after tripping over his opponents feet.

The only real thrill of the fight came in the final round. As McAvoy left his corner, one of his seconds yelled, 'Go in and tear him up.' Jock opened up and slammed a left hook into Petersen's ribs. The response from the Welshman, however, was immediate. He crashed a short right to the chin sending McAvoy heavily to the floor for a count of 'eight'. When he rose, the champion tried desperately to finish it but the smaller man held and mauled his way through to the final bell.

Petersen was a clear points winner, and McAvoy went straight over and congratulated him. It had been a poor fight although the contrast in styles and size were contributory factors. Despite that, Jack looked well below his best form.

The tactics adopted by McAvoy of swerving, swaying, bobbing and weaving, gave Jack little chance to show his true class. Height and reach, instead of being in his favour, were a handicap. Except in the latter stages of the fight, hardly a dangerous punch was thrown by either man.

McAvoy had no complaints about the decision and after the fight said, 'Jack won, no doubt about it, and I want nothing but to pay my tribute to him.'

Pa Petersen had watched the fight from a ringside seat and could not conceal his delight at Jack's victory. 'He's a great boy,' he said, 'but so is McAvoy.'

Predictably, Tommy Farr was quick to comment about the fight. 'It would not have gone half a dozen rounds if McAvoy had opened up,' he said with an air of resentment. 'I hope Jack will give me a fight before the summer is out. Who is there in Britain with greater qualifications for a fight with Petersen than I have?'

* * *

The handling of the Petersen-McAvoy fight was a matter of great concern to the Board of Control, and two weeks later referee, Arthur Myers, was called before the Stewards. He explained that although he cautioned McAvoy on a number of occasions for holding, he could not disqualify him because every time he got inside, Petersen held on.

Myers was then questioned closely concerning his scorecard. He had not scored the final round, failed to total up the points, and for rounds eight to fifteen inclusive had given both boxers five points.

The referee explained that had he continued to score correctly he would have been required to stop the fight in accordance with Board of Control rules because Petersen would have been too far ahead.

The Stewards concluded that there had been a very serious lapse on behalf of Mr. Myers. His name was therefore removed from the Board list of 'A' graded star licence holders who now qualify to officiate world title contests.

After the hearing, the Board issued a statement saying it would no longer sanction a title contest between champions of different weights when, in the opinion of the Board, there were suitable contenders in the higher weight division. In future, the challenger would have to prove to the satisfaction of the controlling body, that he was entitled to a title shot, having defeated leading contenders in the higher weight division.

12

DEVASTATING DEFEATS

Within hours of his victory over Jock McAvoy, Petersen received an offer from Jimmy Johnstone to fight John Henry Lewis in America during the early summer. Johnstone had been keen to get Jack to the States for some time, and saw a light-heavyweight title fight between him and Lewis as an attractive proposition.

The British champion was also wanted by Andy Neiderreiter, a promoter of open air shows at Ebbetsfield, Brooklyn. He offered Jack 25 per cent of the gate, plus two return boat tickets to America, to fight Leroy Haynes over 15 rounds on 7 July. Haynes sprung to prominence the previous month when he beat Primo Carnera in three rounds. As an extra incentive to tempt Jack across the Atlantic, the promoter said the winner would be in line to face the winner of a fight between Joe Louis and Max Schmeling scheduled for August.

Despite bad press over his poor performance against Jock McAvoy, promoters in London were also seeking his services. Through William E. Allen, Harry Levene issued a further challenge on behalf of Larry Gains, offering to make a fight with side-stakes of £250. When Allen put it to him, Jack immediately rejected it.

A promoter who wished to remain anonymous, told the *South Wales Echo* that Petersen was in danger of pricing himself out of big contests by his unreasonable purse demands. There appeared to be some substance to this theory because several promoters in Wales made him offers which he rejected.

In particular, a syndicate of Cardiff businessmen wanted him to top a promotion in June, possibly against the winner of a fight between Tommy Farr and Jim Wilde scheduled for 18 May. Jack was offered $33^{1}/_{3}$ per cent of the gate with a guarantee of £2,000. He declined the offer saying he wanted a minimum of £4,000.

Meanwhile, Jeff Dickson made a determined effort to get

Wembley Stadium Limited to release Petersen from his contract with them. Despite their refusal, they were unable to arrange a fight for him before the contract expired on 15 June 1936. The following week, Sydney Hulls resigned from his position as matchmaker for Wembley, stating that in future he intended to promote fights on his own behalf.

* * *

The failure of Wembley Stadium Limited to secure a fight within the agreed time, entitled Petersen to a forfeit of £1,000, but the promoters were reluctant to pay up. Lawyers were engaged by both sides, and the matter became lengthy and complicated.

Eventually, Jack referred his claim to the Welsh Area of the British Boxing Board of Control who, in February 1937, referred it to Board headquarters in London. After reading an agreement between Jack Petersen and Sydney Hulls dated 26 March 1936, it was decided that the matter would be placed before the Stewards.

At a hearing at the Board of Control offices at 68, Dean Street, Jack placed full particulars of his claim before the Stewards. A total of 36 documents were read and introduced as evidence. The solicitor representing Wembley Stadium Limited, asked that a ruling be given on a question of law. He submitted that the Stewards had no power to arbitrate the case because there was no binding statement or contract. The submission was discussed but rejected by the Stewards.

The case for Wembley was then put. Arthur Elvin gave full details of his negotiations with John Henry Lewis in an attempt to secure Petersen a shot at the world light-heavyweight title. Considerable difficulty arose and it was not possible to stage the contest. He also contacted other prospective opponents but was unable to make a fight for Petersen before the contract expired.

A series of questions were asked of all witnesses, and at the conclusion of the evidence, the hearing was adjourned until 14 April. On that date, the Stewards found in favour of Jack in the amount claimed which was not publicly disclosed. The promoters, however, refused to accept the decision and referred the matter to the Kings Bench Division of the High Court.

The case was eventually listed for hearing on 20 January 1938 as 'PETERSEN V WEMBLEY STADIUM LIMITED', and there was a motion to set aside the award. Mr. A. T. Denning of Counsel appeared on behalf of Wembley, and Sir Patrick Hastings, K.C. represented Petersen.

The court was told that since the decision of the Board of

Control, the two parties had been in communication with the Board, and with each other. Counsel said that it had become clear that the award had been made under a misunderstanding, and the Stewards had intimated their readiness to re-hear the case. It was agreed by both parties that the matter should be referred back to the Board for reconsideration. Mr. Justice Goddard and Mr. Justice Lewis agreed, and the case was taken out of the High Court list.

The matter came before the Board of Control Stewards of Appeal on 17 March 1938, and took the form of a complete re-hearing. Both parties were represented by Counsel, and a total of 54 documents were introduced. Jack Petersen and Arthur Elvin gave evidence, were cross-examined and also asked questions by the Stewards. Both Counsel addressed the Stewards on the law.

After a lengthy retirement, the Stewards issued their findings:

1) The decision and order of the Board are confirmed, and the appeal is dismissed.
2) Wembley Stadium Limited are ordered to pay Jack Petersen £20 in respect of expenses incurred attending the hearing.
3) The Stewards of Appeal certify that there were good and reasonable grounds for the appeal.

Jack had pursued the claim on principle, but in view of the course of events and the length of time taken to bring it to a conclusion, most, if not all of his award, was eaten up by legal fees.

* * *

Before his contract with Wembley Stadium Limited expired, Jack was in quiet negotiation with Leicester promoter, Jim Panter, to defend his British Empire title against Ben Foord. He was at ringside on 15 June when Foord beat Manuel Abrew, and stayed at Leicester overnight. The following morning he accepted Panter's offer of £3,500 to meet Foord at Leicester rugby ground on 17 August. When the contest was announced later that day, it came as a shock to members of the press and most leading figures in boxing.

An application by the promoter for the fight to be for the British title as well as that of the British Empire, was rejected by the Board of Control. The National Union of Boxers took issue with the Board decision, and declared it would recognise the contest as being for both titles by virtue of Foord's period of residence in Britain. A number of national newspapers were also critical of the Board.

The Stewards re-convened, and, after a lengthy discussion,

agreed that the British title would be at stake subject to a further application from the promoter, and agreement being received from Petersen. Jack had no objection, saying he was as surprised as anyone by the Board's original decision.

Rugby Football Ground, LEICESTER

Monday, August 17th, 1936, at 8 p.m.

JAMES PANTER presents the
HEAVY-WEIGHT CHAMPIONSHIPS OF GREAT BRITAIN and the BRITISH EMPIRE

15 3-min. ROUNDS

JACK PETERSEN v. BEN FOORD

(Holder) CARDIFF   (Challenger) SOUTH AFRICA

4 ((3-min.) Rounds Feather-weight Contest
DENNIS HOWARD (BIRMINGHAM)   v.   **CYCLONE WESTON** (LEICESTER)

8 (3-min.) Rounds Welter-weight Contest
ELFRYN MORRIS (WALES)   v.   **LEN WICKWAR** (LEICESTER)

8 (3-min.) Rounds Heavy-weight Contest
BERT IKIN (STOKE-ON-TRENT)   v.   **MAX HODGETTS** (DESBOROUGH)

8 (3-min.) Rounds Light Heavy-weight Contest
REINUS DE BOER (CHAMPION OF HOLLAND)   v.   **CHARLIE BUNDY** (WALES)

8 (3-min.) Rounds Middle-weight Contest
EDDIE MAGUIRE (CHAMPION OF S. AFRICA)   v.   **MOE MOSS** (LONDON)

Seats : 50/-, 36/- 24/-, Special Reserved Ringside Enclosure. **Member's Stand, Centre Blocks, 20/-.** Wing Blocks, 15/- (numbered and reserved). Crumbie Stand, 12/- (numbered and reserved). The above Seats are bookable. Terrace, 7/6 (unreserved) ; Popular Standing, 4/6 (unreserved) ; Pay at gate.

BOOK NOW ! James Panter, 1, Chatham Street, Leicester, Phone 59895. The Midland Holiday Bureau, 53, Granby Street, Leicester, Phone 59377. All Pickfords and Thos. Cooks & Sons Agencies in Wales. Con. Wilson, 65, Sheep Street, Northampton. Jerry Shaw, Newmarket Inn, Derby. Gus Platts, The White Hart, Glass House Street, Nottingham. Jack Sharman, 8, Dalkeith Avenue, School Lane, Kettering. Jim Murphy, Farcroft Hotel, Rookery Road, Handsworth, Birmingham, Phone Northern 0957. Ted Kendall, Seven Stars, Warwick. Joe Jacobs, Haunch of Venison, High Street, Leicester, Phone 228941. And the Usual Ticket Agencies.

Poster advertising contest between Petersen and Foord.

News of the fight came as a shock to fans, particularly in London and Wales, because it had been rumoured that Petersen would meet Max Baer in London during August or September. Scores of letters were received by the *South Wales Echo* from people expressing disappointment over the contest with Foord.

Baer was easing his way back following a defeat by Joe Louis in September 1935. With Harringay Arena opening its doors to boxing, Sydney Hulls travelled to America and offered him $30,000, (£6,000) to meet Petersen in London. Provisional agreement was reached, and Baer's manager, Ancil Hoffman, expressed great surprise when he heard that Jack had agreed to fight Ben Foord.

Tommy Farr was furious at being overlooked again. He had

expected to get the next shot at Jack, bringing with it his long awaited big purse. In a letter to William E. Allen, he said:

> I was surprised to see Foord matched with Petersen. It strikes me that I don't mean a thing when reading your article the other day that Foord had a side-stake waiting to be covered by any of the heavies. My manager, Ted Broadribb, and I have had £200 waiting to be covered for the last three months by Neusel, Petersen or Foord. I am still ready to fight Petersen when and where he likes for a side-stake, and if I am not there at the end, I will give my purse to charity.
>
> Tommy Farr.

Although he was a natural contender, in reality, Tommy had not qualified for a shot at Jack. On 18 May, he had only drawn with Welsh heavyweight champion Jim Wilde in a bitter contest at Swansea. Tommy was, however, given a glimmer of hope when a re-match was agreed for 14 September. Not only would it be for Wilde's Welsh title, but the Board of Control anounced that the contest would be recognised as a final eliminator for the British heavyweight title. On hearing the news, Farr raised his side-stake offer to £500 in a challenge to the winner of Petersen and Foord.

Despite the popularity of Foord in Leicestershire, the fight did not create the interest the promoter had hoped. He expected a heavy demand for ringside seats but was disappointed at the response from fans in London. Petersen's poor showing against McAvoy and confusion over him meeting Baer were thought to be responsible.

Former Welsh light-heavyweight champion, Charlie Bundy, received offers to join both training camps as chief sparring partner. Having assisted Petersen for more than two years, he knew him better than most men. His value was recognised by Foord's manager, Louis Walsh, whose offer was good enough to lure him to their Desborough Camp. Walsh also engaged Bert Ikin who had also worked with the British champion on a number of occasions.

Petersen engaged Johnny Summers of Leeds and Harry Lister from Northumberland as his sparring partners. Lister had built up a formidable record, winning all of his 23 fights in just over a year.

Again much of Jack's training was done behind closed doors at the Lynn Institute. Despite travelling long distances in the hope of getting interviews with the British champion, most journalists went away disappointed.

* * *

Since meeting Petersen in 1934, Foord had improved tremendously, having beaten Eddie Phillips, Jack London, Larry Gains, Tommy Loughran and George Cook who he knocked out in nine rounds at Cardiff. A keen all-round athlete, he was a big powerful fighter who outweighed Jack by almost two stones. He was extremely pumped up for the fight, and once in the ring his cornermen had to restrain him as he stood poised like a gladiator ready for combat.

At the bell, Foord tore into Petersen with determined ferocity. Totally ignoring defence, he bombarded the Welshman with shots from every angle. Although Jack calmly tried to box him off, his judgement was poor and his jabs lacked power.

Although both men were always looking to throw big shots, neither had much success until the latter part of the round when Petersen suddenly landed a hard right to the chin. Foord rocked back on his heels but recovered quickly, and on the bell unleashed two solid left digs to the body. The Welshman gasped but took them well and gave a wry smile as he returned to his corner.

Jack began round two with three sharp lefts to the face, and as Foord forced his way forward a right hook opened a cut on his left ear. The champion was boxing well at this stage but a few seconds before the end of the round, the situation changed dramatically. Petersen appeared to momentarily lose concentration and in doing so left himself open to Foord's crude attacks. Seizing his opportunity, the South African connected with two solid left hooks to the stomach. He quickly smashed a right to the head which opened the old injury above Jack's left eye bringing blood streaming down his face.

Realising it was a bad cut, the champion hung on for all he was worth, Foord became a fighting fury and smashed away relentlessly. At the bell he had to be wrenched away from his opponent and ordered back to his corner. The bell was a welcome sound to the bloodied Welshman who walked head bowed to his corner on unsteady legs.

Realising his damaged eye couldn't hold up for long, Jack was determined to go out fighting. At the start of the third round he met Foord's aggression with two good rights to the head. The South African, however, was ready for him, and with a snarl on his face tore into the Welshman with a battery of heavy punches.

Never a man to retreat from danger, Petersen bravely stood his ground and hit back with his own powerful shots. As they simultaneously landed right swings to the jaw, Foord's knees buckled. He grabbed and held on tightly until referee, Moss Deyong, forced them to break.

Anxious to follow up his advantage, Jack rushed forward but

was caught by a tremendous right which crashed against his chin. Blood gushing from his mouth, he crashed to the floor, his head striking it with a resounding thud. As Jack lay flat on his back, the fight appeared to be over. Suddenly, with tremendous courage, he dragged himself up at the count of 'seven'. Although his legs were very unsteady and his eyes glazed, referee Deyong surprisingly ordered them to box on.

With many people screaming for the fight to be stopped, Jack was a sitting target as Foord tore into him smashing vicious blows to the head. Nothing could stem the tide of leather that was thrown at him.

A vicious right which landed flush on his damaged eye sent him floundering halfway through the ropes. Amazingly, he regained an upright position only for more savage blows to crash into his face. Blood streamed from his eye and spurted from his damaged mouth like a red spray.

With the most incredible bravery, Petersen somehow stayed on his feet gallantly refusing to quit despite his face being beaten to a pulp. He was scarcely recognisable when another tremendous right crashed against his undefended jaw. Only then did Moss Deyong, his shirt saturated in blood, step in and put a sympathetic hand on Jack's shoulder before leading him to his corner.

There were just 15 seconds of the round remaining but Jack was out on his feet. His mouth was so badly damaged that his gum shield could be seen through the torn flesh. He had displayed courage far beyond the call of duty, and won the admiration of everyone in the 25,000 crowd.

As he left the ring, Jack was oblivious to the generous yet sympathetic ovation he received. A towel was wrapped over his head and tied tightly under his lower jaw and neck. It was at first feared he had suffered a fractured jaw, but subsequent examination showed this not to be so.

Within half an hour of his devastating defeat, Jack returned to his hotel and went to bed. He was in no condition to give interviews, but Billy Diamond spoke to anxious reporters and assured them he was okay and would not retire. 'He is determined to come back again,' said Diamond. 'Jack believes that before anyone else, he should be considered for a return with the new champion.'

Back at Cardiff the following afternoon, Jack insisted that his spirit was undaunted. 'We all have to lose at some stage,' he told William E. Allen. 'I will take a rest and then hope that Ben Foord, to whom I tender my sincerest congratulations, will give me a return.'

With typical sportsmanship, Jack made no mention of the sleepless night he endured before the fight. Staying at a hotel in Leicester, he was subjected to knocks on his door, annoymous phone calls to his room throughout the night, and a vacuum cleaner being used in the corridor outside during the early hours. It was apparent that every effort was being made to unsettle him before his big fight against the local hero.

Despite his popularity with the fans, Jack's crushing defeat did not concern some of the promoters. Well schooled by his father in business affairs, he was more than capable of dictating his terms.

There were many occasions since he split with Pa when promoters made him what they considered reasonable offers, only to be rejected. Jack's response was inevitably the same. 'Here are my terms, and I will take nothing less.' Wembley promoter, Arthur Elvin stated publicly that he wanted to put on good quality shows featuring the best men, including Petersen. He could not do so, however, if demands were unreasonable.

Since handling his own affairs, Jack had kept his business plans and negotiations a close secret. Only people very close to him really knew what was going on. Much of what was reported in the national newspapers was therefore speculation.

* * *

In early September, 1936, Jimmy Johnstone, speaking in America, told the Press Association that Petersen had accepted an offer to fight John Henry Lewis over 15 rounds at Madison Square Garden for the world light-heavyweight title. Although no date had been set, Johnstone claimed the fight would definitely take place during the winter.

Another story originating from New York, claimed Jack had asked for a guarantee of £7,000 with an option of 35 per cent of the gate to meet Lewis. Jack was in fact on holiday in Devon at the time, and Billy Diamond assured the British press he would make no decision about future contests until he returned.

Meanwhile, there had been enormous interest in the return contest between Tommy Farr and Jim Wilde at the Vetch Field, Swansea, on 14 September. Farr won by a knockout in round seven in front of a crowd of 20,000 to become the official contender for the British heavyweight title. His manager, Ted Broadribb, immediately contacted Ben Foord's people with a view to staging a defence against Farr, but he was ignored.

A few days later, Sydney Hulls announced that he planned to

stage a return contest between Foord and Petersen at Harringay Arena early in 1937. Farr and Broadribb were furious, and immediately lodged a protest with the Board of Control. Farr claimed he was in possession of a letter from Charles Donmall, General Secretary of the British Boxing Board of Control, confirming that he was officially regarded as Foord's next opponent. On receipt of it, he deposited £500 with the Board in support of his challenge.

Although Tommy was the official contender for Foord's titles, a fight between them was not seen by promoters as a good commercial proposition. On the other hand, Foord against Petersen was a guaranteed sell-out, and Sydney Hulls was determined to stage it. He insisted it was a fight the public wanted.

Despite his insistence that the fight would go ahead, Hulls had to work extremely hard to secure it. He made several trips to Cardiff and also had other meetings with Jack in London trying to persuade him to agree a contract. It was not until late November, however, that the former champion eventually agreed to sign.

'I am happy,' said Jack once everything was agreed. 'I believe I still have the beating of Foord. The fight will give me the opportunity to show my friends and boxing followers that my form at Leicester was all wrong.'

Tommy Farr became very disillusioned because he had beaten Loughran, Olin, and plenty of others as well. He had also won a final eliminator for the British title, but for what? He was seriously thinking of giving up boxing, but when he was suddenly contacted by Len Harvey, things began to look brighter. Len had become matchmaker for Wembley promoter, Arthur Elvin, who wanted to stage a fight between Farr and Petersen despite the fact that Jack was no longer champion.

The prospect of fighting Petersen was the most important thing in the world to Farr. It had become a very personal issue, and by this stage he was unconcerned that the British title would not be at stake.

'I am prepared to meet Petersen anywhere, anytime,' insisted Tommy, 'but now I shall insist on an equitable division of the purse.'

Elvin made Petersen a substantial offer to meet Tommy, but he turned it down saying he was only interested in winning back his titles. Furthermore, he made it clear that he didn't consider he had anything to gain by meeting Tommy at this stage.

The Board of Control, however, supported Farr, and rejected an application by Sydney Hulls for the return fight between Foord and Petersen to be for the British and Empire titles. A statement was issued giving reasons for the rejection:

> The Stewards wished to be first assured that Petersen is the logical contender for such titles. It was therefore decided not to recognise the Foord-Petersen contest as being for the championships mentioned until Petersen has met and defeated Tommy Farr who has already been declared by the Stewards as the official contender for the titles held by Foord.

Jack strongly disagreed with the Board's decision. 'Everybody seems to have had something to say,' he said firmly. 'All I can add is that Farr will have to wait until after the Foord fight.'

A couple of weeks later Jack and Tommy met at a boxing tournament at Greyfriars Hall in aid of Cardiff and District British Legion. Farr made a sporting gesture when he successfully bid three guineas at an auction to obtain a pair of Petersen's boxing gloves. Turning to Jack he said with a smile, 'Now I've got your gloves Jack, perhaps we can at last get down to the real business.'

Jack grinned broadly, but refused to be drawn into a situation with a man known to have a massive chip on his shoulder.

* * *

Many people who saw Jack lose to Ben Foord thought he would never enter the ring seriously again. Newly married and prosperous enough, he was so obviously lacking his usual fitness and vitality. Yet despite the defeats he had suffered he was still the most sought after heavyweight in the country.

A number of American boxers were keen to get engagements in Britain, and his name regularly featured in discussions. Yet whenever attempts were made to get him to talk about future plans, Jack flatly refused to discuss matters.

The return fight with Ben Foord was fixed for 1 February 1937 at Harringay Arena. Jack engaged Danny Davies as his trainer and prepared along entirely different lines to previous fights. He planned to go into the ring against Foord heavier than ever before. To build up the extra poundage he went on a special diet and almost doubled his daily meat ration. He also introduced wrestling into his training, something nearly every champion on a comeback trail resorted to.

To help him prepare, Jack engaged some particularly big men as sparring partners. Max Hodgetts weighed $15^{1}/_{2}$ stones and stood 6 foot 6, Alex Bell weighed 17½ stones, 'Big' Jack Pettifer and Bert Ikin were also recruited.

Just as training reached a peak, Foord went down with influenza and had to pull out. Expecting a new date to be announced, Jack continued training, but Sydney Hulls was anxious not to postpone the Harringay promotion. He therefore offered Jack a third meeting with Walter Neusel.

The Welshman always believed he could beat the German, so he readily accepted. That alone took great courage, but there was an added incentive. Jack knew Hulls still had plans to bring Max Baer to London despite the fact that he wanted a minimum of £8,000.

Determined to find a way to beat Neusel, Jack spent a great deal of time studying a film of their second fight. In the gym, he worked in virtual secrecy, concentrating on punching the heavy bag in search of extra power.

Asked by William E. Allen how he felt about meeting Neusel for a third time, Jack was very guarded. 'It's immaterial to me who I meet,' he replied.

A small select group of boxing personalities and pressmen watched the Welshman's final try-out, but when asked questions he remained very secretive. Danny Davies, who stood beside him, was no more forthcoming. 'You've seen him, use your own judgement,' he snapped when asked how training had gone.

* * *

'Hello Jack, how are you?' said Neusel as the two men came face to face at the weigh-in at the Stadium Club at noon on the day of the fight. Both were smartly dressed in lounge suits, and Neusel wore a sprig of heather in his lapel.

Unusual precautions were taken as the two men went to the scales, with only a few people being allowed to watch. Neusel was in a particularly cheerful mood, and turning to the official in charge of the scales, said, 'You will need a lot of weights for me.'

The German's weight was called as being 14 stones 11¾ and Petersen at 13 stones 11½, bringing gasps from the audience. Yet that evening, different weights were announced by the Master of Ceremonies from the ring; Neusel 14 stones 4, and Petersen 13 stones. It was a strange state of affairs, and although the differences were quoted in the press, no particular issue was raised.

Despite his crushing defeats by Neusel and Foord, Jack remained as popular as ever. Throughout the day, big fight specials steamed out of Cardiff taking his loyal supporters to London. During late afternoon and early evening, traffic around Harringay was almost at a standstill as all roads leading to the great north London arena became choked with traffic and pedestrians.

In the arena, the atmosphere built steadily. There was great patriotism and an air of expectancy that Jack would finally triumph over Neusel. Anything other than victory didn't bear thinking about.

The excitement reached fever pitch as the two boxers emerged from their dressing rooms. Heralded by a fanfare of trumpets, they were cheered all the way to the ring by the capacity crowd of almost 14,000. The roar increased dramatically as Petersen, clad in his green dressing gown emblazoned with the Welsh dragon, climbed through the ropes.

The first two contests between Petersen and Neusel had been full bloodied affairs but they could not compare with this one. Full of action from start to finish, it turned out to be one of the most gruelling heavyweight fights seen in a British ring.

At the opening bell, Neusel shuffled across the ring in a typical continental crouch and attacked with heavy clubbing shots to the body. When he missed with a vicious swing to the head, Petersen hit back. Ignoring screams from Danny Davies of 'Don't hurry, there's plenty of time,' Jack attacked with all the fury shown in his earlier fights.

Neusel was knocked out of his stride as Jack tore into him appearing determined to destroy him in the opening round. The German hardly landed a telling blow for almost a minute, but once he re-grouped his heavy blows began to find the target. By the end of the round, Petersen was already showing signs of distress.

Although the Welshman was quickly off his stool at the start of round two, Neusel took control of the situation and set the pattern of the fight. He launched a ruthless body attack to which Jack had no defence. Sledgehammer blows thudded into his sides and midriff, and heavy single shots smashed into his face. One powerful short left jab brought blood streaming from his nose.

Petersen was driven from corner to corner as the flat-footed Neusel mercilessly drove him backwards. Heavy punches hit home with monotonous ease and precision and the Welshman was in serious trouble. He had to defend desperately for most of the round as Neusel gave him no respite. At the bell he didn't know where he was and needed the shouts of his seconds to identify his corner.

Feverish work by Danny Davies revived the plucky Welshman but he still had to hang on for dear life in the third. Forced to the ropes at the start of the round, he hung on grimly but then cleverly worked his way out of trouble. He was rewarded because as the round wore on, Neusel appeared to tire.

The crowd roared with excitement as a terrific left and right to the chin knocked the German sideways, but their hopes were short-lived. Showing amazing resilience, Neusel fought back strongly to silence the pro-Petersen crowd. A heavy body attack was followed by a vicious right to the head which again brought blood streaming from Jack's nose. Although he took a good right to the head, Neusel battered the Welshman heavily until the bell brought him respite. The crowd rose to him as he returned wearily to his corner because yet again he was displaying incredible coruage.

Neusel went straight after his man at the start of round four, and a right hook opened a cut under Jack's left eye. Blood poured down his cheek but in typical fashion the gutsy Welshman hit back. A two-fisted counter attack shook Neusel and temporarily halted the stream of punches he was throwing.

Making a tremendous effort to turn the fight around, Jack fought for all he was worth and began to rely more on his speed. Plenty of left jabs found the target. Yet fight as he did, he could not check his strong opponent and take control. Although he was very one-paced, Neusel lashed back with solid punches to head and body. His extra weight and strength were beginning to tell and by the end of the round Petersen was gasping for air.

Jack recovered well in the interval and a stream of beautiful left jabs at the start of round five made Neusel look slow and clumsy. A chopping right to the head shook the German and brought the crowd to their feet. This was Petersen at his best and even when trapped in a corner he gallantly fought his way out with vicious hooks from both hands.

Yelled on by the frantic crowd, Jack looked to be turning the fight his way, but Neusel dourly and methodically stuck to his body punching. As the round neared its end, the Welshman was doubled up in pain as heavy blows sank deep into his stomach.

Jack looked refreshed as he came off his stool for the sixth but soon weakened as Neusel again concentrated his attack to the body. Making his extra weight tell, the German crashed blow after blow into the slender Welshman's waistline, and then hurt him badly with a vicious right to the head. The punches went in hard and deep throughout the round and it was amazing that Petersen stayed upright. By the bell he was sagging badly and gasping for air.

Neusel sustained the body attack in the seventh but as the round progressed both men became extremely tired. They mauled and held, prompting referee, Jack Smith, to warn them both. Although Jack tried desperately to box Neusel off, his strength had gone and it was only a question of how long he could survive.

The fight had become very one-sided, and although Petersen tried to use his left jab during the eighth, Neusel just brushed it aside. Knowing the Welshman's punches had lost their sting, he powered forward, head down, sinking more powerful shots into the body.

The dour German went on the attack at the start of round nine and soon had Petersen in desperate trouble. Yet despite the terrible punishment he was taking, Jack refused to drop. Calling on all his reserves of strength he suddenly hurt the German with a terrific right to the temple but could not follow it up. The punch only served to enrage Neusel.

Another savage and relentless attack to Jack's bruised and reddened body had him backing away as virtually every punch found the target. Badly hurt, with blood streaming from his damaged nose and mouth, the Welshman fell into a clinch, gasping for air. As the referee pulled them apart and ordered 'box on', a battery of punches to the head sent Petersen reeling across the ring. At the bell he trudged to his corner an extremely tired man.

Sitting at ringside in evening dress, Pa Petersen looked nervous and apprehensive. The expression on his face showed that he was feeling the punches his son was taking. Realising Jack couldn't take much more he gestured to Danny Davies to throw in the towel. Jack saw his father's signal and angrily rejected it. He believed he still had the punch to beat Neusel and was determined to stay in there until the bitter end.

One last desperate gamble remained. Champagne was tipped over the Welshman's head and as the bell sounded for round ten he was off his stool and straight after the German. Petersen lacked nothing when it came to courage and sheer fighting spirit and was determined to stake all on one last furious attack.

A tremendous right with all the power he could muster, crashed flush on Neusel's chin sending him reeling into the ropes. Jack went after him and although he landed two more rights and several lefts there was insufficient power behind them to seriously hurt the German. Once the fury of the attack had worn off, Jack had nothing further to offer. His last hope had gone.

Neusel re-grouped again, waded forward and pumped clubbing punches to head and body. A right swing went deep into the Welshman's stomach, and as he let out a painful gasp, another fearsome right crashed against his head.

Blood streamed from Petersen's left eye and nose as he was pounded unmercifully. Although he tried desperately to fight back, his punches were brushed aside as the relentless Neusel continued to lumber forward looking to end the fight.

The crowd roared but the cheers were for the incredible courage and bravery of Petersen who was fighting on heart alone. He could barely hold his gloves up and at one stage fell forwards into the ropes and almost out of the ring. As referee, Jack Smith, pushed Neusel away, many people thought he had stopped the fight. As the Welshman pulled himself upright, however, Smith surprisingly ordered them to box on.

It was bad judgement because Jack had no defence and hardly knew where he was. The crowd gasped as a tremendous right from Neusel crashed against his chin sending him reeling across the ring. Arms hanging limply at his sides, the Welshman was a sitting target, but mercifully the towel was thrown in before Neusel could land another punch.

A hush fell over the packed arena but then an almighty roar greeted the winner and increased to deafening proportions when Neusel walked over to Jack and hugged him.

The sad fact was that Petersen had been out-fought and out-punched. Although there had surely never been a greater display of courage in a British ring, that was not enough against a bigger and stronger man whom he could never get the better of. Except during the first few rounds, Jack never seemed to have the slightest chance of victory. He had been only a shadow of the dashing fighter the fans remembered. The earlier beatings at the hands of Neusel and Foord had taken their toll. All that remained was his undying courage.

* * *

Jack made a quiet departure from London the following day aboard the 1.15 pm train from Paddington. Few people recognised him as he strolled along the platform accompanied by Danny Davies and a small group of close friends.

Despite some bruising around both eyes, his cheek and left eye gashed, he did not appear despondent. Before boarding the train he spoke briefly to a *South Wales Echo* reporter. 'You saw the fight for yourself,' said Jack. 'What more can be said. It's all over and I admit defeat.' With that he politely asked to be left alone.

Danny Davies remained in a positive mood and told the reporter Jack would definitely carry on fighting. 'After a good rest, he will be out for blood again, and with all his old courage undiminished,' he remarked.

When Jack arrived at Cardiff, he confirmed what Davies had said. 'I am a very long way from finished,' he insisted, but added that he would take a long rest before deciding on his next fight.

It was not long before Tommy Farr had something to say about the situation. He had been at ringside the night Jack faced Neusel, and had yelled encouragement for his fellow Welshman throughout the fight. He insisted that although he was anxious to meet Ben Foord for the British heavyweight title, he still desperately wanted to fight Jack.

'I have not waited for Neusel to lick him again,' Farr told the *South Wales Echo*. 'I have been challenging him for more than twelve months. Perhaps he will now condescend to meet me.' Farr said he would cover any side-stake Jack agreed to put down.

* * *

A few days later, William E. Allen, writing in the *South Wales Echo*, claimed to have discovered what had been wrong with Jack when he faced Neusel at Harringay. Apparently, the weekend before the fight, he scaled 13 stones 6 stripped to the waist. Everyone in the camp was delighted because they believed the extra poundage could be crucial to Jack's chance of success. When he weighed again a few hours before the fight, however, it was found that he had lost over five pounds in less than 24 hours. No explanation could be found.

Shortly after Allen's story had been released, there was more bad news for Petersen followers. The batterings he had taken from Neusel, and the fearful eye injuries sustained in recent fights, had caused Jack to consult an eye specialist in London. The verdict was ominous. Jack was told that if he continued to box, he risked permanent blindness. In reality, this splendid young fighter was finished at the age of just 25.

13

THE FIGHTING IS OVER

All of Wales was stunned when, at the beginning of April 1937, Petersen announced his retirement from the ring. It marked the end of the career of one of Britain's most popular heavyweights.

'Yes, I am going to retire,' he told a reporter from the *South Wales Argus*. 'It is a great blow because I have loved the game and always enjoyed my fights.'

As usual, Jack had conducted his affairs privately, but when he travelled to London the previous week, he hadn't anticipated such a devastating outcome. Apart from visiting the specialist, he had also planned to meet Sydney Hulls to discuss the possibility of future fights, any one of which would have guaranteed him a minimum purse of £3,000. Instead, he returned to Cardiff broken-hearted.

Less than three weeks earlier, Jack had attended Hulls promotion at Harringay Arena and seen Tommy Farr take the British and Empire titles from Ben Foord. Before the fight he was introduced from the ring, together with Walter Neusel and Buddy Baer. Despite his recent defeats, the rousing reception he received was a clear indication that his popularity had not diminished.

There had been no indication of the problem Jack was facing, and Hulls was stunned when he heard the news. 'His retirement is a severe blow to British boxing,' he remarked. 'He is one of the very best heavyweights, and has been one of my biggest draws.'

Jack was idolised in Wales, and whenever he boxed in London at least three trains would leave Cardiff packed with fans. His retirement was a tremendous disappointment to followers of boxing generally, and over the ensuing weeks he received hundreds of letters and telegrams. Many contained sympathetic messages, whilst others thanked him for the thrills he had given.

Tributes poured in, and one of the most moving came from Len

Harvey. In an interview with the weekly trade paper, *'Boxing'*, he said, 'I am indeed very sorry to hear that Jack is to retire. He was a splendid sportsman, both in and out of the ring. I know he always pleased the public with his plucky fighting. His retirement is a great loss to the British ring.'

Jack and Len would remain the closest of friends for many years to come and frequently meet at public functions and ex-boxers conventions.

Ben Foord was equally complimentary when he heard the news. 'Jack has been the most popular man amongst heavyweights in recent years,' he remarked. 'There was always keen competition when he was champion, and I was one of the fortunate men who secured a fight with a great boxer.'

Jack said goodbye to his endearing fans by boxing a three rounds exhibition with Leicester heavyweight, Max Hodgetts, at the Grand Pavillion, Llandrindod Wells on 2 April. It was an emotional evening, and a crowd of 2,000 warmly greeted the former champion as he climbed into the ring for the last time.

'I am sorry ladies and gentlemen, but this is Jack's last appearance in the ring,' said Master of Ceremonies, Harry Simon.

The announcement came as a shock to many people, and there were cries of 'No, Jack, no,' as the former champion sorrowfully shook his head.

Explaining that the specialist Jack had consulted was adamant he gave up boxing, the M.C. added, 'Jack does not want to quit the game he loves and to which he has brought so much honour and glory to Wales.'

In a response to calls for a speech, Jack reluctantly took the microphone, but was very brief, 'I thank you all,' he said choked with emotion, 'I thank you very much.' As he spoke, the championship belt which he won outright by virtue of his victories over Meen, Pettifer and Doyle, was displayed to his admiring fans.

Jack was broken hearted because he loved everything about the game and loved fighting for fighting's sake. Without further ado he got on with the exhibition because the occasion was becoming too much for him.

After leaving the ring, Jack was too overcome to engage in further conversation about his retirement. 'There is nothing more to say,' he remarked solemnly. 'It has all been said.'

* * *

Behind the scenes Jack had quietly reached agreement with the

Sunday Chronicle to pursue a new career as a boxing correspondent. In an exclusive article on 4 April 1937, he told the world the reasons behind his retirement from boxing:

> ..... my eyes which have suffered from blows received in many fights, have been troubling me for some time. My visit to a London specialist last week confirmed my worst fears. The specialist's words sounded like a death sentence. At first I could scarcely believe his verdict it was so shattering. If I continue to fight, he told me, the ultimate and terrible price might be blindness .....

This was not Jack's first effort at journalism because in 1935, preceeding and following the second Neusel fight, he had written a series of articles in the *News of the World*. Articulate and descriptive, they prompted hundreds of letters from fans requesting photographs and information about various aspects of his career. He replied to as many as he could, but found it almost a full time job.

Jack's first job with the *Sunday Chronicle* was a trip to The Green Man at Blackheath in south London. It was the training camp of fellow Welshman, Tommy Farr, who was hard in training for his forthcoming fight with Max Baer.

During the last two years of his career, Petersen had been subjected to considerable criticism by Farr. Jack, however, never held a grudge against anybody, so he went to Blackheath intent on putting the situation between them into perspective.

Casually dressed in an old pair of baggy plus fours and a faded football sweater, Farr was watching his sparring partners playing darts when the former champion walked in. As their eyes met, Jack realised they were two men of clashing personalities and temperaments. He knew what Tommy was thinking, and was convinced it was not hostility in Farr's eyes as he narrowed them. Nor was there any jealousy. Instead, Jack read resentment at the bad luck which had robbed Tommy of the chance of fighting the one man he always wanted to meet.

When they eventually came together, they shook hands and exchanged pleasantries. Suddenly and abruptly, Farr said, 'Jack, I'm sorry you are leaving the game.' 'Thanks', replied Petersen, but there was something in Farr's eyes which made him suddenly wonder if that was the right response.

'I'm sorry because if there was one man in the world I would like to take a crack at, it is you,' said Farr dourly. 'I have always wanted to fight you Jack. I was always wanting to get at you, but you never gave me the chance, and now the chance has gone.'

Listening to Farr, and looking at him, Jack realised that Max Baer was going to have a much harder fight than many people believed. He summed up his thoughts in the *Sunday Chronicle* the following day:

> ..... if Tommy thought that about me, how must he feel about Baer who has enjoyed the glamour, the limelight and the big money during the years while Tommy has been struggling. Perhaps it's because I'm another Welshman, and he regards me as an especially irritating obstacle. If so, let me say now that I wish him all the success that good fighting can bring. I saw in him all the stubborness of a typical Welsh fighter. Never have I seen such earnestness and such determination to win .....

It was a moving story, written from the heart of a man expressing complete respect for a fellow fighter. Despite Farr's constant criticism of Jack in the past, there was no hint of animosity. It was so typical of Petersen, a man interested only in the positive things in life.

For the first time ever, Jack openly expressed his feelings about his fellow Welshman, and gave his readers a vivid insight into Tommy's difficult background.

In conclusion Jack wrote:

> I was a heavyweight. I had been a champion and I was a natural foe. Although we were neighbours as boys, I hardly spoke three words to Tommy until I met him yesterday. When I saw him working out, I was as sorry as he was that we never fought. It would have been an interesting contest.

On 15 April, Jack was at the ringside at Harringay when Farr convincingly outpointed Baer. The following weekend, he treated *Sunday Chronicle* readers to another moving article, praising Tommy's tremendous achievement.

Two months later, after Farr knocked out Walter Neusel in three rounds, Jack was equally complimentary:

> I fought thirty rounds with Neusel without succeeding in landing a punch like the one with which Farr finished the fight. What a beauty it was. A short right to the chin that didn't travel more than six inches. I was sitting right underneath it, and I gasped because I could see and feel how deadly it would be.

Jack described Farr's victory as a grand vindication for British boxing. 'Farr showed himself to be a great strategist,' he wrote. 'The whole fight was a masterpiece of planning.'

Before the fight, Jack had been introduced from the ring together with Max Schmeling, Max Baer, Len Harvey and Ben Foord. Although he got a wonderful reception, just as he did as a fighter, he felt really sad to know that he was no longer involved.

Shortly after the fight was over, Jack bumped into Schmeling as he was on his way to Farr's dressing room. 'Congratulate Farr for me,' said Max. Jack knew plans were being made to match Tommy with the former world champion, and fancied him to win that one as well. Although for political reasons it didn't take place, Jack believed Tommy could become the next world champion.

His admiration for Farr continued to grow, and in the build-up to Tommy's championship fight against Joe Louis in August 1937, Jack again wrote about him with great passion:

..... There is hardly any doubt in my mind that Tommy Farr will give Joe Louis the biggest surprise he has received since Max Schmeling beat him. In short, I am of the opinion that my fellow countryman is about to become the first heavyweight champion these islands have produced since St. Patrick's Day 1897 .....

Jack proved to be an astute judge of boxing ability because although Farr didn't win, he gave Louis a tremendous fight before losing on points. Yet despite everything Jack wrote and said about him, Tommy never forgave him for not fighting him.

Some years later when they met at a public function, Jack said, 'You don't like me do you?' 'No,' replied Farr bluntly. 'When you had the title, you would never give me a fight, and I don't like anyone who stops me earning my bread and butter.'

Jack always claimed that when he was champion, Farr had done nothing to qualify for a shot at the title. The fact was, Jack was earning incredible money fighting men like Harvey and Neusel. He was an exciting fighter who could command exceptional purses. Farr, on the other hand, was not an attractive fighter. It was only after he became British champion in March 1937, that he shot to prominence.

Had Jack not been forced to retire, a fight between them would almost certainly have broken box office records, especially if staged in the open air in Cardiff. Sadly, the fans were deprived of what could have been the most intriguing heavyweight contest in the history of British boxing.

Such a fight would have guaranteed each man a tremendous purse. That aspect was probably of little concern to Petersen, who it was claimed had amassed at least £30,000 in six years as a professional. Jeff Dickson claimed in *Topical Times* that in 16 months he paid Jack a total of £11,330 for just five fights. Farr, however, had been striving for years to secure a big purse, which is why he never forgave Jack for not fighting him.

* * *

Although he was devasted when told he must quit boxing, Jack received great comfort and re-assurance from his wife who did much to help drive away any despair in his mind. With her support he soon adapted to life outside the ring. Apart from writing his weekly column for the *Sunday Chronicle*, he played a lot of golf which helped him relax and took his mind off the disappointment.

With no strenuous training routine to contend with, Jack also found time for material things. He loved being a father, and spent quality time with his baby son John who was born in June 1936 whilst he was training to meet Ben Foord. Jack spent hours amusing the little boy by making shadow pictures with his hands. A lovely article appeared in the *Sunday Chronicle* showing how he moulded his hands into the shape of a dove, which, with the aid of a light, he made flutter on the wall. Betty created a camel's head which Jack talked to, and a photograph of the three of them showed clearly the deep parental love and the joy of their little boy.

In early January 1938, there were rumours that Petersen was contemplating a comeback. Although newspaper reports varied, it was generally suggested that Sydney Hulls had offered Jack £10,000 for two fights at Harringay. It was also claimed that John Harding of the National Sporting Club had offered him £6,500 for a single contest.

Predictably, Jack was at first rather tight-lipped when approached by the *South Wales Echo*. 'Phew, that's a lot of money,' he remarked expressing surprise at the suggestions, yet remaining totally calm. Although he admitted having spoken to Harding on the telephone, he insisted it was a strictly personal matter. Denying he had received any offer from Hulls, he refused to discuss his future plans.

In another article a few days later, the *Echo* claimed that Jack had turned down an offer of £20,000 from a large syndicate of businessmen. It was stated that Pa Petersen acted as a go-between, and Jack had been asked to sign a contract which would bind him to the syndicate for twelve months. It was proposed that he would have two or three warm-up fights prior to a major contest to be staged at the Glasgow exhibition during the summer of 1938.

Anxious to establish exactly what was occurring, William E. Allen went to see Pa. Despite being a close friend, he was as evasive as Jack, and refused to confirm or deny acting on behalf of a syndicate. 'Nothing could persuade Jack to return to the ring,' insisted Pa, 'although I still think he would give a good account of himself against any present day boxer.'

At the time, Jack was still contracted to the *Sunday Chronicle*. In view of all the speculation about a possible return to the ring, he exclusively told his side of the story in the edition of 9 January. Headlined, 'PETERSEN – I WILL FIGHT AGAIN', Jack said:

> I will certainly return to the boxing game if and when I get a reasonable offer. Why did I refuse my father's offer? Simply because it was not good enough. It was a contract for twelve months but no stipulation was made as to the number of fights. An offer of £6,000 for a single contest which was reported as being made to me the other day, is the type of offer I should consider. A return to the ring might harm my eyes but I shall have to take the risk.

The announcement came as a shock to many people. Jack was an intelligent, level-headed young man, but for him to even contemplate a return to the ring against medical advice was considered extremely irresponsible, especially as he was financially secure.

It was a strange state of affairs because despite his comments in the *Sunday Chronicle*, no further mention was ever made regarding a possible comeback. There was never any suggestion that Jack was in training which throws doubt on whether he was ever serious. In reality, Pa Petersen's remark to William E. Allen, that nothing would ever persuade Jack to return to the ring, looked to be more factual.

Almost nine months elapsed before Jack gave any indication of what went through his mind. It then became clear that despite the fact there may have been a temptation to continue boxing, common sense had prevailed. 'My eyes are worth more to me than all the money in the world,' he wrote in the *Sunday Chronicle* in October 1938. 'I will fight no more. That career is over, and I must look for something else to do.'

* * *

Jack had, by this time, become very positive in his mind. Once he came to terms with the fact that his boxing career was over, he thought of ways by which he could occupy his time, and also serve the community. He was interested in all sports, very keen on health and discipline, and had more than a casual interest in politics.

206

In the 18 months since his retirement he kept himself as fit as he had ever been, and studied every aspect of health. Had Jack not been a fighter, he would have been a doctor, and having grown up at the Lynn Institute, he knew the importance of physical fitness, especially to youngsters. He had learned a great deal from his father, an expert in health, and a student of every faculty of the human body.

'To my father, health has always been almost a religion,' he remarked. 'Before I am finished, I am going to know as much about health as he does.'

Always appreciative of his own good fortune, Jack wished that every boy could have the same opportunities for achieving physical fitness that he did as a youngster. Consequently, if there was ever a lads club in any part of the country he was visiting, he would turn down other invitations to enable him to be amongst the boys and explain to them everything he knew about health.

The Scout Movement also represented everything Jack believed in, and he saw it as being imperative to encourage and maintain good health and discipline in boys. Having been a scout since he was a schoolboy, he never lost touch with it. On one occasion in the 1970's, he travelled from Cardiff to Well End in Hertfordshire especially to attend a County Scout function. Jack took his National Sporting Club belt which he proudly displayed, and thoroughly entertained the gathering of more than 100 with a talk about his career.

Scouting was one of Jack's major interests, and he devoted a lot of spare time to it at various stages of his life. He frequently attended his local scout hut and enjoyed carrying cups of tea at parties, piling up chairs, and doing any of the chores which go with social events.

Jack adored children generally, and wherever he went they followed him. He would frequently take the son of a friend on to his knee and pretend to spar with him, and allow the lad to hit him. He would talk and ask questions about what the boy wanted to do when he grew up.

He hated hearing about children being hurt or becoming ill. A few days before he fought Jack Doyle, Petersen heard that one of his schoolboy fans had badly cut his foot whilst swimming. Lock-jaw had also developed, and the boy was seriously ill at Cardiff Infirmary. Without delay, the champion went to the hospital, and as he entered the ward the boy sat up and became very excited. They talked for a while and had a photograph taken which Jack later autographed. He kept in touch with the situation and was delighted when he knew the boy had recovered.

Jack was extremely keen on the development of schoolboy boxing, and in particular the training it required. Even when he was champion, he went to the Lynn Institute every Saturday morning to give boxing lessons to boys. He had a regular class, and they only wanted to be taught by him.

'Punching the bag is healthy,' he always insisted, 'and the healthier you are, the more you know about your own body.'

In June 1962, Jack contributed to the weekly journal, *'Education'*, in which he discussed boxing as an essential part of physical education. It was his contention that boxing at school provided a skilful and healthy recreation for boys, as opposed to entertainment. 'That is a matter for professional boxers and promoters,' he remarked. He also stressed the importance of teachers of boxing in schools having the well-being of the boys at heart.

Apart from his interest in health and sport, Jack also openly expressed his concern about the state of the country. He believed that much more could be done by both local and national government. He was particularly disturbed to find so many able-bodied men out of work, not just in Cardiff, but throughout the country.

He also expressed dissatisfaction about the National Fitness Movement which had been in progress for some time. 'Its results are not apparent to me,' he remarked, 'and I am surely one man who would see them.'

Jack was concerned at the number of towns throughout the country without swimming baths or gymnasiums, or any health attractions designed to get boys off the streets. In the *Sunday Chronicle*, he wrote:

> That state of affairs might have been alright in the old days before the towns spread all over the countryside, and when there was always a river for a boy to swim in, or an open country he could reach after he was out of school or workshop. Now he must find his daily recreation in the cities, and we must see that it is the right sort.

Jack was a young man with ambition and drive, and his ideas for development were refreshing. Although he was only 27 and had no previous political experience, it was not long before he was invited to stand as a candidate at the Cardiff Municipal Elections on 1 November 1938. The invitation, from the Cardiff Liberal Association, was for him to contest the Plasnewydd ward, but at first he was reluctant to stand.

'It's true, I have been asked to contest the seat but I've given my sponsors the K.O.,' he told the *South Wales Echo*. 'I do not think I shall stand this time.'

The esteem in which Jack was held by people in Cardiff was seen as a potential vote winner. As a result, he received a visit from the Chairman and Secretary of the Liberal Association, and after further discussion he agreed to contest the seat. His nomination was unanimously adopted at a meeting at party headquarters in early October.

Shortly after accepting the invitation, a friend questioned Jack's decision. 'Why start there?' he asked. 'If you are cut out for a political career, why not capitalise what popularity you have and stand for parliament?'

In Jack's opinion, that was bad advice because he believed local politics to be just as important as those from Westminster. He was convinced that electors were taking too little notice of what went on under their noses. Explaining his feelings in the *Sunday Chronicle*, he said:

> I should like to see a great revival in municipal elections. What's the use of grumbling about rates and then staying away from the polling booths on election day. All over the country we hear of the pathetically small percentage of electors going to the polls. If control of the cities falls into the wrong hands, it is the fault of the voters who don't vote.

In the weeks leading up to the elections, Jack worked extremely hard and was received enthusiastically by constituents. Although he failed to get elected, he came within 253 votes of the successful Conservative candidate. He polled 1,631 votes, over 600 more than the Socialist candidate.

* * *

Although Jack's life was changing dramatically, his heart remained firmly in boxing. He began to take great interest in the amateurs, and, quietly behind the scenes, guided young Cardiff University student, Morton F. Llewellyn, to the Welsh amateur heavyweight title in March 1938. As soon as the decision was announced, Jack excitedly climbed into the ring to congratulate his young protégé.

The fact that Petersen remained the idol of boxing crowds in South Wales was repeatedly demonstrated, but rarely more so than on this occasion. As soon as the crowd of 3,000 at the Cardiff Drill Hall were told that he had Llewellyn 'under his wing', they rose as a body and cheered the house down for several minutes. He was mobbed as he left the ring, and his popularity couldn't have been greater if he had won the world title.

Although he had retired from active boxing, it was essential that Jack remained involved in the professional side in some capacity. Not only had he been a fine champion, he was an articultate, mild-mannered man with a good business brain. The Stewards of the British Boxing Board of Control recognised his talents and the esteem in which he was held. So, in the Autumn of 1938, they invited him to become a representative Steward for Wales.

Jack was thrilled and honoured to receive such an invitation, and a few days later described his feelings in his column in the *Sunday Chronicle*:

> The other day, I attended a meeting of the Stewards of the Board of Control for the first time as a representative Steward. I was the youngest man there, and as I sat with the Stewards, it suddenly came to me that this was the true crown of my boxing career. To be invited to sit there was a greater honour than all the titles I had won.
>
> At 27, life is beginning for me again. I am no longer a ring fighter with the roar of the crowd and sound of the gong in my ears, but a man in a man's world tackling a new sort of fight. I expect to find it as enjoyable as the career that ended when I laid down my gloves.

It turned out to be just the beginning of a relationship with the controlling body which Jack would retain for the rest of his life.

* * *

A strong supporter of Churchill, Jack often expressed concern about the state of the world, particularly the imminent threat from Germany. Convinced he had a contribution to make he joined the Territorial Army but didn't say anything to anyone. On 1 March 1939, he was commissioned 2nd Lieutenant in the Royal Armed Service Corps, T.A. On 28 August 1939, he was promoted to Honorary Captain. It was not until after war was declared in September that people became aware of his involvement.

Following the outbreak of the Second World War, Jack, like so many other boxers, joined the regular army. During service he was a Staff Officer with Western Command, and also served with the Border Regiment. After being transferred to Chester his Commanding Officer, General Reynolds, put him in charge of troop development schemes. Many new recruits lacked strength and fitness when they joined the army, and with his experience and dedication in such areas, Jack was seen as the ideal man to devise necessary training schemes.

Troops in the anti-aircraft and searchlight units were, of necessity, more static than field troops, but in order to give them the opportunity for action, a Training School operated on the South Wales coast near Penarth. Jack was Staff Officer in charge of Physical Training for the Division from 23 March 1941, and much of his time was spent giving special instruction to N.C.Os from gun and searchlight units which they in turn could pass on to members of their units.

A 'commando' style assault course was designed and laid out to prepare students for anything they were likely to encounter in active warfare. Many of Jack's ideas and proposals regarding fitness were adopted from those learned from his father at the Lynn Institute.

As a public relations exercise, Jack frequently visited army camps throughout the country to help devise and supervise the running of courses.

Because of the position he held, he was frequently invited to Regimental Headquarters and entertained to dinner by the Commanding Officer. He never knew what to expect, but quite often a boxing exhibition had been arranged without his knowledge. Only at very short notice would he discover that he was expected to box the Regimental Sergeant Training Instructor.

Having been invited to dinner, Jack would have no kit and therefore be obliged to borrow some. He found himself in a position where he couldn't refuse to go through with exhibitions, although it often irritated him that no advance warning had been given.

The P.T.I. was always an extremely fit individual, determined to put on a good show in front of his own men. Although not as fit as in his fighting days, Jack was obliged to go through with it, and invariably needed all the know-how learned in the professional ring.

In order to survive and not lose face, he often went into a clinch early in the proceedings. Then, very quietly, he would explain to his opponent what was expected in an exhibition. Using a high degree of kidology, he explained that as an ex-professional, he did not want to hurt him. It worked every time.

During war-time, Jack did a lot of charity work with E.N.S.A. and worked with many top class entertainers, including the Crazy Gang. He got to know them so well that they often asked him to turn up at venues where they were performing. Then, when on stage, they would look out into the audience shouting, 'Let's see who's in tonight!' Whenever Jack was present, he would be called on to the stage in uniform and introduced as the ex-British heavyweight champion. He always received a rousing reception.

Jack had a number of postings during his army career, including one to Knightsbridge Barracks in London which he disliked intensely. He always wanted to serve abroad but his requests were refused. When the war was over, he applied to become an Army Welfare Officer in order that he could assist personnel being discharged. He was appointed to hold the position for Wales, and was based at Maindy Barracks.

* * *

Early in the morning of 27 February 1945 a boilerman employed at the Lynn Institute found the lifeless body of Pa Patersen in a bath. Scalds on his shoulders indicated that he had entered the water when it was extremely hot. An electric heater lay nearby.

Due to the circumstances of death, an inquest was conducted by the Cardiff City cornoner, Mr. Gerald Tudor. Jack, described as Captain Petersen, attended the hearing and heard evidence that when found, his father's body was touching the heater close to the bath. The verdict returned was one of accidental death by electrocution.

* * *

Jack had a successful army career, spending seven years on active service with the regulars, attaining the rank of Captain. He was with the Territorials for thirteen years, reaching the rank of Major, and spent a great deal of time with the Army Cadet Force for whom he was Staff Training Officer.

Although he had been a highly successful professional fighter, Petersen was always very respectful of all A.B.A. officials. When the war ended, he put a great deal of time into amateur boxing in Wales.

The Glamorgan Army Cadet team became his pride and joy, winning the County Army Cadet championships for five consecutive years between 1945 and 1949. Their success was built on hard work, and motivation by Jack, for whom the boys had tremendous respect. In 1946, he made an appeal through the *South Wales Echo* for Sergeant instructors and assistant instructors to help him in his work. At the time, he was in charge of fourteen battalions of cadets and needed as many volunteers as possible.

The success of the team in 1947 was exceptional. All nine boxers who entered the competition reached the finals at the Royal Albert Hall, and all won. 'Darkie' Hughes also received a trophy for 'best performance', while Tony George added a third Army Cadet championship to his Welsh Senior A.B.A. title.

The team was further rewarded when a special trophy was awarded to it by Gaumont British Picture Corporation Limited and R.K.O. Radio Pictures, in recognition of their success. Accepting the trophy from Dr. D. R. Prosser, editor of *Western Mail*, at a ceremony at the Cardiff Empire, Major Petersen said he was thrilled to be involved with the cadets. 'Their continued success is due to discipline and their own hard work and dedication,' said Jack.

Among the many fine young boxers Jack helped develop were Joe Erskine and Dai Dower who he took to the 1950 Army Cadet championships, and also Howard Winstone. All would progress to win national A.B.A. championships and British professional titles.

Jack's long service, good conduct and significant contribution to the Army, in particular with the Cadet Force, resulted in him being awarded the Territorial Decoration. Referred to in army records as the Efficiency Decoration, it was given for 12 years commissioned service in the Territorial Army. The award was announced in the *London Gazette* of 20 June 1950.

Because of his involvement with boxing, the Army were keen for Jack to continue, and even offered to promote him. His wife, however, wanted him to leave, so he was torn between two loyalties. Although he was an enthusiastic Army Officer who loved his work, he was also a devoted husband and father. He had no real experience in civilian life, and this concerned him, but he had five children, John, Michael, Barbara, David and Robert. They were growing up fast and he needed to spend more time with them which was the deciding factor.

* * *

After leaving the army, Jack spent two years working as a company representative for Brylcream, appearing on advertising posters alongside England cricketer Dennis Compton. He also worked for United Distillers advertising Lemon Hart Rum. Part of that job involved visiting public houses, but he gave it up because he disliked having to associate with people who were getting drunk.

Jack then opened a shop at Barry selling sports and leather goods. Although he kept it going for about three years, it was not a great success. Too many callers only wanted to talk to him or make his acquaintance.

Meanwhile, in December 1951, having retained his interest in politics, Jack stood as the conservative candidate at a by-election for the Plasnewydd ward of the Cardiff City Council. He was elected with a majority of 882 votes, and served until May 1953 when he retired prior to the new elections taking place.

After giving up his shop, Jack became heavily involved in sports administration and over the years held many prestigious positions with sporting bodies. He became Chairman of the Welsh Sports Development Council which was involved in obtaining grants for sports facilities in Wales, including football and rugby pitches, squash courts, etc. Although only a two or three day a week job, it was extremely demanding.

For two years, he was a member of the National Sports Council acting as the Welsh representative. He attended many functions and did a lot of public speaking for which he never charged a fee. Jack did not particularly enjoy this role, preferring instead to be supervising facilities in Wales.

Other positions included Chairman of the National Sports Centre for Wales for three years, the first Chairman of the South East Wales Advisory Committee, and a member of the Welsh Sports Aid Association. From 1971-1984, he was a campaigning member of the Sports Council for Wales with specific responsibility for the South East.

Jack strongly believed that youngsters should become more involved in organised sport, but at the time those below grammar school level had very little opportunity. There was little in life to keep them out of mischief, so he became the leading figure in a campaign to get kids off the streets.

Having been a member of the Gabalfa Amateur Boxing Club when he was a youngster, Jack knew the self-discipline boxing demanded. As an ardent supporter of the sport, he had a number of debates with Dr. Edith Summerskill, one of boxing's most committed opponents. Whether it was on radio or in private, Jack always maintained the same line of argument. He contended that youngsters needed to channel their aggressive instincts positively. Boxing was the one sport which taught them how to do that as well as learning to respect one another and the authority of the referee.

Jack's commitment and dedication won him many awards, including the Sports Council for Wales gold medal for outstanding services to Welsh sport. In January 1970, at the annual dinner of the Boxing Writers Club at the National Sporting Club in London, he was presented with the Joe Bromley award for outstanding services to boxing. One of his proudest moments, however, came when he was elected to the Welsh Sports Hall of Fame in 1989, and enlisted on the Roll of Honour.

In December 1966, the B.B.C. featured Jack in the television series '*This is your Life.*' Presented by Eamonn Andrews, there were telephone link-ups with his sons John in Cyprus and Michael in Berlin. Both were on active service with the British Army but had been unable to get leave to attend their father's special night. Jack's other children, Barbara, David and Robert accompanied him and Betty at the studio.

Guests included old opponents Rhys Howells, who beat Jack as an amateur in 1929 and became a firm friend, and Len Harvey whom he fought three times for the British heavyweight title. Len had also remained a close friend, and was delighted when asked to be a guest on the programme. Incredibly, just as he was about to leave his home in London, Walter Neusel knocked on his door.

'Why didn't you call me to say you were coming?' said Len. 'I'm just off to Cardiff where the B.B.C. are doing a special programme for Petersen.'

'Can I come along as well?' asked Neusel. Len thought it was a great idea because he knew Jack had tremendous respect for the German, and would be delighted to see him. They travelled to Cardiff together and when they arrived at the studio the B.B.C. producer was very excited and invited Walter to be a guest. Jack was visibly emotional when Neusel was introduced, and despite their three vicious battles 30 years earlier, there was genuine warmth between them.

Earlier that year, Petersen and Harvey were guests at a boxing dinner at the World Sporting Club in London. Both received standing ovations as they climbed into the ring to present cheques to the winner and runner-up of the Booth's Gin £2,000 novice heavyweight competition.

Guests included another of Jack's old opponent's, Joseph Goyder, who by this time was Assistant Commissioner of the City of London Police. He sat with Pat Floyd, another former A.B.A. champion who Jack beat as an amateur in 1930.

In February 1972, Jack visited Harvey at his public house, the '*Star & Garter*' at Islington in North London at the request of the B.B.C. Western Service which covered Len's birth place of Plymouth. A programme entitled '*Len's Life*' was being filmed, and Petersen was a prominent feature.

A few weeks earlier, Jack and Len were joined on the same table at the annual Boxing Writers Club dinner at the National Sporting Club, by Larry Gains. They made a formidable gathering, all having previously won the Joe Bromley award for services to the sport. All were in fine health and discussed their fights with great enthusiasm as though they had taken place only weeks earlier. Gains was heard to remark, 'Yes, I lost that one on a cut eye. Besides, it was October and cold. I wasn't used to it.' Petersen and Harvey roared with laughter.

Jack's tremendous services to sport, particularly as regards youth development, were rewarded in June 1978 when he was awarded the Order of the British Empire. He had spent 40 years striving to give youngsters the opportunities he didn't have as a boy.

'My main concern has always been to see that every boy and girl had the opportunities to take part in organised sport, and now I think we are achieving something,' he told the *South Wales Echo*.

By this time, Jack and Betty were living in the village of Itton near Chepstow. 'It's funny, but I reckon I've opened more garden fetes than I ever had ring battles,' he told the *Echo*, 'but what has given me tremendous pleasure in life is the advances in sport over the past six years.'

The announcement of Jack's award raised the issue over the spelling of his family name. Publishing details of the award, the *London Gazette* insisted it was Peterson, although throughout his boxing career it had been Petersen. The *South Wales Echo* reverted to Peterson when reporting the award, claiming it was the spelling Jack used when he joined the army. The newspaper told readers that the family were quite philosophical about it, with two sons using 'en' while the others used 'on'.

About six months earlier, Prime Minister, James Callaghan, invited Jack and Betty to a function at 10, Downing Street. During the course of conversation, the Prime Minister suddenly said, 'You haven't got any honours Jack, why is that?' With typical modesty, Jack replied, 'I've never been offered one. Probably people don't think I'm worth it.'

Callaghan had tremendous respect for Jack, and knew of his contribution to society since retiring from boxing. Although nothing further was said on the subject, Jack always believed the Prime Minister was influential in the award being made.

At the time, Jack had been a campaigning member of the Sports Council for Wales for seven years. His first public engagement since the announcement of his award took place two weeks later, on 16 June. It was the opening day of the course fishing season, and he officially opened Woodstock Pool, a new six acre lake at Newport. The lake, which cost £15,000 to create, was described as being the first man-made lake in South Wales designed especially for course fishing. The Sports Council for Wales had given Newport Angling Association a fifty per cent grant towards the cost of the project.

* * *

On 21 November, accompanied by members of his family, Jack went to Buckingham Palace to receive his O.B.E. A few days later, he was guest of honour at a special luncheon in London organised by the Boxing Writers Club to celebrate his award.

Remarkably upright for a man of 67, he completely held the floor for 45 minutes with a moving speech. He was extremely articulate and witty as he spoke about his career and the many good times he'd had. 'I do hope I'm not boring you,' he remarked at one stage to the amusement of the select gathering.

'It was a pity people like Baroness Summerskill, who only see the bad side of boxing and none of the good, were not present,' said respected author and journalist Frank Butler. 'Jack is the perfect ambassador for the sport.'

Despite his heavy commitment to Welsh sport generally, Jack always remained firmly involved with boxing. He served for many years on the Welsh Area Council of the British Boxing Board of Control before being appointed Chairman in 1974. He held the position for three years.

In April 1975, he was guest of honour at the first ever international convention of ex-boxers to be held in Britain. Hosted by officers and members of the London ex-Boxers Association and staged at West Centre Hotel, Earls Court, the convention President was his friend and former opponent, Larry Gains.

Jack was also delighted to meet up with another old foe, Charlie Smith. They looked like long lost friends as they warmly discussed their fights which took place more than 40 years earlier. In subsequent interviews, Charlie, like everyone else, paid tribute to Jack as 'a real gentleman.'

When the Welsh ex-Boxers Association was formed in 1976, it was appropriate that Petersen was elected as their first President.

In 1973, Jack made boxing history when he became the first ex-boxer to be appointed as an administrative steward by the British Boxing Board of Control. The following year he became Vice-President, and in 1986, was elected President.

Amazingly, the National Sporting Club championship challenge belt which was not presented to Jack following his victory over Harry Crossley in 1932, was presented to the Board of Control at

217

about the time he became President. The story surrounding it's whereabouts is a fascinating one.

In 1937, John Harding, manager of the revived National Sporting Club discovered the belt in the club safe, and donated it as a prize to the winner of a *Daily Mail* sponsored open heavyweight competition. The winner was Jack Smith of Worcester who boxed before and after the second world war. When he emigrated to Masterton, New Zealand, he took the belt with him, but when the Queen visited the country during the 1970's, he presented it to her. Buckingham Palace eventually decided that the Board of Control should have the belt for safe-keeping, and it was handed over at about the same time Petersen became President. It is currently displayed in the boardroom at the headquarters of the sport's governing body.

One of Jack's first public appearances as President was in September 1986 when he attended the Boxing Awards luncheon organised by the Board of Control at the Connaught Rooms in London. In a short speech he said, 'It is a great honour to be appointed the new President of the British Boxing Board of Control. I am very proud to have achieved this by coming up through the ranks so to speak. From fighter to Steward, to Vice-President, then President.'

Jack was an avid reader of the *Old-Timers* column in the weekly journal, '*Boxing News*', and after the luncheon asked writer, Ron Olver, to pass on his sincere regards to Len Harvey's widow. 'Len was a great opponent and a great friend,' he added.

Always conscious of public opinion regarding boxing, Jack used his status to promote the sport at every possible opportunity. Whether it be during speeches at public functions, or in press interviews, he always stressed the need for it to survive as a sport. At the World Boxing Council Convention in London in 1987, he said, 'Boxing has a firm place in our Society and continues to thrill and excite countless millions. It requires a high degree of training, discipline and sportsmanship. Properly run, it is an excellent sport.'

As President of the Board of Control, Jack was always concerned about public relations in boxing. Being extremely conscientious, it worried him that decisions made by the Board were often misconstrued. He was very positive about discipline, particularly in sport. As a fighter, he set an example to others both in and outside the ring. As an administrator, he did everything possible to encourage and maintain high standards within the sport.

14

GOODBYE TO A GENTLEMAN

Throughout his life, Jack was a kind thoughtful man who always had time for others, particularly those less fortunate than himself. The attention he received never changed him, and the way he conducted himself endeared him to people from all walks of life.

His son, David, once described to a newspaper reporter how, as a boy, he would often walk with his father along St. Mary Street in Cardiff. Those walks would seem never ending because every man and woman who recognised the tall, imposing figure, would stop and want to talk boxing. Always the gentleman, Jack ignored nobody because he belonged to the people of Cardiff.

An example of his kindness and dignity can be derived from the day he attended the funeral of former British heavyweight champion, Joe Erskine, at Cardiff in March 1990. As he arrived at the church, Jack was asked if he would give an address. He was privileged to be asked, and although he only spoke for four minutes, he enthralled the massive gathering with his sincerity. What nobody knew was that only the previous day, Jack had been diagnosed as suffering from lung cancer.

As they left the church, a journalist turned to Jack and said, 'If only Erskine had your punch.' With typical modesty, Petersen smiled and said, 'If only I possessed some of his skills.'

Although his health was deteriorating, Jack continued to attend functions whenever invited because he hated letting people down. In October 1990, despite having recently spent a period in hospital, he made a five hour train journey to Manchester where he was guest of honour at the Anglo American Sporting Club. Organised to raise funds for sporting facilities for the under-privileged, the event was chaired by Prince Edward. Many great sporting personalities were present, including Sir Stanley Matthews, but it was Jack Petersen everyone wanted to talk to.

* * *

During his life, Jack attended countless dinners throughout the British Isles, yet there had never been one organised in his honour. The Wales Committee of the Variety Club of Great Britain recognised it was long overdue, and organised a special tribute dinner in his honour at Cardiff City Hall on 19 November 1990.

Attended by more than 350 guests, the event raised over £5,000 for Variety Club charities, but sadly, the guest of honour's chair remained empty. Jack's health had deteriorated further, and a few days earlier he had been admitted to the Princess of Wales hospital at Bridgend.

Despite having undergone an operation for a lung complaint, Jack originally insisted on attending the event. An ambulance was even laid on to take him, but when his wife arrived to collect him, he conceded that it would be too much for him. Jack was a proud man and didn't want people to see him in failing health. Yet, with typical dignity, he expressed a wish that everyone had a thoroughly enjoyable evening. He insisted that Betty joined her daughter, four sons, and other family members, and asked that his eldest son, John, took along the National Sporting Club challenge belt he had won outright.

Among the guests were former world featherweight champion, Howard Winstone, and former British and European flyweight champion, Dai Dower, both of whom boxed under Jack when he was Staff Training Officer for the Glamorgan Army Cadet Force.

The speakers included Lord Tonypandy, Lord Parry of Neyland, and Sir David Hopkin, Chairman of the British Boxing Board of Control, who said he could not have asked for greater support and encouragement than he had received from Jack. 'He's an example to all of us in our lives as well as in sport.' said Sir David. 'We are all privileged to be here to honour a fine boxer, administrator and man.'

Chairman, Lynn Jones, said the Wales Committee were honoured and privileged to pay tribute to one of Wales' greatest sportsmen and ambassadors. 'Jack achieved so much in life, and has put so much back into the sport he loves.'

The following day, Jack's sons visited him in hospital and gave him a full account of the dinner. Typically, he was delighted to hear that everyone had enjoyed themselves.

* * *

Jack did not recover from his illness and died in hospital on 22

November 1990. He was aged 79. As news of his death spread, there was a feeling of real sadness, especially throughout South Wales where people knew of the monumental efforts he made to promote youth sport. Tributes poured in, particularly from the world of boxing.

Obituaries appeared in every national newspaper, although one inaccurately described him as having served with the Royal Air Force. Jack would have been furious, but it brought to mind one of his standard comments; 'You can't always believe what you read in newspapers.'

A moving and accurate description of Jack was portrayed by Dan O'Neil in the *South Wales Echo* on 23 November:

> He was more than a boxer. He was what we call in later years, an idol – someone who transcended sport to become a mythic figure in his own lifetime.

Dai Dower spoke for many people when, on hearing of Jack's passing said, 'He never had a bad word to say about anyone, and nobody ever said a bad word about him.'

Dower always remembered Jack with affection because when he won a schoolboy championship as an eleven year old in 1944, Jack had presented him with his prize.

'I'm only five foot four now, so I was pretty short then,' he remarked. 'Jack got down on his knees and pretended to spar with me.'

Eddie Thomas also had fond memories of Jack from the 1940's. As a 17 year old, he was presented with a prize by the former champion. 'He had put up a cup for the best boxer of the evening, and he presented it to me,' recalled Thomas. 'He was the finest ambassador we have ever had.'

Former Chairman of the Sports Council for Wales, Sir Harry Llewellyn said, 'Jack was a wonderful man who did more for sport than any man I know. He was a great man and a dear friend.'

The following week, All Saints Church at Porthcawl was packed to capacity as people from all walks of life gathered to pay their last respects. It was a moving event as the congregation put whole-hearted power and enthusiasm into the singing of two of Jack's favourite hymns; *'For all the Saints who from their labours rest',* and *'Guide me, O thou great Jehovah.'* The Reverend Canon David John, who officiated, described Jack as 'a giant of a man who made an indelible mark in the field of boxing'.

'Yet it has to be remembered that he was more than a boxer,' continued Canon John. 'He was a wonderful husband, father and grandfather. He was also a friend, and he was a gentleman.'

Among the mourners were the Mayor and Mayoress of Porthcawl, Mr and Mrs W. Nash, the Deputy Mayor, David Newton-Williams, and many well known sporting personalities. Former boxers included Howard Winstone, Dai Dower, Eddie Thomas, Cliff Curvis, Johnny Williams and Eddie Avoth. They were joined by 'star' referees', Jim Brimmell and Adrian Morgan, and members of the Welsh ex-Boxers Association.

Former Welsh Rugby internationals Ken Jones and Bleddwyn Williams attended along with Wilf Wooller, the former Glamorgan cricket captain, and Sports Council Chairman, Ossie Wheatley. The Army Training Corps sent two representatives as a mark of respect for Jack's massive contribution to the Armed Services.

The attendance of such a vast cross-section of society was a clear indication of the esteem in which Jack was held. Those feelings were expressed by his oldest and closest friend, Stan Thomas, a former Chairman of the Welsh Area Council of the British Boxing Board of Control in an interview with the *South Wales Echo*:

> Some of us are fortunate to remember the golden era of Jack Petersen as a boxer supreme. He lifted the hearts of Welshmen everywhere, and as a nation of sportsmen, we adored him.
>
> During the past few months since he became ill, I visited him at his home. There was always the ready smile, the big welcome and the indomitable spirit he showed throughout his life. He was a gallant sporting son of Wales who had an aura of greatness. He fought to the end like the true champion he was.

The funeral service was followed by cremation at Coychurch crematorium, Bridgend attended by gentlemen only. The singing of *'The Lord's my Shepherd'* provided a fitting goodbye to a gentleman.

Later that day, the death was announced of the great Welsh rugby international fly-half, Cliff Jones, who had been a friend of Jack.

* * *

Jack Petersen gave his life to boxing but never regretted a moment of it. He saw the sport from every level, and whatever position he held, he was loved and respected. When he was appointed President of the Board of Control in 1986, there could not have been a better choice. He was articulate in every way and respected by all who came across him.

In Loving Memory

of

John Charles Peterson O.B.E., T.D.

2nd September, 1911
22nd November, 1990

All Saints Church, Porthcawl

Wednesday, 28th November, 1990

12 Noon

Afterwards Gentlemen only at Coychurch Crematorium, Bridgend

Officiating: Canon David John

assisted by: Rev. Albert Parry

John Morris, then General Secretary of the Board, echoed the thoughts of many people within boxing when he said, 'Jack was one of the most remarkable men that we have ever had in boxing. I shall never forget him at Joe Erskine's funeral earlier this year. At that time we didn't know what was wrong, but we knew he was ill.'

By becoming President of the Board, Jack reached the pinnacle of the sport. When the controlling body named their new headquarters in South London 'JACK PETERSEN HOUSE', it was the ultimate tribute.

Today, a fine portrait of the former President hangs in the entrance hall of the Board offices, while other pictures of him are displayed elsewhere in the building.

* * *

Jack spent the last years of his life living at Porthcawl. He and Betty enjoyed a wonderful marriage, and in October 1985 celebrated their golden wedding anniversary. From a very young age, Jack was determined that his family would never suffer the heartbreak he experienced as a child when his parents divorced. Although he was left with some scars, he put the memories behind him and became a wonderful husband, father and grandfather.

It is difficult to imagine that Jack ever made any enemies. Certainly within boxing, former opponents always remembered him with great respect and affection. Despite their gruelling battles he maintained particularly close friendships with Len Harvey and Larry Gains, meeting them regularly at dinners and ex-boxers association functions.

In his later years, Harvey ran the *Star & Garter* pub at Islington in North London, and the last time Jack visited him, Len's health was deteriorating. They talked for a long time about their careers, and in particular their three title fights back in the 1930's. Recalling the occasion in a dinner speech, Jack said that a few days later he received a lovely photo of Len in a boxing pose. It was endorsed: 'To Jack – in memory of our great battles.' 'Wasn't that nice?' said Jack. 'That's one of the great things about boxing. Shake hands at the beginning, shake hands at the end. There's no malice.'

Jack Petersen typified that attitude. He took his knocks but bore no grudges. He was always quick to praise the courage of his opponents and recognise their quality and experience. His descriptions were often vivid but came from the heart. He once described Jack Bridgewater, who had been manager of Harry

224

Crossley, as a man who looked more like a methodist parson than a manager of fighters. Years later, when recalling some memories of his career, Jack remarked, 'Mr. Bridgewater is another official in the game whom I shall always remember with respect. Father also spoke highly of him.'

Anyone who ever met Jack Petersen, knew they were in the presence of a legend. He was a man with charisma who everyone knew because his contribution to sport and youth in Wales had been so great over many years. Although his boxing career was short, it was glorious, and Jack will always be remembered for his outstanding courage and the immense prestige he brought to the British ring. If boxing ever needed to choose a role-model, he would be the obvious choice.

Of the many fine tributes paid to Jack over the years, the most descriptive surely came from Lord Brooks of Tremorfa, at the time an administrative Steward, and now Chairman, of the British Boxing Board of Control:

> Petersen was simply one of the outstanding sports personalities of the twentieth century. Not only did he achieve great things in boxing, but went on to be a first class administrator with the Sports Council for Wales and with the British Boxing Board of Control.
>
> He was a marvellous advert for boxing in particular, and sport in general. He never refused an invitation, and was always prepared to help and give his time. Throughout the sporting world, there was the greatest respect for him.

Lord Brooks' tribute was the perfect summary of a man who ranks high amongst the great Welsh sporting heroes. As a gentleman, he surely has no equal. Long may he rest in peace.

BIBLIOGRAPHY

Books

Butler, Frank, *A History of Boxing in Britain*, Arthur Barker, 1972.

Carpenter, Harry, *Masters of Boxing*, Heinemann, 1964.

Dalby, Barrington, *Come in Barry*, Cassell, 1961.

Deyong, Moss, *Everybody Boo*, Stanley Paul, 1951.

Doughty, Jack, *The Rochdale Thunderbolt*, Pentaman, 1991.

Gains, Larry, *The Impossible Dream*, Leisure, 1976.

Hails, Jack, *Classic Moments in Boxing*, Moorland, 1983.

Haldane, R. A., *Champions & Challengers*, Stanley Paul, 1967.

Helliwell, Arthur, *Private Lives of Famous Fighters*, Day & Mason, 1949.

Odd, Gilbert, *Len Harvey, Prince of Boxers*, Pelham, 1978.

Odd, Gilbert, *Ring Battles of the Century*, Nicholson & Watson, 1948.

Rose, Charlie, *Life's a Knockout*, Hutchinson, 1953.

Taub, Michael, *Jack Doyle, Fighting for Love*, Stanley Paul, 1990

Newspapers

Brighton Evening Argus

Empire News

News of the World

Sporting Chronicle

Sporting Life

South Wales Argus

South Wales Echo

The Star

Sunday Chronicle

Sunday Dispatch

Swansea Evening Post

Western Mail

APPENDIX

Jack Petersen's Fighting Record 1931-1937

Date	Opponent	Result		Venue
1931				
Sept 28	Bill Partridge	W RSF	4	Holborn Stadium
Oct 12	Alf Noble	W KO	1	Holborn Stadium
Oct 19	Jim Campbell	W KO	1	Holborn Stadium
Oct 26	Jeff Wilson	W Ret	4	Holborn Stadium
Nov 2	George Porter	W Pts	6	Holborn Stadium
Nov 9	George Brown	W Pts	6	Holborn Stadium
Nov 13	Joe Mullins	W KO	2	Cardiff) (in private)
Nov 13	Ted Mason	W KO	2	Cardiff) (in private)
Nov 16	Tom Wailes	W RSF	1	Holborn Stadium
Nov 23	Jack Stratton	W Pts	6	Holborn Stadium
Dec 7	George Brown	W Pts	6	Holborn Stadium
Dec 14	Leo Bandias	W Pts	10	Cardiff
Dec 21	Gunner Bennett	W Pts	10	Holborn Stadium
Dec 22	Andrew Partridge	Exh	3	Cardiff
1932				
Jan 11	Jack Newitt	W KO	1	Holborn Stadium
Feb 3	Dick Power	W KO	1	Cardiff
	(Welsh heavyweight title)			
Feb 22	George Slack	W KO	5	Holborn Stadium
Mar 28	Charlie Smith	W KO	15	Cardiff
May 2	Tom Toner	W Disq	5	Crystal Palace
May 23	Harry Crossley	W Pts	15	Holborn Stadium
	(British Light-heavyweight title)			
July 12	Reggie Meen	W KO	2	Wimbledon Stadium
	(British heavyweight title)			
1933				
Jan 2	Hans Schonrath	W Ret	9	Cardiff
Jan 26	Jack Pettifer	W KO	12	Olympia
	(British heavyweight title)			
Feb 23	Ernst Guehring	W Pts	12	Albert Hall
May 16	Heine Muller	W KO	1	Cardiff
June 26	George Cook	W Pts	15	Cardiff

July 12	Jack Doyle	W Disq	2	White City
	(British heavyweight title)			
Nov 30	Len Harvey	L Pts	15	Albert Hall
	(British heavyweight title)			

1934

Jan 15	Charlie Bundy	Exh	4	Holborn Stadium
Jan 29	Charlie Smith	W KO	1	Cardiff
Feb 12	Reggie Meen	W KO	2	Leicester
Feb 26	Harry Crossley	W RSF	10	Cardiff
Mar 8	Ben Foord	W Ret	13	Albert Hall
June 4	Len Harvey	W Ret	12	White City
	(British & Empire heavyweight titles)			
Aug 18	Charlie Bundy	Exh	3	Cardiff
Sept 10	Larry Gains	W Ret	13	White City
	(British Empire heavyweight title)			
Nov 7	Charlie Bundy	Exh	3	Cardiff
Nov 8	Charlie Bundy	Exh	3	Swansea
Nov 8	Jim Wilde	Exh	2	Swansea
Dec 17	George Cook	W Pts	15	Albert Hall
	(British & Empire heavyweight titles)			

1935

Feb 4	Walter Neusel	L Ret	11	Wembley Pool
Jun 25	Walter Neusel	L Ret	10	Wembley Stadium

1936

Jan 29	Len Harvey	W Pts	15	Wembley Pool
	(British & Empire heavyweight titles)			
Apr 23	Jock McAvoy	W Pts	15	Earls Court
	(British & Empire heavyweight titles)			
Aug 17	Ben Foord	L RSF	3	Leicester
	(British & Empire heavyweight titles)			

1937

Feb 1	Walter Neusel	L Ret	10	Harringay
Apr 2	Max Hodgetts	Exh	3	Llandrindod Wells

Claimed record of John Thomas 'Pa' Petersen (Cardiff) – no dates available.

Opponent	Result	Venue
Tommy Watts	W 3	
'Stiff' Condon	W 1	
Charlie James	W 2	Cardiff
'Colonel' Williams	D 4	

– Won a featherweight competition for a silver cup.

– Won 9 stone 12 lb competition, open to Wales.   Scarrotts Booth, Pontypridd.

– Won welterweight competition, open to Wales.   Scarrotts Booth, Pontypridd.

Opponent	Result	Venue
Jim Driscoll	D 6	Cardiff
Kid Davis	D 6	
Brase	W 1	Cardiff
Frank Burge (US)	W 2	
Tommy Price	W 6	
Fred Delaney (Birmingham)	W KO 1*	
Joe Ross (London)	W 6	
Joe White	ND	Badminton Club, Cardiff.
Jack Lewis	ND	Hamburg

* The result of the fight with Fred Delaney is highly suspect because other newspaper reports claim Delaney won by a first round knockout.